Web Mining and Social Networking

Web Information Systems Engineering

and Internet Technologies

Book Series

Series Editor: Yanchun Zhang, Victoria University, Australia

For more titles in this series, please visit
www.springer.com/series/6970

Guandong Xu • Yanchun Zhang • Lin Li

Web Mining and Social Networking

Techniques and Applications

 Springer

Guandong Xu
Centre for Applied Informatics
School of Engineering & Science
Victoria University
PO Box 14428, Melbourne
VIC 8001, Australia
Guandong.Xu@vu.edu.au

Yanchun Zhang
Centre for Applied Informatics
School of Engineering & Science
Victoria University
PO Box 14428, Melbourne
VIC 8001, Australia
Yanchun.Zhang@vu.edu.au

Lin Li
School of Computer Science & Technology
Wuhan University of Technology
Wuhan Hubei 430070
China
cathylilin@whut.edu.cn

ISBN 978-1-4614-2718-6   ISBN 978-1-4419-7735-9 (eBook)
DOI 10.1007/978-1-4419-7735-9
Springer New York Dordrecht Heidelberg London

Printed on acid-free paper

Springer is part of Springer Science+Business Media (www.springer.com)

Dedication to

To Feixue and Jack
From Guandong

To Jinli and Dana
From Yanchun

To Jie
From Lin

Preface

World Wide Web has become very popular in last decades and brought us a powerful platform to disseminate information and retrieve information as well as analyze information, and nowadays the Web has been known as a big data repository consisting of a variety of data types, as well as a knowledge base, in which informative Web knowledge is hidden. However, users are often facing the problems of information overload and drowning due to the significant and rapid growth in amount of information and the number of users. Particularly, Web users usually suffer from the difficulties in finding desirable and accurate information on the Web due to two problems of low precision and low recall caused by above reasons. For example, if a user wants to search for the desired information by utilizing a search engine such as Google, the search engine will provide not only Web contents related to the query topic, but also a large mount of irrelevant information (or called noisy pages), which results in difficulties for users to obtain their exactly needed information. Thus, these bring forward a great deal of challenges for Web researchers to address the challenging research issues of effective and efficient Web-based information management and retrieval.

Web Mining aims to discover the informative knowledge from massive data sources available on the Web by using data mining or machine learning approaches. Different from conventional data mining techniques, in which data models are usually in homogeneous and structured forms, Web mining approaches, instead, handle semi-structured or heterogeneous data representations, such as textual, hyperlink structure and usage information, to discover "nuggets" to improve the quality of services offered by various Web applications. Such applications cover a wide range of topics, including retrieving the desirable and related Web contents, mining and analyzing Web communities, user profiling, and customizing Web presentation according to users preference and so on. For example, Web recommendation and personalization is one kind of these applications in Web mining that focuses on identifying Web users and pages, collecting information with respect to users navigational preference or interests as well as adapting its service to satisfy users needs.

On the other hand, for the data on the Web, it has its own distinctive features from the data in conventional database management systems. Web data usually exhibits the following characteristics: the data on the Web is huge in amount, distributed, hetero-geneous, unstructured, and dynamic. To deal withe the heterogeneity and complexity characteristics of Web data, Web community has emerged as a new efficient Web data management means to model Web objects. Unlike the conventional database management, in which data models and schemas are well defined, Web community, which is a set of Web-based objects (documents and users) has its own logical struc-tures. Web communities could be modeled as Web page groups, Web user clusters and co-clusters of Web pages and users. Web community construction is realized via various approaches on Web textual, linkage, usage, semantic or ontology-based analysis. Recently the research of Social Network Analysis in the Web has become a newly active topic due to the prevalence of Web 2.0 technologies, which results in an inter-disciplinary research area of Social Networking. Social networking refers to the process of capturing the social and societal characteristics of networked structures or communities over the Web. Social networking research involves in the combination of a variety of research paradigms, such as Web mining, Web communities, social network analysis and behavioral and cognitive modeling and so on.

This book will systematically address the theories, techniques and applications that are involved in Web Mining, Social Networking, Web Personalization and Rec-ommendation and Web Community Analysis topics. It covers the algorithmic and technical topics on Web mining, namely, Web Content Mining, Web linkage Mining and Web Usage Mining. As an application of Web mining, in particular, Web Person-alization and Recommendation is intensively presented. Another main part discussed in this book is Web Community Analysis and Social Networking. All technical con-tents are structured and discussed together around the focuses of Web mining and Social Networking at three levels of theoretical background, algorithmic description and practical applications.

This book will start with a brief introduction on Information Retrieval and Web Data Management. For easily and better understanding the algorithms, techniques and prototypes that are described in the following sections, some mathematical nota-tions and theoretical backgrounds are presented on the basis of *Information Retrieval* (IR), *Nature Language Processing, Data Mining* (DM), *Knowledge Discovery* (KD) and *Machine Learning* (ML) theories. Then the principles, and developed algorithms and systems on the research of Web Mining, Web Recommendation and Personaliza-tion, and Web Community and Social Network Analysis are presented in details in seven chapters. Moreover, this book will also focus on the applications of Web min-ing, such as how to utilize the knowledge mined from the aforementioned process for advanced Web applications. Particularly, the issues on how to incorporate Web mining into Web personalization and recommendation systems will be substantially addressed accordingly. Upon the informative Web knowledge discovered via Web mining, we then address Web community mining and social networking analysis to find the structural, organizational and temporal developments of Web communities as well as to reveal the societal sense of individuals or communities and its evo-lution over the Web by combining social network analysis. Finally, this book will summarize the main work mentioned regarding the techniques and applications of

Web mining, Web community and social network analysis, and outline the future directions and open questions in these areas.

This book is expected to benefit both research academia and industry communities, who are interested in the techniques and applications of Web search, Web data management, Web mining and Web recommendation as well as Web community and social network analysis, for either in-depth academic research and industrial development in related areas.

Aalborg, Melbourne, Wuhan   *Guandong Xu*
July 2010   *Yanchun Zhang*
                                                                   Lin Li

Acknowledgements: We would like to first appreciate Springer Press for giving us an opportunity to make this book published in the Web Information Systems Engineering & Internet Technologies Book Series. During the book writing and final production, Melissa Fearon, Jennifer Maurer and Patrick Carr from Springer gave us numerous helpful guidances, feedbacks and assistances, which ensure the academic and presentation quality of the whole book. We also thank Priyanka Sharan and her team, who commit and oversee the production of the text of our book from manuscript to final printer files, providing several rounds of proofing, comments and corrections on the pages of cover, front matter as well as each chapter. Their dedicated work to the matters of style, organization, and coverage, as well as detailed comments on the subject matter of the book adds the decorative elegance of the book in addition to its academic value. To the extent that we have achieved our goals in writing this book, they deserve an important part of the credit.

Many colleagues and friends have assisted us technically in writing this book, especially researchers from Prof. Masaru Kitsuregawa's lab at University of Tokyo . Without their help, this book might not have become reality so smoothly. Our deepest gratitude goes to Dr. Zhenglu Yang, who was so kind to help write the most parts of Chapter 3, which is an essential chapter of the book. He is an expert in the this field. We are also very grateful to Dr. Somboonviwat Kulwadee, who largely helped in the writing of Section 4.5 of Chapter 4 on automatic topic extraction. Chapter 5 utilizes a large amount of research results from the doctoral thesis provided by her as well. Mr. Yanhui Gu helps to prepare the section of 8.2.

We are very grateful to many people who have given us comments, suggestions, and proof readings on the draft version of this book. Our great gratitude passes to Dr. Yanan Hao and Mr. Jiangang Ma for their careful proof readings, Mr. Rong Pan for reorganizing and sorting the bibliographic file.

Last but not the least, Guandong Xu thanks his family for many hours they have let him spend working on this book, and hopes he will have a bit more free time on weekends next year. Yanchun Zhang thanks his family for their patient support through the writing of this book. Lin Li would like to thank her parents, family, and friends for their support while writing this book.

Contents

Part I

Foundation

1

Introduction

1.1 Background

With the dramatically quick and explosive growth of information available over the Internet, World Wide Web has become a powerful platform to store, disseminate and retrieve information as well as mine useful knowledge. Due to the huge, diverse, dynamic and unstructured nature in Web data, Web data research has encountered a lot of challenges, such as heterogeneous structure, distributed residence and scalability issues etc. As a result, Web users are always drowning in an "ocean" of information and facing the problem of information overload when interacting with the Web, for example. Typically, the following problems are often encountered in Web related researches and applications:

(1). Finding relevant information: To find specific information on the Web, a user often either browses Web documents directly or uses a search engine as a search assistant. When the user utilizes a search engine to locate information, he or she often enters one or several keywords as a query, then search engine returns a list of ranked pages based on the relevance to the query. However, there are usually two major concerns associated with the query-based Web search [140]. The first problem is low precision, which is caused by a lot of irrelevant pages returned by search engines. The second problem is low recall, which is due to lack of capability of indexing all Web pages available on the Internet. This causes the difficulty in locating the unindexed information that is actually relevant. How to find more relevant pages to the query, thus, is becoming a popular topic in Web data management in last decade [274].

(2). Finding needed information: Since most of search engines perform in a query-triggered way that is mainly on a basis of one keyword or several keywords entered. Sometimes the results returned by the search engine are not exactly matched with what a user really needs due to the fact of existence of homograph. For example, when one user with information technology background wishes to search for information with respect to "Python" programming language, he/she might be presented with the information of creatural python, one kind of snake rather than programming language, given entering only one "python" word as the query. In other words, semantics of Web data [97] is rarely taken into account in the context of Web search.

G. Xu et al., *Web Mining and Social Networking*,
DOI 10.1007/978-1-4419-7735-9_1, © Springer Science+Business Media, LLC 2011

(3). Learning useful knowledge: With traditional Web search service, query results relevant to query input are returned to Web users in a ranked list of pages. In some cases, we are interested in not only browsing the returned collection of Web pages, but also extracting potentially useful knowledge out of them (data mining oriented). More interestingly, more studies [56, 46, 58] have been conducted on how to utilize the Web as a knowledge base for decision making or knowledge discovery recently.

(4). Recommendation/personalization of information: While a user is interacting with Web, there is a wide diversity of the user's navigational preference, which results in needing different contents and presentations of information. To improve the Internet service quality and increase the user click rate on a specific website, thus, it is necessary for Web developers or designers to know what the user really wants to do, to predict which pages the user would be potentially interested in, and to present the customized Web pages to the user by learning user navigational pattern knowledge [97, 206, 183].

(5). Web communities and social networking: Opposite to traditional data schema in database management systems, Web objects exhibit totally different characteristics and management strategy [274]. Existence of inherent associations amongst Web objects is an important and distinct phenomenon on the Web. Such kind of relationships can be modeled as a graphic expression, where nodes denote the Web objects and edges represent the linking or collaboration between nodes. In these cases, Web community is proposed to deal with Web data, and in some extent, is extended to the applications of social networking.

Above problems greatly suffer the existing search engines and other Web applications, and hereby produce more demands for Web data and knowledge research. A variety of efforts have been contributed to deal with these difficulties by developing advanced computational intelligent techniques or algorithms from different research domains, such as database, data mining, machine learning, information retrieval and knowledge management, etc. Therefore, the evolution of Web has put forward a great deal of challenges to Web researchers and engineers on innovative Web-based data management strategy and effective Web application development.

Web search engine technology [196] has emerged to carter for the rapid growth and exponential flux of Web data on the Internet, to help Web users find desired information, and has resulted in various commercial Web search engines available online such as Yahoo!, Google, AltaVista, Baidu and so on. Search engines can be categorized into two types: one is general-purpose search engines and the other is specific-purpose search engines. The general-purpose search engines, for example, the well-known Google search engine, try to retrieve as many Web pages available on the Internet that is relevant to the query as possible to Web users. The returned Web pages to user are ranked in a sequence according to their relevant weights to the query, and the satisfaction to the search results from users is dependent on how quickly and how accurately users can find the desired information. The specific-purpose search engines, on the other hand, aim at searching those Web pages for a specific task or an identified community. For example, Google Scholar and DBLP are two representatives of the specific-purpose search engines. The former is a search engine for searching academic papers or books as well as their citation information for different disciplines, while the latter is designed for a specific researcher community, i.e. computer science, to provide various research information regarding conferences or journals in computer science domain, such as conference website, abstracts or full text of papers published in computer science journals or conference proceedings. DBLP has become a helpful and practicable tool for researchers or engineers in computer science area to find the needed literature easily, or for authorities to assess the track record of one researcher objectively. No matter which type the search engine is, each search engine owns a background text database, which is indexed by a set of keywords extracted from collected documents. To satisfy higher recall and accuracy rate of the search, Web search engines are requested to provide an efficient and effective mechanism to collect and manage the Web data, and the capabilities to match user queries with the background indexing database quickly and rank the returned Web contents in an efficient way that Web user can locate the desired Web pages in a short time via clicking a few hyperlinks. To achieve these aims, a variety of algorithms or strategies are involved in handling the above mentioned tasks [196, 77, 40, 112, 133], which lead to a hot and popular topic in the context of Web-based research, i.e. Web data management.

1.2 Data Mining and Web Mining

Data mining is proposed recently as a useful approach in the domain of data engineering and knowledge discovery [213]. Basically, data mining refers to extracting informative knowledge from large amount of data, which could be expressed in different data types, such as transaction data in e-commerce applications or genetic expressions in bioinformatics research domain. No matter which type of data it is, the main purpose of data mining is discovering hidden or unseen knowledge, normally in the forms of patterns, from available data repository. Association rule mining, sequential pattern mining, supervised learning and unsupervised learning algorithms are commonly used and well studied data mining approaches in last decades [213].

Nowadays data mining has attracted more and more attentions from academia and industries, and a great amount of progresses have been achieved in many applications. In the last decade, data mining has been successfully introduced into the research of Web data management, in which a board range of Web objects including Web documents, Web linkage structures, Web user transactions, Web semantics become the mined targets. Obviously, the informative knowledge mined from various types of Web data can provide us help in discovering and understanding the intrinsic relationships among various Web objects, in turn, will be utilized to benefit the improvement of Web data management [58, 106, 39, 10, 145, 149, 167].

As known above, the Web is a big data repository and source consisting of a variety of data types as well as a large amount of unseen informative knowledge, which can be discovered via a wide range of data mining or machine learning paradigms. All these kinds of techniques are based on intelligent computing approaches, or so-called computational intelligence, which are widely used in the research of database, data mining, machine learning, and information retrieval and so on.

Web (data) mining is one of the intelligent computing techniques in the context of Web data management. In general, Web mining is the means of utilizing data mining methods to induce and extract useful information from Web data information. Web mining research has attracted a variety of academics and engineers from database management, information retrieval, artificial intelligence research areas, especially from data mining, knowledge discovery, and machine learning etc. Basically, Web mining could be classified into three categories based on the mining goals, which determine the part of Web to be mined: Web content mining, Web structure mining, and Web usage mining [234, 140]. Web content mining tries to discover valuable information from Web contents (i.e. Web documents). Generally, Web content is mainly referred to textual objects, thus, it is also alternatively termed as text mining sometimes [50]. Web structure mining involves in modeling Web sites in terms of linking structures. The mutual linkage information obtained could, in turn, be used to construct Web page communities or find relevant pages based on the similarity or relevance between two Web pages. A successful application addressing this topic is finding relevant Web pages through linkage analysis [120, 137, 67, 234, 184, 174]. Web usage mining tries to reveal the underlying access patterns from Web transaction or user session data that recorded in Web log files [238, 99]. Generally, Web users are usually performing their interest-driven visits by clicking one or more functional Web objects. They may exhibit different types of access interests associated with their navigational tasks during their surfing periods. Thus, employing data mining techniques on the observed usage data may lead to finding underlying usage pattern. In addition, capturing Web user access interest or pattern can, not only provide help for better understanding user navigational behavior, but also for efficiently improving Web site structure or design. This, furthermore, can be utilized to recommend or predict Web contents tailored and personalized to Web users who can benefit from obtaining more preferred information and reducing waiting time [146, 119].

Discovering the latent semantic space from Web data by using statistical learning algorithms is another recently emerging research topic in Web knowledge discovery. Similar to semantic Web, semantic Web mining is considered as a new branch of Web mining research [121]. The abstract Web semantics along with other intuitive Web data forms, such as Web textual, linkage and usage information constitute a multidimensional and comprehensive data space for Web data analysis.

By using Web mining techniques, Web research academia has achieved substantial success in Web research areas, such as retrieving the desirable and related information [184], creating good quality Web community [137, 274], extracting informative knowledge out of available information [223], capturing underlying usage pattern from Web observation data [140], recommending or recommending user customized information to offer better Internet service [238], and furthermore mining valuable business information from the common or individual customers' navigational behavior as well [146].

Although much work has been done in Web-based data management and a great amount of achievements have been made so far, there still remain many open research problems to be solved in this area due to the fact of the distinctive characteristics of Web data, the complexity of Web data model, the diversity of various Web applications, the progress made in related research areas and the increased demands from Web users. How to efficiently and effectively address Web-based data management by using more advanced data processing techniques, thus, is becoming an active research topic that is full of many challenges.

1.3 Web Community and Social Network Analysis

1.3.1 Characteristics of Web Data

For the data on the Web, it has its own distinctive features from the data in conventional database management systems. Web data usually exhibits the following characteristics:

- The data on the Web is huge in amount. Currently, it is hard to estimate the exact data volume available on the Internet due to the exponential growth of Web data every day. For example, in 1994, one of the first Web search engines, the World Wide Web Worm (WWWW) had an index of 110,000 Web pages and Web accessible documents. As of November, 1997, the top search engines claim to index from 2 million (WebCrawler) to 100 million Web documents. The enormous volume of data on the Web makes it difficult to well handle Web data via traditional database techniques.
- The data on the Web is distributed and heterogeneous. Due to the essential property of Web being an interconnection of various nodes over the Internet, Web data is usually distributed across a wide range of computers or servers, which are located at different places around the world. Meanwhile, Web data is often exhibiting the intrinsic nature of multimedia, that is, in addition to textual information, which is mostly used to express contents; many other types of Web data, such as images, audio files and video slips are often included in a Web page. It requires the developed techniques for Web data processing with the ability of dealing with heterogeneity of multimedia data.
- The data on the Web is unstructured. There are, so far, no rigid and uniform data structures or schemas that Web pages should strictly follow, that are common requirements in conventional database management. Instead, Web designers are able to arbitrarily organize related information on the Web together in their own ways, as long as the information arrangement meets the basic layout requirements of Web documents, such as HTML format. Although Web pages in well-defined HTML format could contain some preliminary Web data structures, e.g. tags or anchors, these structural components, however, can primarily benefit the presentation quality of Web documents rather than reveal the semantics contained in Web documents. As a result, there is an increasing requirement to better deal with the unstructured nature of Web documents and extract the mutual relationships hidden in Web data for facilitating users to locate needed Web information or service.

- The data on the Web is dynamic. The implicit and explicit structure of Web data is updated frequently. Especially, due to different applications of Web-based data management systems, a variety of presentations of Web documents will be generated while contents resided in databases update. And dangling links and relocation problems will be produced when domain or file names change or disappear. This feature leads to frequent schema modifications of Web documents, which often suffer traditional information retrieval.

The aforementioned features indicate that Web data is a specific type of data different from the data resided in traditional database systems. As a result, there is an increasing demand to develop more advanced techniques to address Web information search and data management. The recently emerging Web community technology is a representative of new technical concepts that efficiently tackles the Web-based data management.

1.3.2 Web Community

Theoretically, Web Community is defined as an aggregation of Web objects in terms of Web pages or users, in which each object is "losely" related to the other under a certain distance space. Unlike the conventional database management in which data models and schemas are defined, a Web community, which is a set of Web-based objects (documents and users) that has its own logical structures, is another effective and efficient approach to reorganize Web-based objects, support information retrieval and implement various applications. Therefore, community centered Web data management systems provide more capabilities than database-centered ones in Web-based data management.

So far a large amount of research efforts have been contributed to the research of Web Community, and a great deal of successes have been achieved accordingly. According to the aims and purposes, these studies and developments are mainly about two aspects of Web data management, that is, how to accurately find the needed information on the Internet, i.e. Web information search, and how to efficiently and effectively manage and utilize the informative knowledge mined from the massive data on the Internet, i.e. Web data/knowledge management. For example, finding Web communities from a collected data source via linkage analysis is an active and hot topic in Web search and information filtering areas. In this case, a Web community is a Web page group, within which all members share similar hyperlink topology to a specific Web page. These discovered Web communities might be able to help users to find Web pages which are related to the query page in terms of hyperlink structures. In the scenario of e-commerce, market basket analysis is a very popular research problem in data mining, which aims to analyze the customer's behavior pattern during the online shopping process. Web usage mining through analyzing Web log files is proposed as an efficient analytical tool for business organizations to investigate various types of user navigational pattern of how customers access the e-commerce website. Here the Web communities expressed as categories of Web users represent the different customers' shopping behavior types.

1.3.3 Social Networking

Recently, with the popularity and development of innovative Web technologies, for example, semantic Web or Web 2.0, more and more advanced Web data based services and applications are emerging for Web users to easily generate and distribute Web contents, and conveniently share information in a collaborative environment. The core component of the second generation Web is Web-based communities and hosted services, such as social networking sites, wikis and folksonomies, which are characterized by the features of open-communication, decentralization of authority, and freedom to share and self-manage. These newly enhanced Web functionalities make it possible for Web users to share and locate the needed Web contents easily, to collaborate and interact with each other socially, and to realize knowledge utilization and management freely on the Web. For example, the social Web hosted service like *Myspace* and *Facebook* are becoming a global and influential information sharing and exchanging platform and data source in the world. As a result, Social Networks is becoming a newly emerging research topic in Web research although this term has appeared in social science, especially psychology in several decades ago. A social network is a representative of relationships existing within a community [276]. Social Networking provide us a useful means to study the mutual relationships and networked structures, often derived and expressed by collaborations amongst community peers or nodes, through theories developed in social network analysis and social computing [81, 117].

As we discussed, Web community analysis is to discover the aggregations of Web pages, users as well as co-clusters of Web objects. As a result, Web communities are always modeled as groups of pages and users, which can also be represented by various graphic expressions, for example, here the nodes denote the users, while the lines stand for the relationships between two users, such as pages commonly visited by these two users or email communications between senders and receivers. In other words, a Web community could be modeled as a network of users exchanging information or exhibiting common interest, that is, a social network. In this sense, the gap between Web community analysis and social network analysis is becoming closer and closer, many concepts and techniques used and developed in one area could be extended into the research area of the other.

In summary, with the prevalence and maturity of Web 2.0 technologies, the Web is becoming a useful platform and an influential source of data for individuals to share their information and express their opinions, and the collaboration or linking between various Web users is knitting as a community-centered social networking over the Web. From this viewing point, how to extend the current Web community analysis to a very massive data source to investigate the social behavior pattern or evaluation, or how to introduce the achievements from traditional social network analysis into Web data management to better interpret and understand the knowledge discovered, is bringing forward a huge amount of challenges that Web researchers and engineers have to face. Linking the two distinctive research areas, but with immanent underlying connection, and complementing the respective research strengths in a broad range to address the cross-disciplinary research problems of Web social communities and their behaviors is the most motivation and significance of this book.

1.4 Summary of Chapters

The whole book is divided into three parts. Part I (chapter 2-3) introduces the basic mathematical backgrounds, and algorithms and techniques used in this book for Web mining and social network analysis. This part forms a fundamental base for the further description and discussion. Part II (chapter 4-6) covers the major topics on Web data mining, one main aspect of this book. In particular, three kinds of Web data mining techniques, i.e. Web content (text) mining, Web linkage (structure) mining and Web usage mining, are intensively addressed in each chapter, respectively. Part III (chapter 7-8) focuses on the application aspect of this book, i.e. Web community, social networking and web recommendation. In this part, we aim at linking Web data mining with Web community, social network analysis and web recommendation, and presenting several practical systems and applications to highlight the application potentials arising from this inter-disciplinary area. Finally this book concludes the main research work discussed and interesting findings achieved, and outline the future research directions and the potential open research questions within the related areas. The coverage of each chapter presented is particularly summarized as follows:

Chapter 2 introduces the preliminary mathematical notations and background knowledge used. It covers matrix, sequence and graph expression of Web data in terms of Web textual, linkage and usage information; various similarity functions for measuring Web object similarity; matrix and tensor operations such as eigenvector, Singular Value Decomposition, tensor decomposition etc, as well as the basic concepts of Social Network Analysis.

Chapter 3 reviews and presents the algorithms and techniques developed in previous studies and systems, especially related data mining and machine learning algorithms and implementations are discussed as well.

Chapter 4 concentrates on the topic of Web content mining. The basic information retrieval models and and the principle of a typical search system are described first, and several studies on text mining, such as feature enrichment of short text, topic extraction, latent semantic indexing, and opinion mining and opinion spam together with experimental results are presented.

Chapter 5 is about Web linkage analysis. It starts with two well-known algorithms, i.e. HITS and PageRank, followed by the description of Web community discovery. In addition, this chapter presents the materials of modeling and measuring the Web with graph theory, and this chapter also demonstrates how linkage based analysis is used to increase Web search performance and capture the mutual relationships among Web pages.

Chapter 6 addresses another interesting topic in Web mining, i.e. Web usage mining. Web usage mining is to discover Web user access patterns from Web log files. This chapter first discusses how to measure the interest or preference similarity of Web users, and then presents algorithms and techniques of finding user aggregations and user profiles via Web clustering and latent semantic analysis. At the end of this chapter, a number of Web usage mining applications are reported to show the application potential in Web search and organization.

Chapter 7 describes the research issues of Web social networking using Web mining. Web community mining is first addressed to indicate the capability of Web mining in social network analysis. Then it focuses on the topics of temporal characteristics and dynamic evolutions of networked structures in the context of Web social environments. To illustrate the application potential, a real world case study is presented in this chapter along with some informative and valuable findings.

Chapter 8 reviews the extension of Web mining in Web personalization and recommendation. Starting from the introduction the well-known collaborative filtering based recommender systems, this chapter talks about the combination of Web usage mining and collaborative filtering for Web page and Web query recommendation. By presenting some empirical results from developed techniques and systems, this chapter gives the evidenced values of the integration of Web mining techniques with recommendation systems in real applications.

Chapter 9 concludes the research work included in this book, and outlines several active and hot research topics and open questions recently emerging in these areas.

1.5 Audience of This Book

This book is aiming at a reference book for both academic researchers and industrial practitioners who are working on the topics of Web search, information retrieval, Web data mining, Web knowledge discovery and social network analysis, the development of Web applications and the analysis of social networking. This book can also be used as a text book for postgraduate students and senior undergraduate students in Computer Science, Information Science, Statistics and Social Behavior Science.

This book has the following features:

- systematically presents and discusses the mathematical background and representative algorithms for Web mining, Web community analysis and social networking as well;
- thoroughly reviews the related studies and outcomes conducted on the addressed topics;
- substantially demonstrates various important applications in the areas of Web mining, Web community and social behavior and network analysis; and
- heuristically outlines the open research questions of the inter-disciplinary research topics, and identifies several future research directions that readers may be interested in.

2

Theoretical Backgrounds

As discussed, Web data involves in a complex structure and heterogeneous nature. The analysis on the Web data needs a broad range of concepts, theories and approaches and a variety of application backgrounds. In order to help readers to better understand the algorithms and techniques introduced in the book, it is necessary to prepare some basic and fundamental background knowledge, which also forms a solid theoretical base for this book. In this chapter, we first present some theoretical backgrounds and review them briefly.

We first give an introduction of Web data models, particularly the data expressions of textual, linkage and usage. Then the basic theories of linear algebra especially the operations of matrix and tensor are discussed. The two essential concepts and approaches in Information Retrieval - similarity measures and evaluation metrics, are summarized as well. In addition, some basic concepts of social networks are addressed in this chapter.

2.1 Web Data Model

It is well known that the Internet has become a very popular and powerful platform to store, disseminate and retrieve information as well as a data respiratory for knowledge discovery. However, Web users always suffer the problems of information overload and drowning due to the significant and rapid growth in amount of information and the number of users. The problems of low precision and low recall rate caused by above reasons are two major concerns that users have to deal with while searching for the needed information over the Internet. On the other hand, the huge amount of data/information resided over the Internet contains very valuable informative knowledge that could be discovered via advanced data mining approaches. It is believed that mining this kind of knowledge will greatly benefit Web site design and Web application development, and prompt other related applications, such as business intelligence, e-Commerce, and entertainment broadcast etc. Thus, the emerging of Web has put forward a great deal of challenges to Web researchers for Web-based

G. Xu et al., *Web Mining and Social Networking*,
DOI 10.1007/978-1-4419-7735-9_2, © Springer Science+Business Media, LLC 2011

information management and retrieval. Web researcher and engineer are requested to develop more efficient and effective techniques to satisfy the demands of Web users.

Web data mining is one kind of these techniques that efficiently handle the tasks of searching needed information from the Internet, improving Web site structure to improve the Internet service quality and discovering informative knowledge from the Internet for advanced Web applications. In principle, Web mining techniques are the means of utilizing data mining methods to induce and extract useful information from Web information and service. Web mining research has attracted a variety of academics and researchers from database management, information retrieval, artificial intelligence research areas especially from knowledge discovery and machine learning, and many research communities have addressed this topic in recent years due to the tremendous growth of data contents available on the Internet and urgent needs of e-commerce applications especially. Dependent on various mining targets, Web data mining could be categorized into three types of Web content, Web structure and Web usage mining. In the following chapters, we will systematically present the research studies and applications carried out in the context of Web content, Web linkage and Web usage mining

To implement Web mining efficiently, it is essential to first introduce a solid mathematical framework, on which the data mining/analysis is performed. There are many types of data expressions could be used to model the co-occurrence of interactions between Web users and pages, such as matrix, directed graph and click sequence and so on. Different data expression models have different mathematical and theoretical backgrounds, and therefore resulting in various algorithms and approaches. In particular, we mainly adopt the commonly used matrix expression as the analytic scheme, which is widely used in various Web mining context. Under this scheme, the interactive observations between Web users and pages, and the mutual relationships between Web pages are modeled as a co-occurrence matrix, such as in the form of page hyperlink adjacent (inlink or outlink) matrix or session-pageview matrix. Based on the proposed mathematical framework, a variety of data mining and analysis operations can be employed to conduct Web mining.

2.2 Textual, Linkage and Usage Expressions

As described, the starting point of Web mining is to choose appropriate data models. To achieve the desired mining tasks discussed above, there are different Web data models in the forms of feature vectors, engaged in pattern mining and knowledge discovery. According to the three identified categories of Web mining, three types of Web data/sources, namely content data, structure data and usage data, are mostly considered in the context of Web mining. Before we start to propose different Web data models, we firstly give a brief discussion on these three data types in the following paragraphs.

Web content data is a collection of objects used to convey content information of Web pages to users. In most cases, it is comprised of textural material and other types of multimedia content, which include static HTML/XML pages, images, sound and video files, and dynamic pages generated from scripts and databases. The content data also includes semantic or structured meta-data embedded within the site or individual pages. In addition, the domain ontology might be considered as a complementary type of content data hidden in the site implicitly or explicitly. The underlying domain knowledge could be incorporated into Web site design in an implicit manner, or be represented in some explicit forms. The explicit form of domain ontology can be conceptual hierarchy e.g. product category, and structural hierarchy such as yahoo directory etc [206].

Web structure data is a representation of linking relationship between Web pages, which reflects the organizational concept of a site from the viewing point of the designer [119]. It is normally captured by the inter-page linkage structure within the site, which is called linkage data. Particularly, the structure data of a site is usually represented by a specific Web component, called "site map", which is generated automatically when the site is completed. For dynamically generated pages, the site mapping is becoming more complicated to perform since more techniques are required to deal with the dynamic environment.

Web usage data is mainly sourced from Web log files, which include Web server access logs and application server logs [234, 194]. The log data collected at Web access or application servers reflects the navigational behavior knowledge of users in terms of access pattern. In the context of Web usage mining, usage data that we need to deal with is transformed and abstracted at different levels of aggregations, namely Web page set and user session collection. Web page is a basic unit of Web site organization, which contains a number of meaningful units serving for the main functionality of the page. Physically, a page is a collection of Web items, generated statically or dynamically, contributing to the display of the results in response to a user request. A page set is a collection of whole pages within a site. User session is a sequence of Web pages clicked by a single user during a specific period. A user session is usually dominated by one specific navigational task, which is exhibited through a set of visited relevant pages that contribute greatly to the task conceptually. The navigational interest/preference on one particular page is represented by its significance weight value, which is dependent on user visiting duration or click number. The user sessions (or called usage data), which are mainly collected in the server logs, can be transformed into a processed data format for the purpose of analysis via data preparing and cleaning process. In one word, usage data is a collection of user sessions, which is in the form of a weighted vector over the page space.

Matrix expression has been widely used to model the co-occurrence activity like Web data. The illustration of a matrix expression for Web data is shown in Fig.2.1. In this scheme, the rows and columns correspond to various Web objects which are dependent on various Web data mining tasks. In the context of Web content mining, the relationships between a set of documents and a set of keyword could be represented by a document-keyword co-occurrence matrix, where the lows of the matrix represent the documents, while the columns of the matrix correspond to the keywords. The intersection value of the matrix indicates the occurrence of a specific keyword appeared in a particular document, i.e. if a keyword appears in a document, the corresponding matrix element value is 1, otherwise 0. Of course, the element value could also be a precise weight rather than 1 or 0 only, which exactly reflects the occurrence degree of two concerned objects of document and keyword. For example, the element value could represent the frequent rate of a specific keyword in a specific document. Likewise, to model the linkage information of a Web site, an adjacent matrix is used to represent the relationships between pages via their hyperlinks. And usually the element of the adjacent matrix is defined by the hyperlink linking two pages, that is, if there is a hyperlink from page i to page j ($i \neq j$), then the value of the element a_{ij} is 1, otherwise 0. Since the linking relationship is directional, i.e. given a hyperlink directed from page i to page j, then the link is an out-link for i, while an in-link for j, and vice versa. In this case, the ith row of the adjacent matrix, which is a page vector, represents the out-link relationships from page i to other pages; the jth column of the matrix represents the in-link relationships linked to page i from other pages.

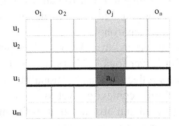

Fig. 2.1. The schematic illustration of Web data matrix model

In Web usage mining, we can model one user session as a page vector in a similar way. As the user access interest exhibited may be reflected by the varying degree of visits on different Web pages during one session, we can represent a user session as a collection of pages visited in the period along with their significant weights. The total collection of user sessions can, then, be expressed a usage matrix, where the ith row is the sequence of pages visited by user i during this period; and the jth column of the matrix represents the fact which users have clicked this page j in the server log file. The element value of the matrix, a_{ij}, reflects the access interest exhibited by user i on page j, which could be used to derive the underlying access pattern of users.

2.3 Similarity Functions

A variety of similarity functions can be used as measuring metrics in vector space. Among these measures, Pearson correlation coefficient and cosine similarity are two well-known and widely used similarity functions in information retrieval and recommender systems [218, 17].

2.3.1 Correlation-based Similarity

Pearson correlation coefficient, which is to calculate the deviations of users' ratings on various items from their mean ratings on the rated items, is a commonly used similarity function in traditional collaborative filtering approaches, where the attribute weight is expressed by a feature vector of numeric ratings on various items, e.g. the rating can be from 1 to 5 where 1 stands for the lest like voting and 5 for the most preferable one. The Pearson correlation coefficient can well deal with collaborative filtering since all ratings are on a discrete scale rather than on an analogous scale. The measure is described below. Given two users i and j, and their rating vectors R_i and R_j, the Pearson correlation coefficient is then defined by:

$$sim(i,j) = corr(R_i, R_j) = \frac{\sum\limits_{k=1}^{n} \left(R_{i,k} - \overline{R_i}\right)\left(R_{j,k} - \overline{R_j}\right)}{\sqrt{\sum\limits_{k=1}^{n} \left(R_{i,k} - \overline{R_i}\right)^2 \sum\limits_{k=1}^{n} \left(R_{j,k} - \overline{R_j}\right)^2}} \tag{2.1}$$

where $R_{i,k}$ denotes the rating of user i on item k, $\overline{R_i}$ is the average rating of user i.

However, this measure is not appropriate in the Web mining scenario where the data type encountered (i.e. user session) is actually a sequence of analogous page weights. To address this intrinsic property of usage data, the cosine coefficient is a better choice instead, which is to measure the cosine function of angle between two feature vectors. Cosine function is widely used in information retrieval research.

2.3.2 Cosine-Based Similarity

Since in a vector expression form, any vector could be considered as a line in a multiple-dimensional space, it is intuitive to define the similarity (or distance) between two vectors as the cosine function of angle between two "lines". In this manner, the cosine coefficient can be calculated by the ratio of the dot product of two vectors with respect to their vector norms. Given two vectors A and B, the cosine similarity is then defined as:

$$sim(A,B) = \cos\left(\overrightarrow{A}, \overrightarrow{B}\right) = \frac{\overrightarrow{A} \cdot \overrightarrow{B}}{\left|\overrightarrow{A}\right| \times \left|\overrightarrow{B}\right|} \tag{2.2}$$

where "·" denotes the dot operation and "×" the norm form.

2.4 Eigenvector, Principal Eigenvector

In linear algebra, there are two kinds of objects: scalars, which are just numbers, and vectors, which can be considered as arrows in a space, and which have both magnitude and direction (though more precisely a vector is a member of a vector space). In the context of traditional functions of algebra, the most important functions in linear algebra are called "linear transformations", and particularly in the context of vector, a linear transformation is usually given by a "matrix", a multi-array of numbers. In order to avoid the confusion in mathematical expression, here the linear transformation of matrix is denoted by $\mathbf{M}(\mathbf{v})$ instead of $f(x)$ where $\mathbf{M}$ is a matrix and $\mathbf{v}$ is a vector.

If A is an n-by-n matrix, then there is a scalar number λ for $\mathbf{A}$ and a nonzero vector $\mathbf{v}$ (called an eigenvector for A associated to λ) so that $\mathbf{Av} = \lambda \mathbf{v}$. The eigenspace corresponding to one eigenvalue of a given matrix is the set of all eigenvectors of the matrix with that eigenvalue.

$$E(\lambda) = \{\mathbf{v} : \mathbf{Av} = \lambda \mathbf{v}\} = \{\mathbf{v} : (\mathbf{A} - \lambda \mathbf{I})\mathbf{v} = 0\} \tag{2.3}$$

The basic equation $\mathbf{Av} = \lambda \mathbf{v}$ can be rewritten as $(\mathbf{A} - \lambda \mathbf{I})\mathbf{v} = 0$. For a given λ, its eigenvectors are nontrivial solutions of $(\mathbf{A} - \lambda \mathbf{I})\mathbf{v} = 0$. When this equation is regarded as an equation in the variable λ, it becomes a polynomial of degree n in λ. Since a polynomial of degree n has at most n distinct answers, this could be transformed to a solving process of at most n eigenvalues for a given matrix. The eigenvalues are arranged in a ordered sequence, and the largest eigenvalue of a matrix is called the principal eigenvalue of the given matrix. Particularly, in some specific applications of matrix decomposition with eigenvalue like in *Principal Component Analysis* (PCA) or *Singular Value Decomposition* (SVD), some eigenvalues after a certain position in the ordered eigenvalue sequence are decreased to very small values such that they are truncated by that certain position and discarded. Then the remaining eigenvalues are left together to form an estimated fraction of matrix decomposition. This estimate is then used to reflect the correlation criterion of approximation of the row and column attributes. In case that eigenvalues are known, they could be used to compute the eigenvector of the matrix, which is also called latent vectors of matrix $\mathbf{A}$.

Eigenvalues and eigenvectors are widely used in a variety of applications that involve in the computation of matrix. In spectral graph theory, for example, an eigenvalue of a graph is defined as an eigenvalue of the graph's adjacency matrix $\mathbf{A}$, or of the graph's Laplacian matrix, which is either $\mathbf{T} - \mathbf{A}$ or $\mathbf{I} - \mathbf{T}^{-1/2}\mathbf{AT}^{1/2}$, where T is a diagonal matrix holding the degree of each vertex. The kth principal eigenvector of a graph is defined as either the eigenvector corresponding to the kth largest eigenvalue of $\mathbf{A}$, or the eigenvector corresponding to the kth smallest eigenvalue of the Laplacian matrix. The first principal eigenvector of the graph is also referred to as the principal eigenvector. In spectral graph applications, principal eigenvectors are usually used to measure the significance of vertices in the graph. For example, in Google's PageRank algorithm, the principal vector is used to calculate the centrality (i.e. hub or authority score) of nodes if the websites over the Internet are modeled as a complete directed graph. Another application is that the second smallest eigenvector can be used to partition the graph into clusters via spectral clustering.

In summary, given the operation of a matrix performed on a (nonzero) vector changing its magnitude but not its direction, then the vector is called an eigenvector of that matrix. The scalar which is used to complete the operation by multiplying the eigenvector is called the eigenvalue corresponding to that eigenvector. For a given matrix, there exist many eigenvalues, each of them could be used to calculate the eigenvectors.

2.5 Singular Value Decomposition (SVD) of Matrix

The standard LSI algorithm is based on SVD operation. The SVD definition of a matrix is illustrated as follows [69]: For a real matrix $A = [a_{ij}]_{m \times n}$, without loss of generality, suppose $m \geq n$, there exists a SVD of A (shown in Fig.2.2)

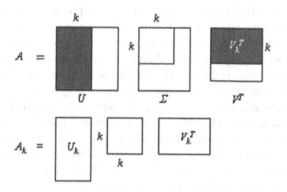

Fig. 2.2. Illustration of SVD approximation

$$A = U \begin{pmatrix} \Sigma_1 \\ 0 \end{pmatrix} V^T = U_{m \times m} \sum\nolimits_{m \times n} V_{n \times n}^T \tag{2.4}$$

where U and V are orthogonal matrices $U^T U = I_m$, $V^T V = I_n$. Matrices U and V can be respectively denoted as $U_{m \times m} = [u_1, u_2, \cdots u_m]_{m \times m}$ and $V_{n \times n} = [v_1, v_2, \cdots v_n]_{n \times n}$, where u_i, $(i = 1, \cdots, m)$ is a m-dimensional vector $u_i = (u_{1i}, u_{2i}, \cdots u_{mi})^T$ and v_j, $(j = 1, \cdots, n)$ is a n-dimensional vector $v_j = (v_{1j}, v_{2j}, \cdots v_{nj})^T$. Suppose $rank(A) = r$ and the single values of A are diagonal elements of σ as follows:

$$\Sigma = \begin{bmatrix} \sigma_1 & 0 & \cdots & 0 \\ 0 & \sigma_2 & \ddots & \vdots \\ \vdots & \ddots & \ddots & 0 \\ 0 & \cdots & 0 & \sigma_n \end{bmatrix} = diag(\sigma_1, \sigma_2, \cdots \sigma_m) \tag{2.5}$$

where $\sigma_i \geq \sigma_{i+1} > 0$, for $1 \leq i \leq r - 1$; $\sigma_j = 0$, for $j \geq r + 1$, that is $\sigma_1 \geq \sigma_2 \geq \cdots \sigma_r \geq \sigma_{r+1} = \cdots = \sigma_n = 0$

For a given threshold $\varepsilon (0 < \varepsilon < 1$, choose a parameter k such that $(\sigma_k - \sigma_{k+1})/\sigma_k \geq \varepsilon$. Then, denote $U_k = [u_1, \cdots, u_k]_{m \times k}$, $V_k = [v_1, \cdots, v_k]_{n \times k}$, $\Sigma_k = diag(\sigma_1, \cdots, \sigma_k)$, and $A_k = U_k \Sigma_k V_k^T$.

As known from the theorem in algebra [69], A_k is the best approximation matrix to A and conveys the maximum latent information among the processed data. This property makes it possible to find out the underlying semantic association from original feature space with a dimensionality-reduced computational cost, in turn, is able to be used for latent semantic analysis.

2.6 Tensor Expression and Decomposition

In this section, we will discuss the basic concepts of tensor, which is a mathematical expression in a multi-dimensional space. As seen in previous sections, matrix is an efficient means that could be used to reflect the relationship between two types of subjects. For example, the author-article in the context of scientific publications or document-keyword in applications of digital library. No matter in which scenario the common characteristics is the fact which each row is a linear combination of values along different column or each column is represented by a vector of entries in row space. Matrix-based computing possesses the powerful capability to handle the encountered problem in most real life problems since sometimes it is possible to model these problems as two-dimensional problems. But in a more complicated sense, while matrices have only two "dimensions" (e.g., "authors" and "publications"), we may often need more, like "authors", "keywords", "timestamps","conferences". This is exactly a high-order problem, which, in fact, is generally a tensor represents. In short, from the perspective of data model, tensor is a generalized and expressive model of high-dimensional space, and of course, a tensor is a generalization of a matrix (and of a vector, and of a scalar). Thus, it is intuitive and necessary to envision all such problems as tensor problems, to use the vast existing work for tensors to our benefit, and to adopt tensor analysis tools into our interested research arenas. Below we discuss the mathematical notations of tensor related concepts and definitions.

First of all, we introduce some fundamental terms in tensor which have different meanings in the context of two-dimensional cases. In particular we use order, mode and dimension to denote the equivalent concepts of dimensionality, dimension and attribute value we often encounter and use in linear algebra. For example a 3rd-order tensor means a three-dimensional data expression. To use the distinctive mathematical symbols to denote the different terms in tensor, we introduce the following notations:

- Scalars are denoted by lowercase letter, a.
- Vectors are denoted by boldface lowercase letters, **a**. The ith entry of **a** is denoted by $\mathbf{a}_i$.
- Matrices are denoted by boldface capital letters, e.g., **A**. The jth column of **A** is donated by $\mathbf{a}_j$ and element by a_{ij}.
- Tensors, in multi-way arrays, are denoted by italic boldface letters, e.g., X. Element (i, j, k) of a 3rd-order tensor X is denoted by X_{ijk}.
- As known, a tensor of order M closely resembles a Data Cube with M dimensions. Formally, we write an Mth order tensor $X \in R^{N_1 \times N_2 \times \cdots N_m}$, where N_i,

$(1 \leq i \leq M)$ is the dimensionality of the ith mode . For brevity, we often omit the subscript $[N_1, \cdots, N_M]$.

Furthermore, from the tensor literature we need the following definitions [236]:

Definition 2.1. *(Matricizing or Matrix Unfolding) [236]. The mode-d matricizing or matrix unfolding of an Mth order tensor* $X \in R^{N_1 \times N_2 \times \cdots N_m}$ *are vectors in* R^{N_d} *obtained by keeping index d fixed and varying the other indices. Therefore, the mode-d matricizing* $X_{(d)}$ *is in* $R^{\Pi_{i \neq d}(N_i) \times N_d}$.

Definition 2.2. *(Mode Product)[236]. The mode product* $X \times_d U$ *of a tensor* $X \in R^{N_1 \times N_2 \times \cdots N_m}$ *and a matrix* $U \in R^{N_d \times N'}$ *is the tensor in* $R^{N_1 \times \cdots \times N_{d-1} \times N' \times N_{d+1} \times \cdots \times N_M}$ *defined by:*

$$X \times_d U(i_1, \ldots, i_{d-1}, j, i_{d+1}, \ldots, i_M) = \sum_{i_d=1}^{N_i} X(i_1, \ldots, i_{d-1}, i_d, i_{d+1}, \ldots, i_M) U(i_d, j) \tag{2.6}$$

for all index values.

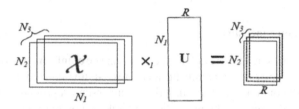

Fig. 2.3. An example of multiplication of a 3rd-order tensor with a matrix

Figure 2.3 shows an example of 3rd order tensor X mode-1 multiplies a matrix U. The process consists of three operations: first matricizing X along mode-1, then doing matrix multiplication of $\times_1$ and U, finally folding the result back as a tensor.

Upon definition 2.1, we can perform a series of multiplications of a tensor $X \in R^{N_1 \times N_2 \times \cdots N_m}$ and $U_i \big|_{i=1}^{M} \in R^{N_i \times D_i}$ as: $X \times_1 U_1 \ldots \times_m U_M \in R^{D_1 \times \cdots \times D_M}$, which can be written as $X \prod_{i=1}^{M} \times_i U_i$ for clarity. Furthermore, we express the following multiplications of all U_j except the i-th i.e. $X \times_1 U_1 \cdots \times_{i-1} U_{i-1} \times_{i+1} U_{i+1} \cdots \times_M U_M$ as $X \prod_{j \neq i} \times_j U_j$.

Definition 2.3. *(Rank-$(R_1, \cdots, R_M)$ approximation). Given a tensor* $X \in R^{N_1 \times \cdots N_M}$, *its best Rank-$D_1, \cdots, D_M$ approximation is the tensor* $\tilde{X} \in R^{D_1 \times \cdots \times D_M}$ *with* rank $(\tilde{X}_{(d)}) = D_d$ *for* $1 \leq d \leq M$, *which satisfies the optimal criterion of least-square-error, i.e.* $\arg \min \|X - \tilde{X}\|_F^2$.

The best Rank-$(R_1, \cdots, R_M)$ approximation is $\tilde{X} = Y \prod\limits_{j=1}^{M} \times_j U_j$, where the tensor Y is the core tensor of approximation, $Y \in R^{N_1 \times \cdots \times N_M}$ and $U_j \big|_{j=1}^{M} \in R^{N_j \times D_j}$ is the projection matrices.

2.7 Information Retrieval Performance Evaluation Metrics

An information retrieval process begins when a user enters a query into the system. A query is a collection of keywords that represent the information needs of the user, for example search terms in Web search engines. In information retrieval a query does not uniquely identify a single object in the information repository. Instead, several objects may match the query, perhaps with different degrees of relevancy. Each information piece is crawled from the Web and stored in the repository, i.e. database with an index or metadata in the IR systems.

Most IR systems compute a numeric score on how well each object in the database matches the query, and rank the objects according to this value. The ranked results are then returned to the user for browsing. Therefore, using various matching and ranking mechanisms results in totally different search results, in turn, arising a great challenging in evaluating the performance of IR systems [17].

2.7.1 Performance measures

Many different measures for evaluating the performance of information retrieval systems have been proposed. Apparently the measures require a collection of documents and a query. All common measures described here assume a ground truth notion of relevancy: every document is known to be either relevant or non-relevant to a particular query [2].

Precision

Precision is the fraction of the documents retrieved that are relevant to the user's information need.

$$\text{precision} = \frac{|\{\text{retrieved documents}\}| \cap |\{\text{relevant documents}\}|}{|\{\text{retrieved documents}\}|} \qquad (2.7)$$

In binary classification, precision is analogous to positive predictive value. Precision takes all retrieved documents into account. It means how many percentages of retrieved documents are relevant to the query.

Recall

Recall is the fraction of the documents that are relevant to the query that are successfully retrieved.

$$recall = \frac{|\{retrieved\ documents\}| \cap |\{relevant\ documents\}|}{|\{relevant\ documents\}|} \tag{2.8}$$

In binary classification, recall is called sensitivity. So it can be considered as the how many percentages of relevant documents are correctly retrieved by the query.

F-measure

The traditional F-measure or balanced F-score is defined by taking both of precision and recall into account:

$$F = \frac{2 \cdot precision \cdot recall}{precision + recall} \tag{2.9}$$

This is also sometimes known as the F_1 measure, because recall and precision are evenly weighted. An ideal search mechanism or IR system requires finding as many relevant documents from all relevant existing in the repository as possible, but sometimes it is not easy to achieve the optimal results simultaneously. Thus F-measure (or sometimes called F-score) gives an overall performance indicator of the system.

Mean Average Precision (MAP)

Precision and recall are single-value metrics based on the whole list of documents returned by the system. For systems that return a ranked sequence of documents, it is desirable to also consider the order in which the returned documents are presented. Average precision reflects ranking relevant documents higher. It is the average of precisions computed at the point of each of the relevant documents in the ranked sequence:

$$MAP = \frac{\sum_{n=1}^{N} P@(n) \cdot rel(n)}{|relevant\ documents|} \tag{2.10}$$

where n is the rank, N the number retrieved, $rel(n)$ a binary function indicating the relevance of page at the given rank n, and $P@(n)$ precision at a given cut-off rank that defined: $P(n) = \frac{|relevant\ retrieved\ documents\ at\ or\ below\ rank\ n|}{n}$

Discounted Cumulative Gain (DCG)

In the cases of using a graded relevance scale of documents rather than a binary value of relevance in a search engine result set, the above metrics could not effectively measure the performance required. To deal with this, in particular, another evaluation quantity i.e. *Discounted Cumulative Gain* (DCG) is proposed to measure the usefulness, or gain, of a document based on its position in the result list. The gain is accumulated cumulatively from the top of the result list to the bottom with the gain of each result discounted at lower ranks.

The premise of DCG is that highly relevant documents should ideally appear higher in a search result list to achieve the bigger accumulated gain. Otherwise it would be penalized as the graded relevance value is reduced logarithmically proportional to the position of the result. The discounted CG accumulated at a particular rank position p is defined as [123]:

$$DCG_p = rel_1 + \sum_{i=2}^{p} \frac{rel_i}{\log_2 i} \tag{2.11}$$

2.7.2 Web Recommendation Evaluation Metrics

There are a number of evaluation measures for Web recommendation, here we list three metrics mostly mentioned in the context of Web usage mining and Web recommendation - Mean Absolute Error, Weighted Average Visit Percentage and Hit Ratio.

Mean Absolute Error (MAE) is a widely used metric in the context of recommender systems, which compares the numerical recommendation scores against the actual user rating for the user-item pair in the test dataset [222]. *MAE* considers the deviation of recommendations against the true user-rating scores and calculates the average of the deviation sum. Given a prediction score p_i for an item with a actual rating score q_i by the user, *MAE* is expressed by

$$MAE = \frac{\sum_{i=1}^{N} |p_i - q_i|}{N} \tag{2.12}$$

The lower the MAE, the more accurately the recommendation systems perform.

The second metric, named the *Weighted Average Visit Percentage* (WAVP) [184], is used to evaluate the quality of user profiling in recommendation systems [258]. This evaluation method is based on assessing each user profile individually according to the likelihood that a user session which contains any pages in the session cluster will include the rest pages in the cluster during the same session. The calculating procedure of *WAVP* metric is discussed as follows: suppose T is one of transaction set within the evaluation set, and for s specific cluster C, let T_c denote a subset of T whose elements contain at least one pageview from C. Moreover, the weighted average visit percentage of T_c may conceptually be determined by the similarity between T_c and the cluster C if we consider the T_c and C as in the form of pageview vector. Therefore, the *WAVP* is computed as:

$$WAVP = \left(\sum_{t \in T_c} \frac{t \cdot C}{|T_c|} \right) \bigg/ \left(\sum_{p \in SCL} wt(p, SCL) \right) \tag{2.13}$$

where *SCL* represents the use session cluster, $wt(p, SCL)$ is the weight of page p in session cluster *SCL*. More details refers to [258].

From the definition of *WAVP*, it is known that the higher the *WAVP* value, the better quality of the obtained user profiles is.

The third metric is called *hit ratio* [128] that measures the effectiveness in the context of top-N Web recommendation. Given a user session in the test set, we extract the first j pages as an active session to generate a top-N recommendation set. Since the recommendation set is in a descending order, we then obtain the rank of $j+1$ page in the sorted recommendation list. Furthermore, for each rank $r > 0$, we sum the number of test data that exactly rank the rth as $Nb(r)$. Let $S(r) = \sum_{i=1}^{r} Nb(i)$, and the hit ratio hr is defined as

$$hr = S(N)/|T| \tag{2.14}$$

where $|T|$ represents the number of testing data in the whole test set.

Thus, hr stands for the hit precision of Web recommendation process. Apparently, the hr is monotonically increasing with the number of recommendation - the bigger value of N (number of recommendations) the more accurate recommendation is.

2.8 Basic Concepts in Social Networks

2.8.1 Basic Metrics of Social Network

In the context of social network analysis, some basic concepts or metrics are well used to analyze the connections or interactions between vertexes in the network. Many measures are defined from the perspectives of psychology, sociology and behavior science. Even with more powerful computing paradigms are introduced into social network analysis, they still form a solid foundation for advanced social network analysis. Let's first look at some of them.

Size

Size means the number of vertexes presented in a network, and is essential to calculate other measures. This parameter can give us a general idea of how large the network is.

Centrality

Centrality gives a rough indication of the social power of a vertex in the network based on how well it impacts the network. "Betweenness", "Closeness" and "Degree" are all measures of centrality.

Density and Degree

In real social networks, the fully connected network is rarely happened instead, the less connected network is more often. In order to measure how dense the vertexes in the network are associated, *Density* measure is introduced. Given a network consisting of n vertexes, the total edges or ties between all possible vertexes are in a size of $n \times (n-1)$. Hence *Density* denotes the ratio of the number of all existing edges to the total possible number of edges in the network. *Degree* is the actual number of edges contained in the network.

Betweenness and Closeness

Betweenness and *Closeness* are both the magnitude measures that reflect the relationships of one vertex to the others in the network.

Clique

Clique represents, in the context of social network, a sub-set of a network in which vertexes are more closely connected to one another than to other members of the network. In some extents, clique is a similar concept to community, which means the members within the same group have a high similarity in some aspects, such as cultural or religious belief, interests or preferences and so on. The clique membership gives us a measure of how likely one vertex in the network belongs to a specific clique or community.

2.8.2 Social Network over the Web

Interactions and relationships between entities can be represented with an interconnected network or graph, where each node represents an entity and each link represents an interaction or a relationship between a pair of entities. Social network analysis is interested in studying social entities (such as people in an organization, called actors) and their interactions and relationships by using their network or graph representations.

The World Wide Web can be thought of as a virtual society or a virtual social network, where each page can be regarded as a social actor and each hyperlink as a relationship. Therefore, results from social network analysis can be adapted and extended for use in the Web context. In fact, the two most influential link analysis methods, PageRank and HITS, are based on the ideas borrowed from social network analysis.

Below, two types of social network analysis, i.e. centrality and prestige, which are closely related to hyperlink analysis and Web search, are introduced. Both of them are measures of degree of prominence of an actor in a social network.

Centrality

Intuitively, important or prominent actors are those that are linked or involved with other actors extensively. Several types of centrality are defined on undirected and directed graphs. The three popular types include degree centrality, closeness centrality, and betweenness centrality. For example, using a closeness centrality, the center of the network is defined based on the distance: an actor i is central if it can easily interact with all other actors. That is, its distance to all other actors is short. Let the shortest distance from actor i to actor j be $d(i, j)$, measured as the number of links in a shortest path. The closeness centrality $C_c(i)$ of an actor i is defined as

$$C_c(i) = (n-1) \Big/ \sum_{j=1,\ldots,n} d(i,j) \qquad (2.15)$$

Prestige

Prestige is a more refined measure of prominence of an actor than centrality in that it distinguishes between the links an actor receives (inlinks) and the links an actor sends out (outlinks). A prestige actor is defined as one who receives a lot of inlinks. The main difference between the concepts of centrality and prestige is that centrality focuses on outlinks while prestige focuses on inlinks. There are several types of prestige defined in the literature. The most important one in the context of Web search is perhaps the rank prestige.

The rank prestige forms the basis of most Web page link analysis algorithms, including PageRank and HITS. The main idea of the rank prestige is that an actor's prestige is affected by the ranks or statuses of the involved actors. Based on this intuition, we can define $P_R(i)$, the rank prestige of an actor i as follows.

$$P_R(i) = A_{1i}P_R(1) + A_{2i}P_R(2) + \cdots + A_{ni}P_R(n) \tag{2.16}$$

where, $A_{ji} = 1$ if j points to i, and 0 otherwise. This equation says that an actor's rank prestige is a function of the ranks of the actors who vote or choose the actor. It turns out that this equation is very useful in Web search. Indeed, the most well known Web search ranking algorithms, PageRank and HITS, are directly related to this equation.

Summary

In this chapter, we briefly include some basic but important concepts and theories used in this book. The mathematical descriptions and formulations are reviewed and summarized in eight sections. This chapter and the successive Chapter 3 form the foundation part of this book.

3

Algorithms and Techniques

Apart from the fundamental theoretical backgrounds talked in Chapter 2, in the context of web data mining, there are a lot of algorithms and approaches developed in a large volume of literatures. These various approaches and techniques are well studied and implemented in different applications and scenarios by research efforts contributed from the expertise of Database, Artificial Intelligence, Information Science, Natural Language Processing, Human Computer Interaction even Social Science. Although these algorithms and techniques are developed from the perspectives of different disciplines, they are widely and diversely explored and applied in the above mentioned areas simultaneously. In this chapter, we bring some well used algorithms and techniques together and review the technical strengths of them. We aim to prepare a solid technology knowledge foundation for further chapters.

3.1 Association Rule Mining

Data mining is to find valid, novel, potentially useful, and ultimately understandable patterns in data [91]. The most important and basic princple in data mining is association rule mining [6].

The purpose of finding association rules is to analyze the co-existence relation between items, which is then utilized to make appropriate recommendation. The issue has attracted a great deal of interest during the recent surge in data mining research because it is the basis of many applications, such as customer behavior analysis, stock trend prediction, and DNA sequence analysis. For example, an association rule "apple $\Rightarrow$ strawberry (90%)" indicates that nine out of ten customers who bought apples also bought strawberry. These rules can be useful for store layout, stock prediction, DNA structure analysis, and so forth.

3.1.1 Association Rule Mining Problem

The problem of association rule discovery can be stated as follows [6]: Let $I = \{i_1, i_2, \ldots, i_k\}$ be a set of items. A subset of I is called an *itemset*. The *itemset*, t_j,

G. Xu et al., *Web Mining and Social Networking*,
DOI 10.1007/978-1-4419-7735-9_3, © Springer Science+Business Media, LLC 2011

Table 3.1. An example database

Tid	Transaction
100	{apple, banana}
200	{apple, pear, strawberry}
300	{pear, strawberry}
400	{banana}
500	{apple, strawberry}

is denoted as $\{x_1 x_2 \ldots x_m\}$, where x_k is an item, i.e., $x_k \in I$ for $1 \leq k \leq m$. The number of items in an itemset is called the *length* of the itemset. An itemset with length l is called an l-itemset. An itemset, $t_a = \{a_1, a_2, \ldots, a_n\}$, is contained in another itemset, $t_b = \{b_1, b_2, \ldots, b_m\}$, if there exists integers $1 \leq i_1 < i_2 < \ldots < i_n \leq m$, such that $a_1 \subseteq b_{i_1}, a_2 \subseteq b_{i_2}, \ldots, a_n \subseteq b_{i_n}$. We denote t_a as a *subset* of t_b, and t_b a *superset* of t_a.

The *support* of an itemset X, denoted as $support(X)$, is the number of transactions in which it occurs as a subset. A k length subset of an itemset is called a k-subset. An itemset is *frequent* if its support is greater than a user-specified minimum support (min_{sup}) value. The set of frequent k-itemsets is denoted $\mathscr{F}_k$.

An association rule is an expression $A \Rightarrow B$, where A and B are itemsets. The support of the rule is given as $support(A \Rightarrow B)=support(A \cup B)$ and the *confidence* of the rule is given as $conf(A \Rightarrow B)=support(A \cup B)/support(A)$ (i.e., the conditional probability that a transaction contains B, given that it contains A). A rule is *confident* if its confidence is greater than a user-specified minimum confidence (min_{conf}).

The associate rule mining task is to generate all the rules, whose supports are greater than min_{sup}, and the confidences of the rules are greater than min_{conf}. The issue can be tackled by a two-stage strategy [7]:

- Find all frequent itemsets. This stage is the most time consuming part. Given k items, there can be potentially 2^k frequent itemsets. Therefore, almost all the works so far have focused on devising efficient algorithms to discover the frequent itemsets, while avoiding to traverse unnecessary search space somehow. In this chapter, we mainly introduce the basic algorithms on finding frequent itemsets.
- Generate confident rules. This stage is relatively straightforward and can be easily completed.

Almost all the association rule mining algorithms apply the two-stage rule discovery approach. We will discuss in more detail in the next few sections.

Example 1. Let our example database be the database D shown in Table 3.1 with $min_{sup}=1$ and $min_{conf}=40\%$. Table 3.2 shows all frequent itemsets in D. Table 3.3 illustrates all frequent and confident association rules. For the sake of simplicity and without loss of generality, we assume that items in transactions and itemsets are kept sorted in the lexicographic order unless stated otherwise.

Table 3.2. Frequent itemsets

Itemset	Included Transactions	Support
{}	{100, 200, 300, 400, 500}	5
{apple}	{100, 200, 500}	3
{banana}	{100, 400}	2
{pear}	{200, 300}	2
{strawberry}	{200, 300, 500}	3
{apple, banana}	{100}	1
{apple, pear}	{200}	1
{apple, strawberry}	{200, 500}	2
{pear, strawberry}	{200, 300}	2
{apple, pear, strawberry}	{200}	1

Table 3.3. Frequent and confident association rules

Rule	Support	Confidence
{apple} $\Rightarrow$ {strawberry}	2	67%
{banana} $\Rightarrow$ {apple}	1	50%
{pear} $\Rightarrow$ {apple}	1	50%
{pear} $\Rightarrow$ {strawberry}	2	100%
{strawberry} $\Rightarrow$ {apple}	2	67%
{strawberry} $\Rightarrow$ {pear}	2	67%
{apple, pear} $\Rightarrow$ {strawberry}	1	100%
{apple, strawberry} $\Rightarrow$ {pear}	1	50%
{pear, strawberry} $\Rightarrow$ {apple}	1	50%
{pear} $\Rightarrow$ {apple, strawberry}	1	50%

3.1.2 Basic Algorithms for Association Rule Mining

Apriori

Agrawal et al. [6] proposed the first algorithm (i.e., AIS) to address the association rule mining issue. The same authors introduced another algorithm named Apriori based on AIS in their later paper [8] by introducing the monotonicity property of the association rules to improve the performance. Mannila et al. [177] presented an independent work with a similar idea.

Apriori applies a two-stage approach to discover frequent itemsets and confident association rules.

- **Frequent Itemset Discovery**. To find all frequent itemsets, Apriori introduces a candidate generation and test strategy. The basic idea is that it first generates the candidate k-itemsets (i.e., k is 1 at the beginning and is incrementd by 1 in the next cycle), then these candidates will be evaluated whether frequent or not.

Specifically, the algorithm first scans the dataset and the frequent 1-itemsets are found. To discover those frequent 2-itemsets, Apriori generates candidate 2-itemsets by joining 1-itemsets. These candidates are evaluated by scanning the original dataset again. In a similar way, all frequent $(k+1)$-itemsets can be found based on already known frequent k-itemsets.

To improve the performance by avoiding to generating too many yet unnecessary candidates, Apriori introduced a monotonicity property that a $(k+1)$-itemset becomes a candidate only if all its k-subset are frequent. As demonstrated by the authors [8] and many later works, this simple yet efficient strategy largely reduces the candidates to be evaluated.

The frequent itemset mining of the Apriori algorithm is presented in Algorithm 3.1. The algorithm is executed in a breadth-first search manner. To generate the candidate itemsets with length $k+1$, two k-itemsets with the same $k-1$-prefix are joined together (lines 10-11). The joined itemset can be inserted into C_{k+1} only if all its k-subsets are frequent (line 12).

To test the candidate k-itemsets (i.e., count their supports), the database is scanned sequentially and all the candidate itemsets are tested whether are included in the transaction scanned. By this way, the corresponding support is accumulated (lines 5-7). Finally, frequent itemsets are collected (line 8).

Algorithm 3.1: Apriori - Frequent Itemset Mining

Input: A transaction database D, a user specified threshold min_{sup}
Output: Frequent itemsets F
$C_1 = \{1\text{-itemsets}\}$;
$k=1$;
While $C_k \neq$ NULL do
    // Test candidate itemsets
    for transaction $T \in D$ do
        for candidate itemsets $X \in C_k$ do
            If $X \subseteq T$ then X.support++;
        end
    end
    $F_k = F_k \cup X$, where $X.support \geq min_{sup}$;
    // Generate candidate itemsets
    For all $\{i_1, \ldots i_{k-1}, i_k\}, \{i_1, \ldots i_{k-1}, i_k'\} \in F_k$ such that $i_k < i_k'$ do
        $c = \{i_1, \ldots i_{l-1}, i_k, i_k'\}$;
        If all k-subsets of c are frequent then $C_{k+1} = C_{k+1} \cup c$;
    end
    k++;
end

- **Association Rule Mining.** Given all frequent itemsets, finding all frequent and confident association rules are straightforward. The approach is very similar to

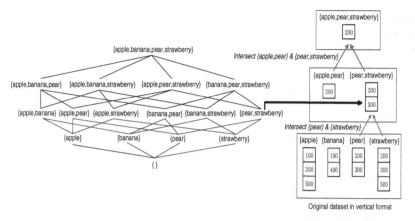

Fig. 3.1. Eclat mining process (vertical dataset, support count via intersection)

the frequent itemset mining algorithm. Because the cost on finding frequent itemsets is high and accounts for most of the whole performance on discovering associate rules, almost all research so far has been focused on the frequent itemset generation stage.

Eclat

There are many algorithms had been proposed based on Apriroi idea, in which Eclat [270, 268] is distinct that it is the first one which proposed to generate all frequent itemsets in a depth-first manner, while employs the vertical database layout and uses the intersection based approach to compute the support of an itemset.

Figure 3.1 illustrates the key idea of Eclat on candidate support counting. While first scanning of the dataset, it converts the original format (i.e., Table 3.1) into vertical TID list format, as shown in Figure 3.1. For example, the TID list of itemset $\{apple\}$ is $\{100, 200, 500\}$, and indicates the transactions that the itemset exist in the original dataset.

To count the support of k-candidate itemset, the algorithm intersects its two (k-1)-subset to get the result. For example, as shown in Figure 3.1, to count the support of the itemset $\{pear, strawberry\}$, it intersects the TID lists of $\{pear\}$ and $\{strawberry\}$, resulting in $\{200, 300\}$. The support is therefore 2.

To reduce the memory used to count the support, Eclat proposed to traverse the lattice (as shown in Figure 3.1) in a depth-first manner. The pseudo code of the Eclat algorithm is presented in Algorithm 3.2.

Algorithm 3.2: Eclat - Frequent Itemset Mining

Input: A transaction database D, a user specified threshold min_{sup}, a set of atoms of

a sublattice S
Output: Frequent itemsets F
Procedure Elat(S)
For all atoms $A_i \in S$
    $T_i = \emptyset$;
    For all atoms $A_j \in S$, with $j > i$ do
        $R = A_i \cup A_j$;
        $L(R) = L(A_i) \cap L(A_j)$;
        If $support(R) \geq min_{sup}$ then
            $T_i = T_i \cup \{R\}$;
            $F_{|R|} = F_{|R|} \cup \{R\}$;
        end
    end
end
For all $T_i \neq \emptyset$ do Eclat(T_i);

The algorithm generates the frequent itemsets by intersecting the tid-lists of all distinct pairs of atoms and evaluating the support of the candidates based on the resulting tid-list (lines 5-6). It calls recursively the procedure with those found frequent itemsets at the current level (line 11). This process terminates when all frequent itemsets have been traversed. To save the memory usage, after all frequent itemsets for the next level have been generated, the itemsets at the current level can be deleted.

FP-growth

Han et al. [107] proposed a new strategy that mines the complete set of frequent itemsets based on a trie-like structure (i.e., FP-tree). The algorithm applies the divide and conquer approach.

FP-tree construction: FP-tree is constructed as follows [107]: create the root node of the FP-tree, labeled with "null". then, scan the database and obtain a list of frequent items in which items are ordered with regard to their supports in descending order. Based on this order, the items in each transaction of the database are reordered. Note that each node n in the FP-tree represents a unique itemset X, i.e., scanning itemset X in transactions can be seen as traversing in the FP-tree from the root to n. All the nodes except the root store a counter which keeps the number of transactions that share the node.

    To construct the FP-tree, the algorithm scans the items in each transaction, one at a time, while searching the already existing nodes in FP-tree. If a representative node exists, then the counter of the node is incremented by 1. Otherwise, a new node is created. Additionally, an item header table is built so that each item points to its occurrences in the tree via a chain of node-links. Each item in this header table also stores its support.

Frequent Itemset Mining (FP-growth): To obtain all frequent itemset, Han et al. [107] proposed a pattern growth approach by traversing in the FP-tree, which retains all the itemset association information. The FP-tree is mined by starting from each frequent length-1 pattern (as an initial suffix pattern), constructing its conditional pattern base (a sub-database, which

Table 3.4. An example database for FP-growth

Tid	Transaction	Ordered Transaction
100	{a, b, d, e, f}	{b, d, f, a, e}
200	{b, f, g}	{b, f, g}
300	{d, g, h, i}	{d, g}
400	{a, c, e, g, j}	{g, a, e}
500	{b, d, f}	{b, d, f}

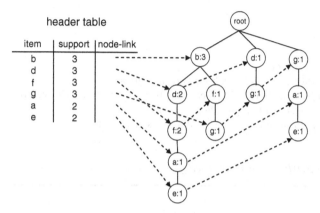

Fig. 3.2. FP-tree of the example database

consists of the set of prefix paths in the FP-tree co-occurring with the suffix pattern), then constructing its conditional FP-tree and performing mining recursively on such a tree. The pattern growth is achieved by the concatenation of the suffix pattern with the frequent patterns generated from a conditional FP-tree.

Example 2. Let our example database be the database shown in Table 3.4 with min_{sup}=2. First, the supports of all items are accumulated and all infrequent items are removed from the database. The items in the transactions are reordered according to the support in descending order, resulting in the transformed database shown in Table 3.4. The FP-tree for this database is shown in Figure 3.2. The pseudo code of the FP-growth algorithm is presented in Algorithm 3.3 [107].

Although the authors of the FP-growth algorithm [107] claim that their algorithm does not generate any candidate itemsets, some works (e.g., [102]) have shown that the algorithm actually generates many candidate itemsets since it essentially uses the same candidate generation technique as is used in Apriori but without its prune step. Another issue of FP-tree is that the construction of the frequent pattern tree is a time consuming activity.

Algorithm 3.3: FP-growth

Input:A transaction database D, a frequent pattern tree $FP\text{-}tree$, a user specified threshold min_{sup}
Output: Frequent itemsets $\mathcal{F}$

Method: *call* FP-growth *FP-tree*, null
Procedure FP-growth(*Tree*, α):
If *Tree* contains a single prefix-path
    Let *P* be the single prefix-path part of *Tree*;
    Let *Q* be the multipath part with the top branching node replaced by a *null* root;
    For each combination β of the nodes in *P* do
        Generate pattern $\beta \cup \alpha$ with *support*=minimum support of nodes in β;
        Let *freq_pattern_set*(*P*) be the set of patterns generated;
    end
end
else
    Let *Q* be *Tree*;
end
For each item $a_i \in Q$ do
    generate pattern $\beta = a_i \cup \alpha$ with *support*=a_i.*support*;
    construct β's conditional pattern-base and then β' conditional FT-tree *Tree*$_\beta$;
    If *Tree*$_\beta \neq \emptyset$ then call Fp-growth(*Tree*$_\beta, \beta$);
    Let *freq_pattern_set*(*Q*) be the set of patterns generated;
end
return
(*freq_pattern_set*(*P*)$\cup$*freq_pattern_set*(*Q*)$\cup$(*freq_pattern_set*(*P*)$\times$*freq_pattern_set*(*Q*)));

3.1.3 Sequential Pattern Mining

The sequential mining problem was first introduced in [11]; two sequential patterns examples are: "80% of the people who buy a television also buy a video camera within a day", and "Every time Microsoft stock drops by 5%, then IBM stock will also drop by at least 4% within three days". The above patterns can be used to determine the efficient use of shelf space for customer convenience, or to properly plan the next step during an economic crisis. Sequential pattern mining is also very important for analyzing biological data [18] [86], in which a very small alphabet (i.e., 4 for DNA sequences and 20 for protein sequences) and long patterns with a typical length of few hundreds or even thousands frequently appear.

Sequence discovery can be thought of as essentially an association discovery over a temporal database. While association rules [9, 138] discern only intra-event patterns (itemsets), sequential pattern mining discerns inter-event patterns (sequences). There are many other important tasks related to association rule mining, such as correlations [42], causality [228], episodes [176], multi-dimensional patterns [154, 132], max-patterns [24], partial periodicity [105], and emerging patterns [78]. Incisive exploration of sequential pattern mining issue will definitely help to get the efficient solutions to the other research problems shown above.

Efficient sequential pattern mining methodologies have been studied extensively in many related problems, including the general sequential pattern mining [11, 232, 269, 202, 14], constraint-based sequential pattern mining [95], incremental sequential pattern mining [200], frequent episode mining [175], approximate sequential pattern mining [143], partial periodic pattern mining [105], temporal pattern mining in data stream [242], maximal and closed sequential pattern mining [169, 261, 247]. In this section, due to space limitation, we focus on introducing the general sequential pattern mining algorithm, which is the most basic one because all the others can benefit from the strategies it employs, i.e., Apriori heuristic and projection-based pattern growth. More details and survey on sequential pattern mining can be found in [249, 172].

Sequential Pattern Mining Problem

Let $I = \{i_1, i_2, \ldots, i_k\}$ be a set of items. A subset of I is called an *itemset* or an *element*. A *sequence*, s, is denoted as $\langle t_1, t_2, \ldots, t_l \rangle$, where t_j is an itemset, i.e., $(t_j \subseteq I)$ for $1 \leq j \leq l$. The *itemset*, t_j, is denoted as $(x_1 x_2 \ldots x_m)$, where x_k is an item, i.e., $x_k \in I$ for $1 \leq k \leq m$. For brevity, the brackets are omitted if an *itemset* has only one item. That is, *itemset* (x) is written as x. The number of items in a sequence is called the *length* of the sequence. A sequence with length l is called an *l-sequence*. A sequence, $s_a = \langle a_1, a_2, \ldots, a_n \rangle$, is contained in another sequence, $s_b = \langle b_1, b_2, \ldots, b_m \rangle$, if there exists integers $1 \leq i_1 < i_2 < \ldots < i_n \leq m$, such that $a_1 \subseteq b_{i_1}, a_2 \subseteq b_{i_2}, \ldots, a_n \subseteq b_{i_n}$. We denote s_a a *subsequence* of s_b, and s_b a *supersequence* of s_a. Given a sequence $s = \langle s_1, s_2, \ldots, s_l \rangle$, and an item α, $s \diamond \alpha$ denotes that s concatenates with α, which has two possible forms, such as *Itemset Extension* (*IE*), $s \diamond \alpha = \langle s_1, s_2, \ldots, s_l \cup \{\alpha\} \rangle$, or *Sequence Extension* (*SE*), $s \diamond \alpha = \langle s_1, s_2, \ldots, s_l, \{\alpha\} \rangle$. If $s' = p \diamond s$, then p is a *prefix* of s' and s is a *suffix* of s'.

A *sequence database*, S, is a set of tuples $\langle sid, s \rangle$, where sid is a sequence_id and s is a sequence. A tuple $\langle sid, s \rangle$ is said to contain a sequence β, if β is a *subsequence* of s. The support of a sequence, β, in a sequence database, S, is the number of tuples in the database containing β, denoted as $support(\beta)$. Given a user specified positive integer, ε, a sequence, β, is called a frequent sequential pattern if $support(\beta) \geq \varepsilon$.

Existing Sequential Pattern Mining Algorithms

Sequential pattern mining algorithms can be grouped into two categories. One category is Apriori-like algorithm, such as Apriori-all [11], GSP [232], SPADE [269], and SPAM [14], the other category is projection-based pattern growth, such as PrefixSpan [202].

AprioriALL

Sequential pattern mining was first introduced by Agrawal in [11] where three Apriori based algorithms were proposed. Given the transaction database with three attributes customer-id, transaction-time and purchased-items, the mining process were decomposed into five phases:

- **Sort Phase:** The original transaction database is sorted based on the customer and transaction time. Figure 3.3 shows the sorted transaction data.
- **L-itemsets Phase:** The sorted database is first scanned to obtain those frequent (or *large*) 1-itemsets based on the user specified support threshold. Suppose the minimal support is 70%. In this case the minimal support count is 2, and the result of large 1-itemsets is listed in Figure 3.4.

Customer ID	Transaction Time	Items Bought
100	July 3 '07	apple
100	July 6 '07	strawberry
100	July 8 '07	banana, strawberry
100	July 10 '07	pear
100	July 12 '07	apple, banana, strawberry
100	July 16 '07	apple
100	July 21 '07	pear
200	July 4 '07	banana
200	July 7 '07	strawberry, pear
200	July 9 '07	apple
200	July 10 '07	strawberry
200	July 15 '07	banana, pear
300	July 13 '07	pear
300	July 15 '07	banana, strawberry
300	July 21 '07	apple, strawberry
300	July 24 '07	strawberry, pear

Fig. 3.3. Database Sorted by Customer ID and Transaction Time

Large Itemsets	Mapped To
apple	a
banana	b
strawberry	c
pear	d

Fig. 3.4. Large Itemsets

Customer ID	Customer Sequence
100	< ac(bc)d(abc)ad >
200	< b(cd)ac(bd) >
300	< d(bc)(ac)(cd) >

Fig. 3.5. Transformed Database

- **Transformation Phase:** All the large itemsets are mapped into a series of integers and the original database is converted by replacing the itemsets. For example, with the help of the mapping table in Figure 3.4, the transformed database is obtained, as shown in Figure 3.5.
- **Sequence Phase:** Mine the transformed database and find all frequent sequential patterns.
- **Maximal Phase:** Prune those patterns which are contained in other sequential patterns. In other words, only maximum sequential patterns are remained.

Since most of the phases are straightforward, researches focused on the sequence phase. AprioriAll [11] was first proposed based on the Apriori algorithm in association rule mining [9]. There are two steps to mine sequential patterns, i.e., candidate generation and test.

The candidate generation process is similar to the AprioriGen in [9]. The Apriori property is applied to prune those candidate sequences whose subsequence is not frequent. The difference is that when the authors generate the candidate by joining the frequent patterns in the

Table 3.5. AprioriAll Candidate Generation L_3 to C_4

Large 4-sequences	Candidate 5-sequences
$\langle b(ac)d \rangle$	$\langle (bc)(ac)d \rangle$
$\langle bcad \rangle$	$\langle d(bc)ad \rangle$
$\langle bdad \rangle$	$\langle d(bc)da \rangle$
$\langle bdcd \rangle$	$\langle d(bc)(ad) \rangle$
$\langle (bc)ad \rangle$	
$\langle (bc)(ac) \rangle$	
$\langle (bc)cd \rangle$	
$\langle c(ac)d \rangle$	
$\langle d(ac)d \rangle$	
$\langle dbad \rangle$	
$\langle d(bc)a \rangle$	
$\langle d(bc)d \rangle$	
$\langle dcad \rangle$	

previous pass, different order of combination make different candidates. For example: from the items, a and b, three candidates $\langle ab \rangle$, $\langle ba \rangle$ and $\langle (ab) \rangle$ can be generated. But in association rule mining only $\langle (ab) \rangle$ is generated. The reason is that in association rule mining, the time order is not taken into account. Obviously the number of candidate sequences in sequential pattern mining is much larger than the size of the candidate itemsets in association rule mining during the generation of candidate sequences. Table 3.5 shows how to generate candidate 5-sequences by joining large 4-sequences. By scanning the large 4-itemsets, it finds that the first itemsets $\langle (bc)ad \rangle$ and second itemsets $\langle (bc)(ac) \rangle$ share their first three items, according to the join condition of Apriori they are joined to produce the candidate sequence $\langle (bc)(ac)d \rangle$. Similarly other candidate 5-sequences are generated.

The check process is simple and straightforward. Scan the database to count the supports of those candidate sequences and then the frequent sequential patterns can be found.

AprioriAll is a the first algorithm on mining sequential patterns and its core idea is commonly applied by many later algorithms. The disadvantages of AprioriAll are that too many candidates are generated and multiple passes over the database are necessary and thus, the cost of computation is high.

GSP

Srikant and Agrawal generalized the definition of sequential pattern mining problem in [232] by incorporating some new properties, i.e., time constraints, transaction relaxation, and *taxonomy*. For the time constraints, the *maximum gap* and the *minimal gap* are defined to specified the gap between any two adjacent transactions in the sequence. When testing a candidate, if any gap of the candidate falls out of the range between the maximum gap and the minimal gap, then the candidate is not a pattern. Furthermore, the authors relaxed the definition of transaction by using a *sliding window*, that when the time range between two items is smaller than the sliding window, these two items are considered to be in the same transaction. The taxonomy is used to generate multiple level sequential patterns.

Table 3.6. GSP Candidate Generation L_4 to C_5

Large 4-sequences	Candidate 5-sequences after joining	Candidate 5-sequences after pruning
$\langle b(ac)d \rangle$	$\langle (bc)(ac)d \rangle$	$\langle (bc)(ac)d \rangle$
$\langle bcad \rangle$	$\langle d(bc)ad \rangle$	$\langle d(bc)ad \rangle$
$\langle bdad \rangle$	$\langle d(bc)da \rangle$	
$\langle bdcd \rangle$	$\langle d(bc)(ad) \rangle$	
$\langle (bc)ad \rangle$		
$\langle (bc)(ac) \rangle$		
$\langle (bc)cd \rangle$		
$\langle c(ac)d \rangle$		
$\langle d(ac)d \rangle$		
$\langle dbad \rangle$		
$\langle d(bc)a \rangle$		
$\langle d(bc)d \rangle$		
$\langle dcad \rangle$		

In [232], the authors proposed a new algorithm which is named GSP to efficiently find the generalized sequential patterns. Similar to the AprioriAll algorithm, there are two steps in GSP, i.e., candidate generation and test.

In the candidate generation process, the candidate k-sequences are generated based on the frequent $(k-1)$-sequences. Given a sequence $s = \langle s_1, s_2, \ldots, s_n \rangle$ and subsequence c, c is a contiguous subsequence of s if any of the following conditions holds: (1) c is derived from s by dropping an item from either s_1 or s_n; (2) c is derived from s by dropping an item from an element s_j that has at least 2 items; and (3) c is a contiguous subsequence of $\hat{c}$, and $\hat{c}$ is a contiguous subsequence of s. Specifically, the candidates are generated in two steps:

- **Join Phase:** Candidate k-sequences are generated by joining two $(k-1)$-sequences that have the same contiguous subsequences. When we join the two sequences, the item can be inserted as a part of the element or as a separated element. For example, because $\langle d(bc)a \rangle$ and $\langle d(bc)d \rangle$ have the same contiguous subsequence $\langle d(bc) \rangle$, then we know that candidate 5-sequence $\langle d(bc)(ad) \rangle$, $\langle d(bc)ad \rangle$ and $\langle d(bc)da \rangle$ can be generated.
- **Prune Phase:** The algorithm removes the candidate sequences which have a contiguous subsequence whose support count is less than the minimal support. Moreover, it uses a hash-tree structure [199] to reduce the number of candidates.

The candidate generation process for the example database is shown in Figure 3.6. The challenge issue for GSP is that the support of candidate sequences is difficult to count due to the introduced generalization rules, while this is not a problem for AprioriAll. GSP devises an efficient strategy which includes two phases, i.e., forward and backward phases. The process of checking whether a sequence d contains a candidate sequence s is shown as follows (which are repeated until all the elements are found).

- **Forward Phase:** it looks for successive elements of s in d, as long as the difference between the end-time of the element and the start-time of the previous element is less than the maximum gap. If the difference is greater than the maximum gap, it switches to the backward phase. If an element is not found, then s is not contained in d.

a		b		c		d	
SID	TID	SID	TID	SID	TID	SID	TID
100	1	100	3	100	2	100	4
100	5	100	5	100	3	100	7
100	6	200	1	100	5	200	2
200	3	200	5	200	2	200	5
300	3	300	2	200	4	300	1
				300	2	300	4
				300	3		
				300	4		

Fig. 3.6. Vertical Id-List

SID	(Item, TID) pairs
100	(a, 1) (c, 2) (b, 2) (c, 2) (d, 4) (a, 5) (b, 5) (c, 5) (a, 6) (d, 7)
200	(b, 1) (c, 2) (d, 2) (a, 3) (c, 4) (b, 5) (d, 5)
300	(d, 1) (b, 2) (c, 2) (a, 3) (c, 3) (c, 4) (d, 4)

Fig. 3.7. Vertical to Horizontal Database

- **Backward Phase:** it tries to pull up the previous element. Suppose s_i is the current element and end-time$(s_i)=t$. It checks whether there are some transactions containing s_{i-1} and the corresponding transaction-times are larger than the maximum gap. Since after pulling up s_{i-1}, the difference between s_{i-1} and s_{i-2} may not satisfy the gap constraints, the backward pulls back until the difference of s_{i-1} and s_{i-2} satisfies the maximum gap or the first element has been pulled up. Then the algorithm switches to the forward phase. If all the elements can not be pulled up, then d does not contain s.

The taxonomies are incorporated into the database by extending sequences with corresponding taxonomies. Original sequences are replaced by their extended versions. The number of rules becomes larger because the sequences become denser and redundant rules are produced. To avoid uninteresting rules, the ancestors are firstly precomputed for each item and those are not in the candidates are removed. Moreover, the algorithm does not count the sequential patterns that contain both the item and its ancestors.

SPADE

SPADE [269] is an algorithm proposed to find frequent sequences using efficient lattice search techniques and simple joins. All the patterns can be discovered by scanning the database three times. It divides the mining problem into smaller ones to conquer and at the same time makes it possible that all the necessary data is located in memory. The SPADE algorithm, which is developed based on the idea of Eclat [270], has largely improved the performance of sequential pattern mining [269].

The key idea of SPADE can be described as follows. The sequential database is first transformed into a vertical id-list database format, in which each id is associated with its corresponding customer sequence and transaction. The vertical version of the original database (as shown in Figure 3.3) is illustrated in Figure 3.6. For example, we know that the id-list of item

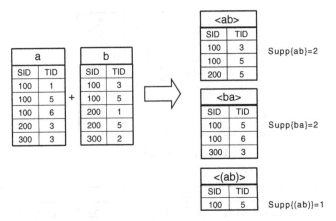

Fig. 3.8. Temporal join in SPADE algorithm

a is (100, 1), (100, 5), (100, 6), (200, 3), and (300, 3), where each pair (SID:TID) indicates the specific sequence and transaction that a locates. By scanning the vertical database, frequent 1-sequences can be easily obtained. To find the frequent 2-sequences, the original database is scanned again and the new vertical to horizontal database is constructed by grouping those items with SID and in increase order of TID, which is shown in Figure 3.7. By scanning the database 2-length patterns can be discovered. A lattice is constructed based on these 2-length patterns, and the lattice can be further decomposed into different classes, where those patterns that have the same prefix belong to the same class. Such kind of decomposition make it possible that the partitions are small enough to be loaded into the memory. SPADE then applies temporal joins to find all other longer patterns by enumerating the lattice [269].

There are two path traversing strategies to find frequent sequences in the lattice: *breadth first search* (BFS) and *depth first search* (DFS). For BFS, the classes are generated in a recursive bottom up manner. For example, to generate the 3-length patterns, all the 2-length patterns have to be obtained. On the contrary, DFS only requires that one 2-length pattern and one k-length pattern to generate a (k+1)-length sequence (assume that the last item of the k-pattern is the same as the first item of the 2-pattern). Therefore, there is always a trade-off between BFS and DFS: while BFS needs more memory to store all the consecutive 2-length patterns, it has the advantage that more information is obtained to prune the candidate k-sequences. All the k-length patterns are discovered by temporal or equality joining the frequent (k-1)-length patterns which have the same (k-2)-length prefix. The Apriori property pruning technique is applied in SPADE.

Figure 3.8 illustrates one example of temporal join operations in SPADE. Suppose we have already got 1-length patterns, a and b. By joining these two patterns, we can test the three candidate sequences, ab, ba and (ab). The joining operation is indeed to compare the SID, TID pairs of the two (k-1)-length patterns. For example, the pattern b has two pairs {100,3}, {100,5} which are larger than (behind) the pattern a's one pair ({100,1}), in the same customer sequence. Hence, $\langle ab \rangle$ should exist in the same sequence. By the same way, other candidate sequences' support can be accumulated, as illustrated on the right part of Figure 3.8.

SID	TID	{a}	{b}	{c}	{d}
100	1	1	0	0	0
100	2	0	0	1	0
100	3	0	1	1	0
100	4	0	0	0	1
100	5	1	1	1	0
100	6	1	0	0	0
100	7	0	0	0	1
200	1	0	1	0	0
200	2	0	0	1	1
200	3	1	0	0	0
200	4	0	0	1	0
200	5	0	1	0	1
300	1	0	0	0	1
300	2	0	1	1	0
300	3	1	0	1	0
300	4	0	0	1	1

Fig. 3.9. Bitmap Vertical Table

SPAM

Ayres et al. [14] proposed SPAM algorithm based on the key idea of SPADE. The difference is that SPAM utilizes a bitmap representation of the database instead of $\{SID, TID\}$ pairs used in the SPADE algorithm. Hence, SPAM can perform much better than SPADE and others by employing bitwise operations.

While scanning the database for the first time, a vertical bitmap is constructed for each item in the database, and each bitmap has a bit corresponding to each itemset (element) of the sequences in the database. If an item appears in an itemset, the bit corresponding to the itemset of the bitmap for the item is set to one; otherwise, the bit is set to zero. The size of a sequence is the number of itemsets contained in the sequence. Figure 3.9 shows the bitmap vertical table of that in Figure 3.5. A sequence in the database of size between 2^k+1 and 2^{k+1} is considered as a 2^{k+1}-bit sequence. The bitmap of a sequence will be constructed according to the bitmaps of items contained in it.

To generate and test the candidate sequences, SPAM uses two steps, S-step and I-step, based on the lattice concept. As a depth-first approach, the overall process starts from S-step and then I-step. To extend a sequence, the S-step appends an item to it as the new last element, and the I-step appends the item to its last element if possible. Each bitmap partition of a sequence to be extended is transformed first in the S-step, such that all bits after the first bit with value one are set to one. Then the resultant bitmap of the S-step can be obtained by doing ANDing operation for the transformed bitmap and the bitmap of the appended item. Figure 3.10 illustrates how to join two 1-length patterns, a and b, based on the example database in Figure 3.5. On the other hand, the I-step just uses the bitmaps of the sequence and the appended item to do ANDing operation to get the resultant bitmap, which extends the pattern $\langle ab \rangle$ to the candidate $\langle a(bc) \rangle$. The support counting becomes a simple check how many bitmap partitions not containing all zeros.

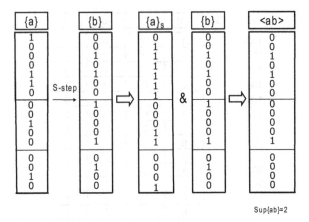

Fig. 3.10. SPAM S-Step join

The main drawback of SPAM is the huge memory consumption. For example, although an item, α, does not exist in a sequence, s, SPAM still uses one bit to represent the existence of α in s. This disadvantage restricts SPAM as a best algorithm on mining large datasets in limit resource environments.

PrefixSpan

PrefixSpan was proposed in [201]. The main idea of PrefixSpan algorithm is to apply database projection to make the database smaller for next iteration and improve the performance. The authors claimed that in PrefixSpan there is no need for candidates generation [201][1]. It recursively projects the database by already found short length patterns. Different projection methods were introduced, i.e., *level-by-level* projection, *bi-level* projection, and *pseudo* projection.

The workflow of PrefixSpan is presented as follows. Assume that items within transactions are sorted in alphabetical order (it does not affect the result of discovered patterns). Similar to other algorithms, the first step of PrefixSpan is to scan the database to get the 1-length patterns. Then the original database is projected into different partitions with regard to the frequent 1-length pattern by taking the corresponding pattern as the prefix. For example, Figure 3.11 (b) shows the projected databases with the frequent (or large) 1-length patterns as their prefixes. The next step is to scan the projected database of γ, where γ could be any one of the 1-length patterns. After the scanning, we can obtain the frequent 1-length patterns in the projected database. These patterns, combined with their common prefix γ, are deemed as 2-length patterns. The process will be executed recursively. The projected database is partitioned by the k-length patterns, to find those $(k+1)$-length patterns, until the projected database is empty or no more frequent patterns can be found.

The introduced strategy is named *level-by-level* projection. The main computation cost is the time and space usage when constructing and scanning the projected databases, as shown

---

[1] However, some works (e.g., [263, 264]) have found that PrefixSpan also needs to test the candidates, which are existing in the projected database.

Large Itemsets	Projected Database
a	<c(bc)d(abc)ad> <c(bd)> <(_c)(cd)>
b	<(_c)d(abc)ad> <(cd)ac(bd)> <(_c)(ac)(cd)>
c	<c(bc)d(abc)ad> <(_d)ac(bd)> <(ac)(cd)>
d	<(abc)ad> <ac(bd)> <(bc)(ac)(cd)>

Customer ID	Customer Sequence
100	<ac(bc)d(abc)ad>
200	<b(cd)ac(bd)>
300	<d(bc)(ac)(cd)>

(a) Example Database   (b) Projected Database

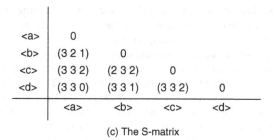

(c) The S-matrix

Fig. 3.11. PrefixSpan Mining Process

in Figure 3.11 (b). To improve the efficiency, another strategy named *bi-level* projection was proposed to reduce the cost of building and scanning the projected databases [202]. The difference between the two projection strategies is that, in the second step of bi-level projection, a $n \times n$ triangle matrix (called S-matrix) is constructed by scanning the database again, as shown in Figure 3.11 (c). This matrix represents all the supports of 2-length candidates. For example, $M[\langle d \rangle, \langle a \rangle] = (3, 3, 0)$ indicates that the supports of $\langle da \rangle$, $\langle ad \rangle$, and $\langle (ad) \rangle$ are 3, 3, and 0, respectively. The original database is then projected with regard to the frequent 2-length patterns in the S-matrix and the projected databases are scanned, respectively. The process recursively follows such a projection and scanning manner to find all the patterns. This strategy, however, seems to be not always optimal, as stated in [202].

A further optimization named *pseudo projection* was proposed in [201] to make the projection more efficient when the projected database can be loaded into the memory. The strategy is fulfilled by employing a pair of pointer and offset to indicate the position of each projection database instead of copying the data each time. The drawback is that the size of the (projected) database can not be too large.

In a brief summary, PrefixSpan improves the performance of mining sequential patterns by using database projection .It scans smaller projected databases in each iteration. The main problem of PrefixSpan, however, is that it is time consuming on scanning the projected database, which may be very large if the original dataset is huge.

3.2 Supervised Learning

Supervised learning (or called *classification*) is one of the major tasks in the research areas such as machine learning, artificial intelligence, data mining, and so forth. A supervised learning algorithm commonly first trains a classifier (or inferred function) by analyzing the given training data and then classify (or give class label to) those test data. One typical example for supervised learning in web mining is that if we are given many already known web pages with labels (i.e., topics in Yahoo!), how to automatically set labels to the new web pages.

In this section, we briefly introduce some most commonly used techniques for supervised learning. More kinds of strategies and algorithms can be found in the comprehensive books [33, 53].

3.2.1 Nearest Neighbor Classifiers

Among the various approaches for supervised learning, the Nearest Neighbor (*NN*) classifier can obtain good performance with consistency. The basic intuition behind it is that similar samples should be classified into the same class. The similarity metric can be any possible type, such as Euclidean distance, cosine measure, Jaccard Similarity, and so forth. An appropriate metric may be chosen based on the specific type of the data.

When building a NN classifier, the training samples are indexed by some index techniques (i.e., R-tree, *kd*-tree, etc) with their assigned class labels. Given a test sample s_t, it looks for the k training ones that most similar to s_t with the help of the index. The class that most frequently exists in the k samples is set to be the class of s_t. Note that the value of k is a tuned constant. The best choice of k depends on the data, where the commonly larger value of k weakens the effect of noise, while makes the boundaries of different classes closer.

To make the classifier more appropriate for real applications, weight information can be embedded to contribute to the total count (or score) of a specific class [53]. For the training sample s which has the label l_s, it computes the count $score(s, s_t)$ with weight value, where s_t is the test sample. The label of the class with the maximum score is then assigned to s_t. Another possible strategy is that a so-called per-class offset o_l can be employed to contribute to the total similarity score. The value of o_l can be trained based on the given data with regard to different class. These two strategies can be integrated and shown as follows.

$$score(c, s_t) = o_l + \sum_{s \in kNN(s_t)} score(s, s_t) \qquad (3.1)$$

where $kNN(s_t)$ represents the k training samples most similar to s_t.

The main advantage of the NN classifier is that the approach can be easily implemented and with fine tuned parameters, the accuracy of the classification can be comparable well with other strategies. The main disadvantage of the NN classifier is that the performance of the responding time and space consumption may be not satisfactory because the size of the training data is commonly very large and the cost of operations conducted on the index can not be neglected.

3.2.2 Decision Tree

Decision tree classifier is one of the commonly used and powerful methods for supervised learning. The advantage of decision tree is that it can represent rules, which may be easily understood by people. In this section, the related issues of decision tree will be briefly introduced. More comprehensive survey and tutorial can be found in [215, 111, 1].

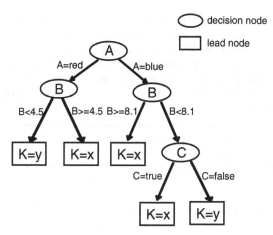

Fig. 3.12. An example of decision tree

When conducting some supervised learning task, common users may not necessary explore the intrinsic reason and mechanism of how the model works. Yet for some other tasks (e.g., manufacturing, marketing, etc), understanding the reason of how decision is made is an essential part, which can be used by domain experts to construct more effective and efficient frameworks.

Decision tree classifier is represented as a tree-like structure (i.e., Figure 3.12) [1], where each node is either of the following two types:

- A leaf node. It presents the target attribute with its value.
- An intermediate node (or called decision node). Test on the node can result in a decision which branch of the node will be searched next.

When conducting classification, we need to search from the root of the tree and move down while testing the decision node. Finally we can reach a leaf node which presents the class of the test sample.

The idea of decision tree classification is based on a typical inductive approach. There are some essential requirements for decision trees.

- Attribute-value description. Samples are represented in terms of a set of attributes. If the data space is continuous, then we need to convert the samples to discrete ones.
- Predefined and discrete classes. We need to provide the supervised classes of the data. It should be easily to judge whether one sample belong to a class or not.
- Sufficient data. Large amount of data is preferred to build a decision tree.

Decision tree construction

There are many algorithms developed to build decision trees and most are devised based on the core idea that applies top-down and greedy search in the space of possible decision trees. The first decision tree building algorithm is may be ID3 [209], which is based on the idea of

Concept Learning System (CLS) [83]. A later famous algorithm developed based on ID3 is C4.5 [210]. In this section we briefly introduce the ID3 algorithm.

The intuitive idea of ID3 is that it searches the training data and looks for the attribute that can best separate the samples. If the attribute perfectly groups them then the algorithm terminates. Otherwise it will operate on m (a tunable constant) subsets to get the optimal attribute in a recursive manner. Greedy search is applied in the algorithm. The pseudo code of ID3 is shown in Algorithm 3.4 [1].

Algorithm 3.4: ID3 Decision Tree Algorithm

Input: A set of non-target attributes R, the target attribute C, a training set S
Output: A decision tree
If S is empty then
    Return a single node with value Failure;
end
If S consists of records all with the same value for the target attribute then
    Return a single leaf node with that value;
end
If R is empty then
    Return a single node with the value of the most frequent of the values of the target attribute that are found in records of S;
end
Let A be the attribute with largest $Gain(A,S)$ among attributes in R;
Let $\{a_j | j = 1, 2, \ldots, m\}$ be the values of attribute A;
Let $\{S_j | j = 1, 2, \ldots, m\}$ be the subsets of S consisting respectively of records with value a_j for A;
Return a tree with root labeled A and arcs labeled $a_1, a_2, \ldots a_m$ going respectively to the trees $(ID3(R-A,C,S1), ID3(R-A,C,S2), \ldots, ID3(R-A,C,S_m))$;
Recursively apply ID3 to subsets $\{S_j | j = 1, 2, \ldots, m\}$ until they are empty;

The main advantages of the decision tree classifier are [215]: (1) complex decisions can be divided into many simpler local decisions and this merit especially benefits those data with high-dimensional spaces; (2) a sample is only tested on certain subsets of classes, which improves the efficiency compared with the traditional single-stage learners that each sample is tested on all the classes; and (3) it can flexibly choose different subset of features during the tree traversing while the traditional single-stage learners only select one subset features. This merit on flexibility may improve the performance [186].

The main drawbacks of the decision tree classifier are: (1) if there are huge number of classes, the tree would may become too large to be searched efficiently, while at the same time the memory usage may be very high; (2) errors may be accumulated as we traverse the tree. There is a trade-off between the accuracy and the efficiency and thus, for any given accuracy an efficiency bound should be hold; and (3) it is not easy to optimize the decision tree yet the performance of the classifier strongly depends on how well the tree is built.

3.2.3 Bayesian Classifiers

Bayesian Classifiers is another one of the commonly used and popular approaches for supervised learning. In this section, the strategy will be briefly introduced. For more comprehensive detail about Bayesian learning model refer [182, 33, 53].

The key idea of Bayesian learning is that the learning process applies Bayes rule to update (or train) the prior distribution of the parameters in the model and computes the posterior distribution for prediction. The Bayes rule can be represented as:

$$Pr(s|D) = \frac{Pr(D|s)P(s)}{Pr(D)} \tag{3.2}$$

where $Pr(s)$ is the priori probability of the sample s, $Pr(D)$ is the priori probability of the training data D, $Pr(s|D)$ is the probability of s given D, and $Pr(D|s)$ is the probability of D given s.

We give an example to illustrate the Bayesian learning process with analysis [53]. Note that for simplicity and without loss of generality, we assume that each sample can be labeled by one class label or a set of class labels. The sample generation process can be modeled as: (1) each class c has an associated prior probability $Pr(c)$, with $\sum_c Pr(c) = 1$. The sample s first randomly chooses a class label with the corresponding probability; and (2) based on the class-conditional distribution $Pr(s|c)$ and the chosen class label c, we can obtain the overall probability to generate the sample, i.e., $Pr(c)Pr(s|c)$. The posterior probability of s generated from class c is thus can be deduced by using Bayes's rule

$$Pr(c|s) = \frac{Pr(c)Pr(s|c)}{\sum_\gamma Pr(\gamma)Pr(s|\gamma)} \tag{3.3}$$

where γ crosses all the classes. Note that the probability $Pr(s|c)$ can be determined by two kinds of parameters: (1) the priori domain knowledge unrelated to the training data; and (2) the parameters which belong to the training samples. For simplicity, the overall parameters are denoted as Θ and thus, Equation 3.3 can be extended as

$$Pr(c|s) = \sum_\Theta Pr(c|s,\Theta)Pr(\Theta|S) = \sum_\Theta \frac{Pr(c|\Theta)Pr(s|c,\Theta)}{\sum_\gamma Pr(\gamma|\Theta)Pr(s|\gamma,\Theta)} Pr(\Theta|S) \tag{3.4}$$

The sum may be taken to an integral in the limit for a continuous parameter space, which is the common case. In effect, because we only know the training data for sure and are not sure of the parameter values, we are summing over all possible parameter values. Such a classification framework is called *Bayes optimal*.

Generally, it is very difficult to estimate the probability $Pr(\Theta|S)$ due to the limitation on computing ability. Therefore, a practical strategy named *maximum likelihood estimate (MLE)* is commonly applied and $argmax_\Theta Pr(\Theta|S)$ is computed.

The advantages of Bayesian classifiers are: (1) it can outperform other classifiers when the size of training data is small; and (2) it is a model based on probabilistic theory, which is robust to noise in real data. The limitation of Bayesian classifiers is that they are typically limited to learning classes that occupy contiguous regions of the instance space.

Naive Bayes Learners

Naive Bayesian classifier is one basic type of the Bayesian learners with an assumption that all the attributes are conditionally independent given the value of the class C. By independence we mean probabilistic independence, that is, A is independent of B given C whenever $Pr(A|B,C) = Pr(A|C)$ for all possible values of A, B and C, whenever $Pr(C)>0$.

The pseudo code of Naive Bayesian classifier is shown in Algorithm 3.5 [182].

Algorithm 3.5: Naive Bayesian learning algorithm

Naive_Bayes_Learn(*samples*)
For each target value v_j do
    $\hat{Pr}(v_j) \leftarrow$ estimate $\hat{Pr}(v_j)$;
    For each attribute value a_i of each attribute a do
        $\hat{Pr}(a_i|v_j) \leftarrow$ estimate $\hat{Pr}(a_i|v_j)$;
    end
end

Classify_New_Instance(x))
    $v_{NB} = argmax_{v_j \in V}\hat{Pr}(v_j)\prod_{a_i \in x}\hat{Pr}(a_i|v_j)$;

3.2.4 Neural Networks Classifier

Neural network (NN) classifier, or *artificial neural network (ANN)* classifier, is one of the classic methods used for supervising learning [182, 33]. A Neural network can be commonly represented as a format of graph, which consists of densely interconnected elements. The elements are called neurons [1].

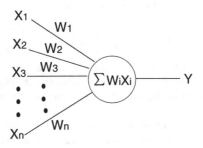

Fig. 3.13. An example neural network

Figure 3.13 illustrates one example of neural network. The input is a number of values $X_1,X_2,\ldots,X_n$ at the left side and the output is Y at the right side, both of which are in the continuous space (i.e., commonly is between 0 and 1). The neuron in the middle of the network first counts the weighted sum of the inputs, then adjusts by subtracting some threshold θ, finally transfers the result to a non-linear function f (e.g., sigmoid) to compute and output. In summary, the process can be modeled as follows.

$$Y = f(\sum_{i=1}^{N} W_i X_i - \theta) \qquad (3.5)$$

The distribution of the sigmoid function is shown in Figure 3.14.

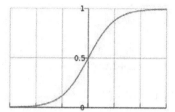

Fig. 3.14. A sigmoid function (extracted from [2])

where W_i is the weight of the element i. Outputs of some neurons may be the inputs of some other neurons. In a multi-layer perceptron topology of NN classifier, neurons are arranged in distinct layers as illustrated in Figure 3.15. Output of each layer is connected to input of nodes in the next layer, i.e., inputs of the first layer (input layer) are the inputs to the network, while the outputs of the last layer form the output of the network.

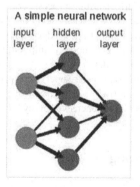

Fig. 3.15. An example perceptron topology (extracted from [2])

Training Neural Network

When training a neural network, the inputs are [3]: (a) a series of examples of the items to be classified; and (2) their proper classifications or targets. Such input can be viewed as a vector: $< X_1, X_2, \ldots, X_n, \theta, t >$, where t is the target or true classification. The neural network uses these to modify its weights, and it aims to match its classifications with the targets in the training set. Weight modification follows a learning rule. The pseudo code of training neural network is shown in Algorithm 3.6.

Algorithm 3.6: Training neural network algorithm

```
fully_trained = FALSE;
While fully_trained != TRUE do
    fully_trained = TRUE;
    For each training_vector = < X₁,X₂,...,Xₙ,θ,target > do
```
$$a = (X_1 * W_1) + (X_2 * W_2) + \ldots + (X_n * W_n) - \theta;$$
```
    y = sigmoid(a);
        If y != target then fully_trained = FALSE;
        For each Wᵢ do
            MODIFY_WEIGHT( Wᵢ);
        end
    end
    If fully_trained then BREAK;
end
```

The advantage of Neural nets is that it performs very well on difficult, non-linear domains, where it becomes more and more difficult to use Decision tree, or Rule induction systems, which cut the space of examples parallel to attribute axes. One of disadvantages in using Neural nets for data mining is a slow learning process, compared top for example Decision trees. This difference can very easily be several orders of magnitude. Another disadvantage is that neural networks do not give explicit knowledge representation in the form of rules, or some other easily interpretable form. The model is implicit, hidden in the network structure and optimized weights, between the nodes.

In addition to the above commonly used supervised learning methods, there are many others developed, such as *Discriminative Classification, Maximum Entropy Learners, SVM*, and so forth. Refer [33] for a more comprehensive survey.

3.3 Unsupervised Learning

In this section, we will introduce major techniques of unsupervised learning (or clustering). Among a large amount of approaches that have been proposed, there are three representative unsupervised learning strategies, i.e., k-means, hierarchical clustering and density based clustering.

3.3.1 The k-Means Algorithm

K-means clustering algorithm was first proposed in [173, 110]. In briefly, k-means clustering is a top-down algorithm that classifies the objects into k number of groups with regard to attributes or features, where k is a positive integer number and specified apriori by users. The grouping is done by minimizing the sum of squares of distances between object and the corresponding cluster centroid.

The key idea of k-means is simple and is as follows: In the beginning the number of clusters k is determined. Then the algorithm assumes the centroids or centers of these k clusters. These centroids can be randomly selected or designed deliberately. There may be existing one special case that the number of objects is less than the number of clusters. If so, each object is treated as the centroid of a cluster and allocated a cluster number. If the number of data is greater than the number of clusters, the algorithm computes the distance (i.e., Euclidean distance) between each object and all centroids to get the minimum distance.

Because the location of the real centroid is unknown during the process, the algorithm needs to revise the centroid location with regard to the updated information (i.e., minimum distance between new objects and the centroids). After updating the values of the centroids, all the objects are reallocated to the k clusters. The process is repeated until the assignment of objects to clusters ceases to change much, or when the centroids move by negligible distances in successive iterations. Mathematically the iteration can be proved to be convergent.

The pseudo code of the k-means algorithm is presented in Algorithm 3.7.

Algorithm 3.7: The k-means algorithm

Input: A dataset D, a user specified number k
Output: k clusters
Initialize cluster centroids (randomly);
While not convergent
    For each object o in D do
        Find the cluster c whose centroid is most close to o;
        Allocate o to c;
    end
    For each cluster c do
        Recalculate the centroid of c based on the objects allocated to c;
    end
end

3.3.2 Hierarchical Clustering

Hierarchical clustering constructs a hierarchy of clusters that can be illustrated in a tree structure which is also known as a *dendrogram*. Each node of the dendrogram, including the root, represents a cluster and the parent-child relationship among them enables us to explore different levels of clustering granularity.

There are mainly two types of algorithms for hierarchical clustering: one is in an agglomerative bottom-up manner that the algorithm starts with all the objects and successively combines them into clusters; the other is in a divisive top-down manner that the algorithm starts with one whole cluster which includes all objects and recursively splits the clusters into smaller ones. The second type can be seen as a reverse procedure of the first one and hence, we mainly introduce the former in this section.

Hierarchical Agglomerative Clustering

Hierarchical Agglomerative Clustering is typically visualized as a dendrogram as shown in Figure 3.16, which is an example on hierarchical clustering 10 objects. Each horizontal line in the dendrogram indicates a merging of two sub-clusters. The value of the horizontal line (i.e., on y-coordinate) is the similarity between the two sub-clusters merged. The bottom layer of the dendrogram indicates that each object is viewed as a singleton cluster. By moving up from the bottom layer to the top one, the dendrogram allows us to reconstruct the intermediate merges that resulted in the resultant hierarchy of clusters. The pseudo code of the Hierarchical Agglomerative Clustering (HAC) algorithm is presented in Algorithm 3.8.

Algorithm 3.8: The hierarchical agglomerative clustering algorithm

---

Input: A dataset D
Output: A hierarchy tree of clusters
Allocate each object o in D as a single cluster;
Let C be the set of the clusters;
While $|C| > 1$ do
    For all clusters $X, Y \in C$ do
        Compute the between-cluster similarity $S(X,Y)$;
    end
    $Z=X \cup Y$, where $S(X,Y)$ is the minimum;
    Remove X and Y from C;
    $C=C \cup Z$;
end

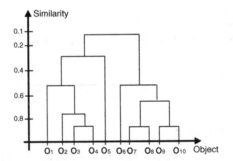

Fig. 3.16. An example dendrogram consists of 10 objects

In a brief summary, the advantages of the hierarchical clustering are [29]: (1) enable flexibility with regard to the level of granularity; (2) ease of dealing with any form of similarity metric; and (3) applicability to any attribute type. The disadvantages of the hierarchical clustering are summarized as: (1) vagueness at judging when to terminate; and (2) the fact that most hierarchical algorithms do not revisit intermediate clusters with the purpose of their improvement.

3.3.3 Density based Clustering

K-means and hierarchical clustering algorithms generally perform well on grouping large data, yet they are awkward on discovering clusters of arbitrary shapes and moreover, their performance is sensitive to the outliers in the data. To address these issues, density based clustering strategies have been proposed, in which DBSCAN is a representative one.

The DBSCAN algorithm was first introduced by Ester et al. [89]. The authors grouped the objects by recognizing the density of them. Given a pre-defined density threshold Eps, those areas with a higher density compared with Eps are considered as qualified clusters and the others are treated as outliers or noise. With the help of the inherent characteristic of cluster density, DBSCAN can discover any kind of arbitrary shape of clusters. Figure 3.17 illustrates some example datasets in which the arbitrary clusters are identified by the DBSCAN algorithm [89].

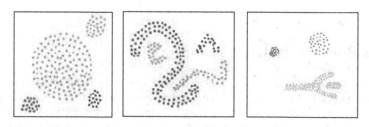

Fig. 3.17. Some clusters identified by DBSCAN in three datasets [89]

There are two main parameters in DBSCAN: Eps, the radius that bound the neighborhood region of an object; and $MinPts$, the minimum number of objects that must exist in the object's neighborhood region. The key idea of the DBSCAN algorithm is that, given the two parameters, the neighborhood (determined by Eps) of each object in a cluster has to contain the objects whose total number is greater than $MinPts$. In other words, the density of the cluster should exceed some threshold. The pseudo code of DBSCAN is presented in Algorithm 3.9 [89, 2].

Algorithm 3.9: The DBSCAN algorithm

Input: A set of objects D, the radius Eps, the threshold number $MinPts$ of neighbor objects
Output: lusters
$C=\emptyset$;
For each unvisited object o in D do
    $o.visited$=true;
    N = GetNeighbors(o,Eps);
    If $|N| < MinPts$ then
        $o.attribute$=noise;
    end
    C=next cluster;
    ExpandCluster($o, N, C, Eps, MinPts$);
end

```
// Function to expand the cluster;
Procedure ExpandCluster(o, N, C, Eps, MinPts):
    C=C ∪ o;
    For each object o' in N do
        If o'.visited=false then
            o'.visited=true;
            N' = GetNeighbors(o', eps);
            If |N'| ≥ MinPts then N = N ∪ N';
        end
        If o' is not member of any cluster then
            C=C ∪ o';
        end
end
```

3.4 Semi-supervised Learning

In the previous two sections, we have introduced the learning issues on the labeled data (supervised learning or classification), and the unlabeled data (unsupervised learning or clustering). In this chapter, we will present the basic learning techniques when both of the two kind of data are given. The intuition is that large amount of unlabeled data is easier to obtain (e.g., pages crawled by Google) yet only a small part of them could be labeled due to resource limitation. The research is so-called *semi-supervised learning* (or *semi-supervised classification*), which aims to address the problem by using large amount of unlabeled data, together with the labeled data, to build better classifiers.

There are many approaches proposed for semi-supervised classification, in which the representatives are self-training, co-training, generative models, graph-based methods. We will introduce them in the next few sections. More kinds of strategies and algorithms can be found in [278, 59].

3.4.1 Self-Training

The idea of self-training (or self-teaching, bootstrapping) appeared long time ago and the first well-known paper on applying self-training to tackle the machine learning issue may be [265]. It is now a common approach for semi-supervised classification.

The basic idea of self-training is that: a classifier c is first trained based on the labeled data L (which has small size). Then we use the classifier c to classify the unlabeled data U. Those confident (judged by a threshold) unlabeled data U' with the corresponding label class, are extracted from U and inserted into L. The two dataset, labeled and unlabeled, are updated and the procedure is repeated. The pseudo code of self-training is shown in Algorithm 3.10.

Algorithm 3.10: The self-training algorithm

Input: A labeled dataset L, an unlabeled dataset U, a confident threshold t
Output: All data with labeled class
Initial a classifier c;

While Unlabeled data $U \neq \emptyset$ do
    Train the classifier c based on L;
    Use c to classify the data in U;
    $X=\emptyset$;
    For each data $d \in U$ do
        If $d.confident \geq t$ then $X=X \cup d$;
    end
    $L=L+X$;
    $U=U-X$;
end

In a brief summary, the advantages of the self-training approach are: (1) the method is intuitive and simple can be wrapped to other more complex classifiers; and (2) it can be applied to many real applications, i.e., word sense disambiguation [265]. The disadvantage of the self-training is that the early error could be accumulated and enlarged in the later procedures.

3.4.2 Co-Training

Blum et al. [37] first proposed the co-training algorithm based on the idea of self-training by employing two classifiers. In the paper, the authors have made such assumptions that the features of data can be partitioned into two independent subsets (w.r.t class) and each subset can be used to train a good classifier. The process of the algorithm thus can be fulfilled as a dual training of the two classifiers to each other.

The pseudo code of self-training is shown in Algorithm 3.11 [53].

Algorithm 3.11: The co-training algorithm

Input: A labeled dataset L, an unlabeled dataset U, a confident threshold t
Output: All data with labeled class
Split features into two sets, F_1 and F_2;
Initial two classifiers c_1 and c_2;
For ach data $d \in L$ do
    Project d to the two feature sets, F_1 and F_2, resulting in d_1 and d_2;
    Train c_1 based on d_1 and c_2 based on d_2;
end
While Unlabeled data $U \neq \emptyset$ do
    // Train c_2 by c_1;
    Use c_1 to classify U in the feature space F_1;
    $X_1=\emptyset$;
    For each data $d \in U$ do
        If $d.confident \geq t$ then $X_1=X_1 \cup d$;
    end
    $d_2=d_2 \cup X_1$;
    // Train c_1 by c_2;
    Use c_2 to classify U in the feature space F_2;
    $X_2=\emptyset$;
    For each data $d \in U$ do
        If $d.confident \geq t$ then $X_2=X_2 \cup d$;

```
    end
    d₁=d₁ ∪X₂;
    Train c₁ based on d₁ and c₂ based on d₂;
    U=U-X₁-X₂;
end
```

The advantages of the co-training approach are: (1) the method is simple and based on self-training, and it can be wrapped to other more complex classifiers; and (2) it is not so sensitive to the early error compared with self-training. The disadvantage of the co-training is that the assumption seems to be too strong that the features of a dataset can not always be partitioned independently into two subsets.

3.4.3 Generative Models

The key idea of generative model based on semi-supervised learning approach is that, we construct an appropriate model which can best "match" the data and as a result, the classification can be easily done. The essential part for constructing the model is to find the proper values of the model parameters.

There is an assumption that both the labeled and the unlabeled datasets have the same kind of model with similar parameters. One common strategy used is to employ EM-like (i.e., expectation maximization [72]) algorithm to estimate the most like values of the parameters.

Generally, the model to be chosen is application oriented and can be different according to different users, e.g., mixture of Gaussian, naive Bayes, and so forth. Algorithm 3.12 shows an example pseudo code of combining naive Bayes model and EM procedure [192, 53].

Algorithm 3.12: The generative model based algorithm

Input: A labeled dataset L, an unlabeled dataset U
Outpot: All data with labeled class
Build the initial model M based on L;
For i=0,1,2,... while results are not satisfactory do
    For each data $d \in U$ do
        E-step: estimate $Pr(c|d,M)$ using a naive Bayes classifier, where c is a cluster;
    end
    For each cluster c do
        M-step: estimate θ_c to build the next model M_{i+1}, where θ is the parameter vector;
    end
end

The advantages of the generative model based approach are: (1) the method is clear and embedded in a probabilistic framework; and (2) is very effective if the model is correct to match the data. The main drawbacks of the co-training are: (1) the appropriate model is difficult to choose and a wrong model may weaken the effectiveness of the approach; (and 2) EM is prone to local maxima. If global maximum is very different from local maximum, then the effectiveness of the method is weakened.

3.4.4 Graph based Methods

Graph based semi-supervised approaches commonly conduct their learning processes in a graph, where each node represents one data (or example) in the labeled and unlabeled datasets. The edge between two nodes indicates the similarity of the nodes. It has been until recently that the semi-supervised researchers have begun to shift toward developing strategies that utilize the graph structure obtained by capturing similarities between the labeled and unlabeled data. In this section, we will make a brief introduction on this issue. Refer to [278] for a more comprehensive survey. Studies on other related issues of graph-based semi-supervised learning can be also found in [59, 277], to name a few.

Blum et al. may propose the first graph based approach for semi-supervised learning. The intuitive idea is that the graph is minimum cut and then the nodes in each remaining connecting component should have the same label. The same author extended the work [36] by introducing a novel strategy called majority voting to conduct the minimum cut. Both of these works assume that prediction function on the unlabeled data is discrete.

To generalize the assumption, Zhu et al. [279] proposed to tackle the issue when the prediction function is continuous. They found that the function with the lowest energy has the harmonic property by conducting experiments on graph with Gaussian random fields. Therefore, the authors proposed a label propagation approach to conduct semi-supervised learning on the graph with the harmonic property. Other interesting and important works on graph based semi-supervised learning include [26, 27, 275, 229].

Although the research on proposing effective approaches on graphs are important for semi-supervised learning, it is also very critical to build the graph that can best match the data. There are some distinct methods introduced [278]:

- knowledge from experts. In [19], the authors used domain knowledge to construct graphs for video surveillance. Without the knowledge, the graphs can not be built appropriately.
- Neighbor graphs. In [4], Carreira-Perpinan and Zemel constructed graphs from multiple minimum spanning trees by conducting perturbation and edge removal. The difficulty is that how to choose the bandwidth of the Gaussian. Zhang and Lee (2006) proposed a strategy to tune the bandwidth for each feature dimension.
- Local fit. In [272], the authors conducted LLE-like (i.e., locally linear embedding) operations on the data points while letting the weights of LLE be non-negative, which will be used as graph weights. Hein and Maier [115] proposed that a preprocessing is necessary that the noisy data should be removed first. Then the graph can be constructed from the remaining better data. The accuracy is therefore can be improved.

3.5 Markov Models

Markov model is one of the well-known approaches because of its broad applications, such as speech recognition, financial forecasting, gene prediction, cryptanalysis, natural language processing, data compression, and so forth. The common point of these applications is that their goal is to predict or recover a data sequence that is not immediately observable. For a concrete example, i.e., stock price prediction, people always want to "guess" the trend of some stock, i.e., whether its price will go up in the next day.

In fact, Markov model may be the simplest and most effective mathematical model for analyzing such kind of time-series processes, while the class of Markov model makes it rich enough to tackle all of these applications.

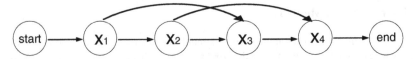

Fig. 3.18. A second-order Markov chain of observations $\{x_n\}$

3.5.1 Regular Markov Models

For the stock prediction problem, one naive solution could be that we ignore the time aspect of the historic data, but only count the frequency of each instance (i.e., up or down) to predict the next possible instance. Yet this approach does not consider the correlated relationship between those neighboring events. It is naturally to think that the most recent event contributes more than the older ones to predict future instance. For example, if we know that the price of a stock often behaves in a continuous trend, then given the fact that today's price has been up, we can draw a conclusion that tomorrow's price will most likely go up. This scenario may let us to consider Markov models in which we assume that future predictions are independent of all but the most recent observations.

Specifically, if we assume that the nth event is independent of all previous observations except the most recent one (i.e., $n-1th$ event), then the distribution could be shown as

$$p(x_n|x_1,\ldots,x_{n-1}) = p(x_n|x_{n-1}), \tag{3.6}$$

where $p(x_i)$ denotes the probability of the event x_i happens. This is also called the *first-order* Markov chain. If the distributions $p(x_n|x_{n-1})$ are assumed to be the same all the time, then the model is named as *homogeneous* Markov chain.

In a similar way, if we allow more early events to contribute to the prediction, then the model should be extended to higher-order Markov chain. For example, we can obtain a *second-order* Markov chain, by assuming that the nth event is independent of all previous observations except the most recent two (i.e., $n-2th$ and $n-1th$ events). It can be illustrated as in Figure 3.18. The distribution is shown as follows.

$$p(x_n|x_1,\ldots,x_{n-1}) = p(x_n|x_{n-2},x_{n-1}), \tag{3.7}$$

We can extend the model to an Mth-*order* Markov chain in which the conditional distribution for an event depends on its previous M events. By this strategy, the knowledge of correlation between more neighboring events can be flexibly embedded into the model. Nevertheless, on the other hand, this solution has the trade-off that more cost of computation will be introduced. For example, suppose the events are discrete with S states. Then the conditional distribution $p(x_n|x_{n-M},\ldots,x_{n-1})$ in a Mth-order Markov chain will be used to generate the joint distribution and the number of parameters will becomes $S^{M-1}(S-1)$. As the value of M becomes larger, the number of parameters will becomes exponentially and the computation cost may be huge.

If the event variables is in a continuous space, then linear-Gaussian conditional distributions is appropriate to use, or we can apply a neural network which has a parametric model for the distribution. Refer to [211, 33, 182] for more detail. In the next section, we will introduce the *hidden Markov model*, or *HMM* [84], which deals with the situation that the state variables are latent and discrete.

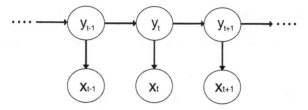

Fig. 3.19. A hidden Markov model with observations $\{x_n\}$ and latent states $\{y_n\}$

3.5.2 Hidden Markov Models

A *hidden Markov model* (*HMM*) is a statistical model in which the system being modeled is assumed to be a Markov process with unobserved state [2]. In a regular Markov model (as introduced in the last section), the state can be visible to the observer directly and thus, the only parameter in the model is the state transition probability. However, in a hidden Markov model, the state can not be directly visible (i.e., hidden), but the event (or observation, output) which is dependent on the state, is visible. In other words, the state behaves like a *latent variable*, where the latent variable is discrete. The hidden Markov model can be illustrated in a graph, as shown in Figure 3.19.

The intuitive idea of HMM is that, because every state has a probability distribution over the possible output, the output sequence generated by an HMM provides some related information about the state sequence.

Hidden Markov models are especially known for their application in temporal pattern recognition such as speech [125], handwriting [187], natural language processing [179], musical score following, partial discharges and bioinformatics [141].

Suppose that the hidden state behaves like a discrete multinomial variable y_n and it controls how to generate the corresponding event x_n. The probability distribution of y_n is dependent on the previous latent variable y_{n-1} and thus, we have a conditional distribution $p(y_n|y_{n-1})$. We assume that the latent variables having S states so that the conditional distribution corresponds to a set of numbers which named *transition probabilities*. All of these numbers together are denoted by T and can be represented as $T_{jk} \equiv p(y_{nk} = 1|y_{n-1,j} = 1)$, where we have $0 \leq T_{jk} \leq 1$ with $\sum_k T_{jk} = 1$. Therefore, the matrix T has $S(S-1)$ independent parameters. The conditional distribution can be computed as

$$p(y_n|y_{n-1},T) = \prod_{k=1}^{S} \prod_{j=1}^{S} T_{jk}^{y_{n-1,j}y_{nk}}. \tag{3.8}$$

Note that for the initial latent variable y_1, because it does not have a previous variable, the above equation can be adapted as $p(y_1|\pi) = \prod_{k=1}^{S} \pi_k^{y_{1k}}$, where π denotes a vector of probabilities with $\pi_k \equiv p(y_{1k} = 1)$ and $\sum_k \pi_k = 1$.

Emission probabilities are defined as the conditional distributions of the output $p(x_n|y_n,\phi)$, where ϕ is a set of parameters controlling the distribution. These probabilities could be modeled by conditional probabilities if x is discrete, or by Gaussians if the elements of x are continuous variables. The emission probabilities can be represented as

$$p(x_n|y_n,\phi) = \prod_{k=1}^{S} p(x_n|\phi_k)^{y_{nk}}. \tag{3.9}$$

Here we discuss a special model, named *homogeneous* model. The word "homogeneous" means that the matrix T and the ϕ are always the same for the model no matter what kind of conditional and emission distributions. As such, we can obtain the joint probability distribution over both latent variables and observations as

$$p(X,Y|\theta) = p(y_1|\pi) \left[\prod_{n=2}^{N} p(y_n|y_{n-1}, T) \right] \prod_{m=1}^{N} p(x_m|y_m, \phi). \qquad (3.10)$$

where $X = \{x_1, \ldots, x_N\}$, $Y = \{y_1, \ldots, y_N\}$, and $\theta = \{\pi, T, \phi\}$ denotes the set of parameters controlling the model. Note that the emission probabilities could be any possible type, e.g., Gaussians, mixtures of Gaussians, and neural networks, since the emission density $p(x|y)$ can be directly obtained or indirectly got by using Bayes' theorem based on the models.

There are many variants of the standard HMM model, e.g., *left-to-right* HMM [211], *generalized* HMM [142], *generalized pair* HMM [195], and so forth. To estimate the parameters of an HMM, the most commonly used algorithm is named Expectation Maximization (EM) [72]. Several algorithms have been later proposed to further improve the efficiency (or training HMM), such as *forward-backward* algorithm [211], and *sum-product* approach. Readers can refer to [211, 33, 182] for more details.

3.6 K-Nearest-Neighboring

K-Nearest-Neighbor (*k*NN) approach is the most often used recommendation scoring algorithm in many recommender systems, which is to compare the current user activity with the historic records of other users for finding the top k users who share the most similar behaviors to the current one. In conventional recommender systems, finding k nearest neighbors is usually accomplished by measuring the similarity in rating of items or visiting on web pages between current user and others. The found neighboring users are then used to produce a prediction of items that are potentially rated or visited but not done yet by the current active user via collaborative filtering approaches. Therefore, the core component of the *k*NN algorithm is the similarity function that is used to measure the similarity or correlation between users in terms of attribute vectors, in which each user activity is characterized as a sequence of attributes associated with corresponding weights.

3.7 Content-based Recommendation

Content-based recommendation is a textual information filtering approach based on users historic ratings on items. In a content-based recommendation, a user is associated with the attributes of the items that rated, and a user profile is learned from the attributes of the items to model the interest of the user. The recommendation score is computed by measuring the similarity of the attributes the user rated with those of not being rated, to determine which attributes might be potentially rated by the same user. As a result of attribute similarity comparison, this method is actually a conventional information processing approach in the case of recommendation. The learned user profile reflects the long-time preference of a user within a period, and could be updated as more different rated attributes representing users interest are observed. Content-based recommendation is helpful for predicting individuals preference since it is on a basis of referring to the individuals historic rating data rather than taking others preference into consideration.

3.8 Collaborative Filtering Recommendation

Collaborative filtering recommendation is probably the most commonly and widely used technique that has been well developed for recommender systems. As the name indicated, collaborative recommender systems work in a collaborative referring way that is to aggregate ratings or preference on items, discover user profiles/patterns via learning from users historic rating records, and generate new recommendation on a basis of inter-pattern comparison. A typical user profile in recommender system is expressed as a vector of the ratings on different items. The rating values could be either binary (like/dislike) or analogous-valued indicating the degree of preference, which is dependent on the application scenarios. In the context of collaborative filtering recommendation, there are two major kinds of collaborative filtering algorithms mentioned in literature, namely memory-based and model-based collaborative filtering algorithm [117, 193, 218].

3.8.1 Memory-based collaborative recommendation

Memory-based algorithms use the total ratings of users in the training database while computing recommendation. These systems can also be classified into two sub-categories: user-based and item-based algorithms [218]. For example, user-based kNN algorithm, which is based on calculating the similarity between two users, is to discover a set of users who have similar taste to the target user, i.e. neighboring users, using kNN algorithm. After k nearest neighboring users are found, this system uses a collaborative filtering algorithm to produce a prediction of top-N recommendations that the user may be interested in later. Given a target user u, the prediction on item i is then calculated by:

$$p_{u,i} = \frac{\sum_{j=1}^{k} \left(R_{j,i} sim\left(u,j\right) \right)}{\sum_{j=1}^{k} sim\left(u,j\right)} \tag{3.11}$$

Here $R_{j,i}$ denotes the rating on item i voted by user j, and only k most similar users (i.e. k nearest neighbors of user i) are considered in making recommendation.

In contrast to user-based kNN, item-based kNN algorithm [218, 126] is a different collaborative filtering algorithm, which is based on computing the similarity between two columns, i.e. two items. In item-based kNN systems, mutual item-item similarity relation table is constructed first on a basis of comparing the item vectors, in which each item is modeled as a set of ratings by all users. To produce the prediction on an item i for user u, it computes the ratio of the sum of the ratings given by the user on the items that are similar to i with respect to the sum of involved item similarities as follows:

$$p_{u,i} = \frac{\sum_{j=1}^{k} \left(R_{u,j} sim\left(i,j\right) \right)}{\sum_{j=1}^{k} sim\left(i,j\right)} \tag{3.12}$$

Here $R_{u,j}$ denotes the prediction of rating given by user u on item j, and only the k most similar items (k nearest neighbors of item i) are used to generate the prediction.

3.8.2 Model-based Recommendation

A model-based collaborative filtering algorithm is to derive a model from the historic rating data, and in turn, uses it for making recommendation. To derive the hidden model, a variety of statistical machine learning algorithms can be employed on the training database, such as Bayesian networks, neural networks, clustering and latent semantic analysis and so on. For example, in a model-based recommender system, named *Profile Aggregations based on Clustering Transaction* (PACT) [184], clustering algorithm was employed to generate aggregations of user sessions, which are viewed as profiles via grouping users with similar access taste into various clusters. The centroids of the user session clusters can be considered as access patterns/models learned from web usage data and used to make recommendation via referring to the web objects visited by other users who share the most similar access task to the current target user.

Although there exist of different recommendation algorithms in recommender systems, however, it is easily found that these algorithms are both executing in a collaborative manner, and the recommendation score is dependent on the significant weight.

3.9 Social Network Analysis

A social network is a social structure consisting of individuals (or organizations) called nodes and ties that connecting nodes by different types of interdependency, such as friendship, affiliation relationship, communication mode or relationship of religions, interest or prestige. Social network analysis aims to reveal or visualize the relationships resided in the network via network theory. Basically the graph theory is a common principle that used to conduct the analysis. Since the social network compounds the complicated interaction behaviors between various individuals from the different aspects, the analysis is not a easy job with only the traditional means, and the resulting graph-based structure is often very *complex*. Social network analysis is studied in social science areas such as psychology, sociology, behavior science and organization science discipline in several decades ago [23, 221, 250].

Nowadays the emergence of web-based communities and hosted services such as social networking sites, Wikis and folksonomies, brings in tremendous freedom of Web autonomy and facilitate collaboration and knowledge sharing between users. Along with the interaction between users and computers, social media are rapidly becoming an important part of our digital experience, ranging from digital textual information to diverse multimedia forms. These aspects and characteristics constitute of the core of second generation of Web. The close involvement of computing intelligence science has injected the social network analysis research a lot of new methodologies and technologies, resulting in the social network analysis became a very active and hot topic in the web research.

3.9.1 Detecting Community Structure in Networks

One of the main tasks in social network analysis is to capture the community structure of networks. Community structure has been recognized as an important statistical feature of networked systems over the past decade. Generally, a community within a network is a subgraph whose nodes are densely connected within itself but less connected with the rest of the network. From this perspective, therefore, finding such group of nodes in a network could be treated as a clustering problem, i.e. satisfying the criterion that the nodes within each cluster have dense connections each other but less linkings with others in other clusters. As discussed in section 3.3. Basically there are two categories of clustering algorithms, namely agglomerative clustering (or hierarchical clustering), which starts from the individual isolated nodes and aggregate them which are close or similar enough to each other, producing aggregated groups, and divisive clustering, which assigns each node into separate clusters continuously by following some optimization rules, such as k-means or k-nodes [106]. In the category of divisive clustering, the partition could be executed in a hard or soft way. The previous one means one node can only belong to one unique cluster [106, 191], while the latter one specifies that one node could be assigned into more than one clusters but with varying memberships [271].

Although the detection solution of community structure is straightforward, devising an efficient algorithm for detecting the community structure in a complex network is highly nontrivial. A number of algorithms for detecting the communities have been developed in different applications [252, 191, 271, 190].

Modularity Function Q for Community Structure Detection

Newman and Girvan [191] has developed a new approach of community structure detection. They introduced a procedure of two stages. First it runs the iterative removal of edges from the network to split it into communities, the removed edges are identified by using any one of a number of possible "betweenness" measures. Second, these measures are, iteratively updated after each removal. The partition operation ceases until the optimization condition is reached. In order to choose an appropriate community number to ensure the strength of community structure, a *modularity* function Q for monitoring community structure is proposed to provide a effective means quantitatively measuring the 'goodness' of the clusters discovered. The modularity of a particular division of a network is computed based on the differences between the actual number of edges within a community in the division and the expected number of such edges if they are partitioned randomly. Hence, finding the underlying community structure hidden in a network is equivalent to a process of determining the optimal modularity value over the all possible divisions of the network.

Formally, given an undirected graph or network $G(V,E)$, where V is the node set and E the edge set. The symmetric weight of each edge represents the "betweenness" between two nodes i and j, i.e. $W = [w_{ij}]$, $w_{ij} \geq 0$. The modularity function Q is given by

$$Q(P_k) = \sum_{c=1}^{k} \left[\frac{L(V_c, V_c)}{L(V,V)} - \left(\frac{L(V_c,V)}{L(V,V)} \right)^2 \right] \qquad (3.13)$$

where P_k is a division of nodes into k groups and $L\left(V', V''\right) = \Sigma_{i \in V', j \in V''} w_{ij}$. The Q function measures the quality of a given community structure organization of a network and provides a objective metric for detecting the optimal community number k according to the maximum Q value. To improve the scalability of the modularity function Q calculation, a variety of variant algorithms are proposed, such as the fast agglomerative greedy algorithm [190].

Updated Modularity Function using Fuzzy C-means Clustering

Zhang et al. proposed an updated version of modularity function Q [271]. The main idea in the work is to replace the "hard division" with the "soft division" by using fuzzy c-means clustering. Given k communities existing in the network, we define a corresponding $n \times k$ soft division matrix $U_k = [u_1, \cdots, u_k]$ with $0 \leq u_{ic} \leq 1$ for each $c = 1, \cdots, k$ and $\sum_{c=1}^{k} u_{ic} = 1$

for each $i = 1, \cdots, n$. With the introduction of fuzzy assignment, we can further define the membership of each community as $\overline{V}_c = \{i | u_{ic} > \lambda, i \in V\}$, where λ is a threshold which is used to determine a soft division to a final clustering The new modularity function Q is reformulated as

$$\overline{Q}(U_k) = \sum_{c=1}^{k} \left[\frac{A(\overline{V}_c, \overline{V}_c)}{A(V,V)} - \left(\frac{A(\overline{V}_c, V)}{A(V,V)} \right)^2 \right] \qquad (3.14)$$

where U_k is a fuzzy division of the nodes into k clusters and

$$A(\overline{V}_c, \overline{V}_c) = \sum_{i \in \overline{V}_c, j \in \overline{V}_c} \left((u_{ic} + u_{jc})/2 \right) w_{ij}$$

$$(\overline{V}_c, V) = A(\overline{V}_c, \overline{V}_c) + \sum_{i \in \overline{V}_c, j \in V \backslash \overline{V}_c} \left((u_{ic} + (1 - u_{jc}))/2 \right) w_{ij}$$

and $A(V,V) = \sum_{i \in V, j \in V} w_{ij}$. Eq.3.14 gives a generalization of the Newman's Q function.

With the updated modularity function Q, Zhang et al. [271] proposed a new algorithm for detecting the community structure by combining the spectral and fuzzy c-mean clustering. The detailed algorithm description is stated as follows [271].

- Spectral mapping: (i) Compute the diagonal matrix $D = (d_{ii})$, where $d_{ii} = \sum_k a_{ik}$ (ii) Form the eigenvector matrix $E_k = [e_1, e_2, \cdots, e_k]$ by computing the top K eigenvectors of the generalized eigensystem $Ax = tDx$.
- Fuzzy c-means: for each value of k, $2 \leq k \leq K$: (i) Form the matrix $E_k = [e_2, e_3, \cdots, e_k]$ from the matrix E_k. (ii) Normalize the rows of E_k to unit length using Euclidean distance norm. (iii) Cluster the row vectors of E_k using fuzzy c-means or any other fuzzy clustering method to obtain a soft assignment matrix U_k.
- Maximizing the modular function: Pick the k and the corresponding fuzzy partition U_k that maximizes $\overline{Q}(U_k)$.

The main purpose of the updated modularity function is to detect the overlapping of the community structure in a network. In Fig.3.20, an example is presented to illustrate the detection of community structure overlapping along with calculated modularity function Q values by using k-means and fuzzy spectral clustering.

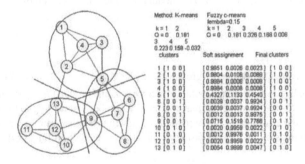

Fig. 3.20. An example of the overlapping detection of community structure using fuzzy spectral clustering [271]

3.9.2 The Evolution of Social Networks

Another important aspect of social networks is the dynamic and evolutionary changes of the network structure over time. Since the social network is an explicit demonstration of relationships or interactions of individuals within a network environment, the networked communities may evolve over time, due to changes to individual roles, social status even the personal preferences in the network. Hence the analysis of these communities (memberships, structure and temporal dynamics) is emerging as an interesting and important research issue within the social network analysis research areas.

There are a variety of approaches and algorithms proposed to address the dynamic evolution of social networks. These algorithms are usually categorized into two main families. The first one is using an additional temporal dimension along with the traditional networked-graphs [236, 15]. In these approaches, the ordinary two-way graph model is expanded into a three-way tensor model by adding a temporal dimension. The networks at different timestamps are modeled as an individual networked graph, which is expressed as a matrix. As such a set of networked graphs at a sequence of time stamps consists of a three-way data cube, in which each slice of the data cube is corresponding to a networked graph at a specific time stamp. Intuitively, a tensor representation is a better means to capture the relationships of nodes in the network along with a temporal feature. Some developed algorithms in tensor analysis have been successfully applied in the analysis of community structure evolutions. The basic idea behind these algorithms is the approximation optimization theory, which is executed by a tensor decomposition process.

For a given tensor expression modeling the sequence of network structures, $tensX$, the process is to find a best rank k approximation tensor $\overline{X}$, which satisfies the criterion of minimization of $\left\|X - \overline{X}\right\|_F$, where $X \in R^{N_1 \times \cdots \times N_m}$ and $\overline{X} \in R^{R_1 \times \cdots \times R_m}$. The best approximation tensor, $\overline{X}$, is decomposed into the product of a core tensor Y of two projection matrices of row and colume avriables U_1 and U_2, as shown in Fig.3.21. The core tensor Y conveys the community structures as well as the temproal evolutions over time, and the projection matrices U_1 and U_2 carry the aggregation property of individual nodes to various community structures.

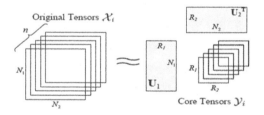

Fig. 3.21. The illustration of tensor decomposition [236]

The second category of temporal analysis of dynamic community structures is the simultaneous discovery of community structure and dynamic evolution. Apart from the classic community detection and dynamic evolution analysis algorithms, such kind of approaches take both two requests together into account when conducting social network analysis. The hypnosis in these approaches is that the evolution of community structures in a network from one stage to its consecutive stage will not change dramatically, instead, follows the routine that the incurring cost will be minimized. This assumption is quite reasonable in real world that the evolution of real observations is gradually and properly in a longitudinal manner.

In [164], Lin et al. proposed a framework for analyzing communities and their evolution in dynamic networks. In their approach, they first introduced a cost function to measure the quality of community structure at a certain time t and assumed the forming of stable community structure is really dependent on the minimization of the cost function. In particular, the cost function consists of two aspects - a snapshot cost and a temporal cost:

$$cost = \alpha \cdot CS + (1 - \alpha) \cdot CT \tag{3.15}$$

The snapshot cost is then determined by the distribution difference between the real similarity matrix of nodes within the network and the calculated similarity matrix of the formed community structures. That is, the snapshot cost is the KL-divergence between the above mentioned similarity matrix. On the other hand, the temporal cost indicates the distribution difference between the similarity matrices at two consecutive time stamps using the same formula. Combining these two types of cost gives the whole cost measure, which is used to guide the community structure detection. Hence the analysis of community structures and their evolutions is converted to an optimization problem of finding appropriate communities that minimizes the whole cost. To solve the optimization problem, an iterative algorithm is devised to alternatively update the requested community structures until an optimization solution is reached. More details is referred to [164].

Summary

In this chapter, we review and summarize some commonly used algorithms and techniques in the applications of web data mining, web recommendation and social network analysis. The mathematical formulations and algorithmic descriptions are elaborately organized into nine sections. It is expected that this chapter provides a technically detailed reference resource for readers to proceed the further chapters.

Part II

Web Mining: Techniques and Applications

4

Web Content Mining

In recent years the growth of the World Wide Web exceeded all expectations. Today there are several billions of HTML documents, pictures and other multimedia files available via Internet and the number is still rising. But considering the impressive variety of the Web, retrieving interesting contents has become a very difficult task. Web Content Mining uses the ideas and principles of data mining and knowledge discovery to screen more specific data. The use of the Web as a provider of information is unfortunately more complex than working with static databases. Because of its very dynamic nature and its vast number of documents, there is a need for new solutions that are not depending on accessing the complete data on the outset. Another important aspect is the presentation of query results. Due to its enormous size, a Web query can retrieve thousands of resulting Web pages. Thus meaningful methods for presenting these large results are necessary to help a user to select the most interesting content. In this chapter we will discuss several basic topics of Web document representation, Web search, short text processing, topic extraction and Web opinion mining.

4.1 Vector Space Model

The representation of a set of documents as vectors in a common vector space is known as the vector space model and is fundamental to a host of information retrieval operations ranging from scoring documents on a query, document classification and document clustering. We first develop the notion of a document vector that captures the relative importance of the terms in a document.

Towards this end, we assign to each term in a document a weight for that term, that depends on the number of occurrences of the term in the document. We would like to compute a score between a query term and a document based on the weight of t in d. The simplest approach is to assign the weight to be equal to the number of occurrences of term t in document d. This weighting scheme is referred to as term frequency and is denoted $tf_{t,d}$, with the subscripts denoting the term and the document in order.

Raw term frequency as above suffers from a critical problem: all terms are considered equally important when it comes to assessing relevancy on a query. In fact certain terms have little or no discriminating power in determining relevance. For instance, a collection of documents on the auto industry is likely to have the term auto in almost every document. To this end, we introduce a mechanism for attenuating the effect of terms that occur too often in the

G. Xu et al., *Web Mining and Social Networking,*
DOI 10.1007/978-1-4419-7735-9_4, © Springer Science+Business Media, LLC 2011

collection to be meaningful for relevance determination. An immediate idea is to scale down the term weights of terms with high collection frequency, defined to be the total number of occurrences of a term in the collection. The idea would be to reduce the weight of a term by a factor that grows with its collection frequency.

Instead, it is more commonplace to use for this purpose the document frequency df_t, defined to be the number of documents in the collection that contain a term t. This is because when trying to discriminate between documents for the purpose of scoring it is better to use a document-level statistic (such as the number of documents containing a term) than to use a collection-wide statistic for the term.

How is the document frequency df of a term used to scale its weight? Denoting as usual the total number of documents in a collection by N, we define the inverse document frequency of a term t as follows:

$$idf_t = log\frac{N}{df_t}. \tag{4.1}$$

Thus the idf of a rare term is high, whereas the idf of a frequent term is likely to be low.

We now combine the definitions of term frequency and inverse document frequency, to produce a composite weight for each term in each document. The $tf-idf$ weighting scheme assigns to term t a weight in document d given by

$$tf-idf_t = tf_{t,d} \times idf_t. \tag{4.2}$$

In other words, $tf-idf$ assigns to term t a weight in document d that is

(1) highest when occurs many times within a small number of documents (thus lending high discriminating power to those documents);
(2) lower when the term occurs fewer times in a document, or occurs in many documents (thus offering a less pronounced relevance signal);
(3) lowest when the term occurs in virtually all documents.

At this point, we may view each document as a vector with one component corresponding to each term in the dictionary, together with a weight for each component that is given by Equation 4.1. For dictionary terms that do not occur in a document, this weight is zero. This vector form is crucial to score and rank in Web content mining.

To compensate for the effect of document length, the standard way of quantifying the similarity between two documents d_1 and d_2 is to compute the cosine similarity of their vector representations $V(d_1)$ and $V(d_2)$

$$sim(d_1,d_2) = \frac{V(d_1) \cdot V(d_2)}{|V(d_1)||V(d_2)|}, \tag{4.3}$$

where the numerator represents the dot product (also known as the inner product) of the vectors $V(d_1)$ and $V(d_2)$, while the denominator is the product of their Euclidean lengths.

As we know, an information retrieval (or IR for short) process begins when a user enters a query into the system. Queries are formal statements of information needs, for example, search strings in Web search engines. In information retrieval a query does not uniquely identify a single document in the collection. Instead, several documents may match the query, perhaps with different degrees of relevancy.

To compute the relevancy, we can also view a query as a vector. By viewing a query as a "bag of words", we are able to treat it as a very short document. As a consequence, we can use the cosine similarity between the query vector and a document vector as a measure of the score of the document for that query. The resulting scores can then be used to select the top-scoring documents for a query in information retrieval. Thus we have

$$score(q,d) = \frac{V(q) \cdot V(d)}{|V(q)||V(d)|}.$$

(4.4)

A document may have a high cosine score for a query even if it does not contain all query terms. The top ranking documents are then shown to the user. The process may then be iterated if the user wishes to refine the query.

4.2 Web Search

The World Wide Web has become a new communication medium with informational, cultural, social and evidential values after a few decades since its inception. Search engines are widely used for Web information access and they are making more information easily accessible than ever before. Although the general Web search today is still performed and delivered predominantly through search algorithms, e.g., Google's PageRank [196], the interests in helping Web users effectively get their desired Web pages have been growing over the recent years.

Web search has its root in information retrieval, a field of study that helps the user find needed information from a large collection of text documents. Traditional IR assumes that the basic information unit is a document, and a large collection of documents are available to form the text database. On the Web, the documents are Web pages.

It is safe to say that Web search is the single most important application of IR. To a great extent, Web search also helped IR. Indeed, the tremendous success of search engines has pushed IR to the center stage. Search is, however, not simply a straightforward application of traditional IR models. It uses some IR results, but it also has its unique techniques and presents many new problems for IR research.

4.2.1 Activities on Web archiving

The World Wide Web has been perceived as a modern human artifact with cultural, societal, historical, and evidential significance. Web information is being created, changed, and modified by governments, companies, organizations, groups, and individuals continuously at a rapid rate. To prevent the Web information from disappearing into past, many national libraries and non-profit organizations have initiated Web Archiving projects with different scopes and scales. In the remaining of this section, we will summarize some current activities on Web archiving.

UNESCO Charter on the Preservation of the Digital Heritage

In 2003, UNESCO announced a campaign to preserve the 'digital heritage'. The draft Charter on the preservation of the digital heritage, in which each member state was obliged to preserve digital materials (text, audio, images, Web pages, etc.) for the future generations, was submitted to the UNESCO executive board in 2003. The purpose of the Charter is to focus worldwide attention on the issues at stake, and to encourage responsible action wherever it can be taken.

The Internet Archive

The Internet Archive is a non-profit organization founded in 1996 with the purpose of offering permanent global access to historical collections that exist in digital format. Pioneering in archiving the World Wide Web, the Internet Archive includes not only Web pages but also texts, audio, moving images, software, etc. It is the largest Web archiving organization based on a crawling approach which strives to collect and maintain snapshots of the entire Web.

At the time of this writing, Web information collected by the Internet Archive consists of more than 110 billion URLs downloaded from over 65 million Web sites (corresponding to about 2 PB of raw data). It includes Web pages captured from every domain name on the internet, and encompasses over 37 languages.

LiWA - Living Web Archives (the European Web Archives)

LiWA[1] is a non-profit organization founded in 2004. The goal of the LiWA project is to foster free online access of European cultural heritage and develops an open Web archive. Research efforts of LiWA focus on improving fidelity, temporal coherence, and long-term viability of Web archives.

The enhancement of archiving fidelity and authenticity will be achieved by devising methods for capturing all types of Web information content, crawler traps detection, Web spam and noise filtering. The improvement of Archives' coherence and integrity will be supported by a set of methods and tools for dealing with temporal issues in Web archive construction. To support long term interpretability of the content in the Archive, problems related to terminology and semantic evolutions will also be addressed.

4.2.2 Web Crawling

Web Crawling Bascis

A Web crawler (also known as a Web spider or a Web robot) is a program or an automated script which browses the Web in a methodical, automated manner. In general, the crawler starts with a list of URLs to visit, called the seeds. As the crawler visits these URLs, it extracts all the hyperlinks in the page and adds them to the list of URLs to visit, called the crawl frontier. The URLs from the frontier are recursively visited according to a set of crawl policies or strategies. This process is repeated until the crawl frontier is empty or some other criteria are met.

Because the Web is dynamic and is evolving at a rapid rate, there is a continuous need for crawlers to help Web applications keep up-to-date as Web information (both page content and hyperlinks) is being added, deleted, moved, or modified. Web crawlers are used in many applications such as business intelligence (e.g. collect information about competitors or potential collaborators), monitoring websites and pages of interest, and malicious applications (e.g. e-mail harvesting). The most important application of crawlers is in support of search engines. Web crawlers are used by search engines to collect pages for building search indexes. Well known search engines such as Google, Yahoo!, and MSN run highly efficient universal crawlers engineered to gather all pages irrespective of their content. Other crawlers, sometimes called preferential crawlers, are designed to download only pages of certain types or topics.

Basically, a crawler starts from a set of seed pages (URLs) and then uses the hyperlinks within the seed pages to fetch other pages. The links in the fetched pages are, in turn, extracted and the corresponding pages are visited. The process repeats until some objective is met e.g. a sufficient number of pages are fetched. Web crawling can be thought of as a graph search

---

[1] http://www.liwa-project.eu/

algorithm. The Web can be viewed as a directed graph with pages as its nodes and hyperlinks as its edges. A crawler starts traversing the Web graph from a few of the nodes (i.e. seeds) and then follows the edges to reach other nodes. The process of fetching a page and extracting the hyperlinks within it is analogous to expanding a node in graph search.

Different Types of Crawlers:

Context-focused crawlers [76] are another type of focused crawlers. The context-focused crawlers also use naïve Bayesian classifier as a guide, but in this case the classifiers are trained to estimate the link distance between a crawled page and a set of relevant target pages. The intuition behind this is based on the fact that sometimes relevant pages can be found by knowing what kinds of off-topic pages link to them. For example, suppose that we want to find information about "machine learning". We might go to the home pages of computer science departments to look for the home page of a faculty staff who is working on the topic which may then lead to relevant pages and papers about "machine learning". In this situation, a typical focused crawler discussed earlier would give the home pages of the computer science department and the faculty staffs a low priority and may never follow its links. However, if the context-focused crawler could estimate that pages about "machine learning" are only two links away from a page containing the keywords "computer science department", then it would give the department home page a higher priority.

C. C. Aggarwal et al. [5] introduce a concept of "intelligent Web crawling" where the user can specify an arbitrary predicate (e.g. keywords, document similarity, and so on anything that can be implemented as a function which determines documents relevance to the crawl based on URL and page content) and the system adapts itself as the crawl progresses in order to maximize the harvest rate. It is suggested that for some types of predicates the topical locality assumption of focused crawling (i.e. relevant pages are located close together) might not hold. In those cases the URL string, actual contents of pages pointing to the relevant one or something else might do a better job at predicting relevance. A probabilistic model for URL priority prediction is trained using information about content of inlinking pages, URL tokens, short-range locality information (e.g. "the parent does not satisfy predicate X but the children does") and sibling information (i.e. number of sibling pages matching the predicate so far). D. Bergmark et al. [28] proposed a modified "tunneling" enhancement to the best-first focused crawling approach. Since relevant information can sometimes be located only by visiting some irrelevant pages first and since the goal is not always to minimize the number of downloaded pages but to collect a high-quality collection in a reasonable amount of time; they propose to continue crawling even if irrelevant pages are found. With statistical analysis they find out that a longer path history does have an impact on relevance of pages to be retrieved in future (compared to just using the current parent pages relevance score) and construct a document distance measure that takes into account parent page's distance (which is in turn based on the grandparent page's distance etc).

S. Chakrabarti et al. [57] enhanced the basic focused crawler framework by utilizing latent information in the HREF of the source page to guess the topic of the HREF of the target relevant page. In this improved framework, page relevance and URL visit priorities are decided separately by two classifiers. The first classifier, which evaluates page relevance, can be anything that outputs a binary classification score. The second classifier (also called "apprentice learner"), which assigns priority for unvisited URLs, is a simplified reinforcement learner. The apprentice learner helps assign a more accurate priority score to an unvisited URL in the frontier by using DOM features on its source pages. This leads to a higher harvest rate.

Experimental results showed that the new system can cut down fraction of false positive by 30-90%.

While most of focused crawlers found in the literature use the naïve Bayesian classification algorithm to assign priority scores for unvisited URLs, G. Pant and P. Srinivasan [198] have shown strong evidence that classification based on SVM or neural networks can yield significant improvements in terms of the quality of crawled pages.

4.2.3 Personalized Web Search

The simple and yet friendly Web user interfaces provided by those search engines allow users to pose search queries simply in terms of keywords. However, the difficulty in finding only those which satisfy an individual's information goal increases. This is because search engines primarily rely on the matching of the keywords to the terms in the desired documents to determine which Web pages will be returned given a search query. The main limitation with keyword-based search queries is two folds. First, due to the ambiguity of user needs, some keywords have different meanings in different context, such as mouse trap, Jaguar, Java and so on. Present search engines generally handle search queries without considering user preferences or contexts in which users submit their queries. Furthermore, users often fail to choose proper terms that best express their information needs. Ambiguous keywords used in Web queries, the diverse needs of users, and the limited ability of users to precisely express what they want to search in a few keywords have been widely recognized as a challenging obstacle in improving search quality.

Currently, encoding human search experiences and personalizing the search result delivery through ranking optimization is a popular approach in recent data engineering field to enhancing the result quality of Web search and user experience with the Web today. We categorize the research efforts on personalized search into three classes of strategies: 1) query modification or augmentation [61, 226], 2) link-based score personalization [113, 124, 170, 196, 208, 213], and 3) search result re-ranking [62, 79, 158, 161, 159, 168, 226, 239, 241].

A general process of search result re-ranking is to devise efficient mechanisms to re-order search results by personalized ranking criteria. Such criteria are typically derived from the modeling of users' search behavior and interests. More specifically speaking, there are two kinds of context information we can use to model search experience and capture user search histories. One is short-term context, which emphasizes that the most recent search is most directly close to the user's current information need [170, 225, 226]. Successive searches in a session usually have the same information need. Detecting a session boundary, however, is a difficult task. The other is long-term context, which generally assumes that users will hold their interests over a relatively long time. It means that any search in the past may have some effect on the current search [62, 168, 207, 241]. These studies commonly used all available contexts as a whole to improve the search result quality and ranking. Preliminary discussion on this problem in [239] is in the context of only exploiting long-term search history of users.

Therefore, one important component of personalized search result re-ranking is learning users' interests (preferences). There have been many schemes of building user profiles to figure user preferences from text documents. We notice that most of them model user profiles represented by bags of words without considering term correlations [32, 148, 230, 255]. A kind of a simple ontology is a taxonomic hierarchy, particularly constructed as a tree structure, which has been widely accepted to overcome the drawbacks of the bag of words in [62, 134, 135, 189, 219, 231, 240].

In learning user preferences, some topics will become more interesting to the user, while the user will completely or to varying degrees, lose interest in other topics. Studies [32, 148, 255] suggest that relevance feedback and machine learning techniques show promise in adapting to changes of user interests and reducing user involvements, while still overseeing what users dislike and their interest degradation. In [148] a two-level approach is proposed to learn user profiles for information filtering. While the lower level learns the stationary user preferences, the higher level detects changes of user preferences. In [255] a multiple three-descriptor representation is introduced to learn changes in multiple interest categories, and it also needs positive and negative relevance feedback provided by users explicitly.

4.3 Feature Enrichment of Short Texts

The task of classifying textual data that has been culled from sites on the World Wide Web is both difficult and intensively studied. Applications of various machine learning techniques that attempt to solve this problem include categorization of Web pages into sub-categories for search engines, and classification of news articles by subject. Nowadays, there are many short texts on the Internet, such as Web search queries, short messages, opinions and so on. The typical application of short texts is the query suggestion service provided by commercial search engines such as "Related search terms" in Google, "Search Assist" in Yahoo!, and "Related Searches" in Bing Search.

In short text case, traditional text processing approaches cannot work well because short text documents usually have little overlap in their feature terms. In this section, we make use of query suggestion to state the problems of short texts. We categorize the research efforts on related query suggestion into the following three classes of strategies according to the feature space source used by them:

(1) Query term based suggestion is easily applicable, which intuitively considers the candidate queries having common words with a current input query to be related. However, the very small word overlap between short Web queries makes it hard to accurately estimate their similarity. One reason is probably that a term may be meant for different meanings by different users (i.e. polysemy), e.g., apple is related to fruit or computer. The other reason is that different terms may have a similar meaning (i.e. synonymy), e.g., car and automobile. Moreover, the common words cannot give useful hints for users to refine their input queries. Therefore, many current studies focus on how to improve the performance of this naive suggestion strategy and find topically related queries.

(2) Pseudo relevance based suggestion induces the similarity between the two queries by enriching query expressions with additional features (e.g., terms and URLs) from the top results returned by search engines [100, 160, 262]. It assumes that the meaning of a query is potentially relevant to its top search results. The pseudo relevance reflects the viewpoints of general search engines, but contains no evidence of individual users' judgments [178].

(3) Implicit relevance based suggestion extracts the additional features (e.g., terms and URLs) from the clicked search results of Web logs to calculate query-to-query similarity [16, 21, 25, 156, 171, 180, 253, 262]. It attracts more researchers' interests than pseudo relevance because the click choices made by a large number of users do suggest a certain level of relevance from the viewing point of actual users.

Although the query term based suggestion strategy is the simplest and does not require any external sources, its suggestion results are always unsatisfactory. To improve the suggestion precision, the latter two strategies are widely used. At first glance, implicit relevance based suggestion is more practical than pseudo relevance based one since it reflects the real opinions

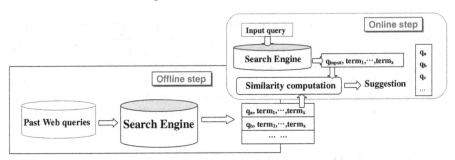

Fig. 4.1. Framework of the traditional pseudo relevance based suggestion using the term feature space

of Web users, but it has a critical drawback. If the input query by a user is totally new to current Web logs, its click information is not accessible from the Web query logs for query similarity computation. In this case, pseudo relevance can be used to expand the expressions of queries by features extracted from the top search results returned by search engines. Two traditional feature spaces are terms and URLs of these search results.

Suppose that we have already obtained a set of candidate queries which are past queries submitted by previous users. The task of query suggestion is to suggest the most related candidates for an target input query. In Figure 1 we illustrate the overview of the traditional pseudo relevance based suggestion which uses the term feature space.

In the offline step, the top search results of past queries are retrieved by a search engine, and terms are extracted from the search result pages. In this manner, each past query is represented by the terms of its search result pages. In the online step, the same process is used to get the term expression of an input query. The query to query similarity is computed based on their term expressions. The past queries with the highest similarity scores are recommended to users. Pseudo relevance based suggestion using the URL feature space works in a similar way shown in Figure 1. The only difference is placing the terms with URLs in query expression.

If we use terms of search results as features. We can obtain the following vector expression: $V(q_i) = \{t_1, t_2, \cdots, t_k\}$. The similarity function can be the well-known cosine coefficient, defined as

$$Sim(q_i, q_j) = \frac{V(q_i) \cdot V(q_j)}{|V(q_i)||V(q_j)|}. \tag{4.5}$$

URLs can also be used to express queries and compute query-to-query similarity. Let q_i and q_j be two queries, and $U(q_i)$ and $U(q_j)$ be the two sets of URLs returned by a search engine (here i.e., Google) in response to the two queries q_i and q_j respectively. In this case, Jaccard is an intuitive and suitable similarity measure, defined as:

$$Jaccard(q_i, q_j) = \frac{|U(q_i) \cap U(q_j)|}{|U(q_i) \cup U(q_j)|}. \tag{4.6}$$

The value of the defined similarity between two queries lies in the range [0, 1]: 1 if they are exactly the same URLs, and 0 if they have no URLs in common.

After the feature enrichment of a query, we can apply traditional text processing approaches on the enriched queries, such as text classification, text clustering, topic detection and so forth.

4.4 Latent Semantic Indexing

We now discuss the approximation of a term-document matrix C by one of lower rank using the SVD as discussed in Chapter 2. The low-rank approximation to C yields a new representation for each document in the collection. We will cast Web search queries into this low-rank representation as well, enabling us to compute query-document similarity scores in this low-rank representation. This process is known as latent semantic indexing (generally abbreviated LSI).

Recall the vector space representation of documents and queries introduced in Section 4.1. This vector space representation enjoys a number of advantages including the uniform treatment of queries and documents as vectors, the induced score computation based on cosine similarity, the ability to weight different terms differently, and its extension beyond document retrieval to such applications as clustering and classification. The vector space representation suffers, however, from its inability to cope with two classic problems arising in natural languages: synonymy and polysemy. Synonymy refers to a case where two different words (say car and automobile) have the same meaning. Because the vector space representation fails to capture the relationship between synonymous terms such as car and automobile - according each a separate dimension in the vector space. Could we use the co-occurrences of terms (whether, for instance, charge occurs in a document containing steed versus in a document containing electron) to capture the latent semantic associations of terms and alleviate these problems?

Even for a collection of modest size, the term-document matrix C is likely to have several tens of thousand of rows and columns, and a rank in the tens of thousands as well. In latent semantic indexing (sometimes referred to as latent semantic analysis (LSA)), we use the SVD to construct a low-rank approximation C_k to the term-document matrix, for a value of k that is far smaller than the original rank of C. In the experiments, k is generally chosen to be in the low hundreds. We thus map each row/column (respectively corresponding to a term/document) to a k-dimensional space; this space is defined by the k principal eigenvectors (corresponding to the largest eigenvalues) of CC^T and $C^T C$. Note that the matrix C_k is itself still an $M \times N$ matrix, irrespective of k.

Next, we use the new dimensional LSI representation as we did the original representation to compute similarities between vectors. A query vector q is mapped into its representation in the LSI space by the transformation

$$q_k = \sum_k^{-1} U_k^T q. \tag{4.7}$$

Now, we may use cosine similarities as in Section 4.1 to compute the similarity between a query and a document, between two documents, or between two terms. Note especially that Equation 4.7 does not in any way depend on being a query; it is simply a vector in the space of terms. This means that if we have an LSI representation of a collection of documents, a new document not in the collection can be "folded in" to this representation using Equation 4.7. This allows us to incrementally add documents to an LSI representation. Of course, such incremental addition fails to capture the co-occurrences of the newly added documents (and even ignores any new terms they contain). As such, the quality of the LSI representation will degrade as more documents are added and will eventually require a re-computation of the LSI representation.

The fidelity of the approximation of C_k to leads us to hope that the relative values of cosine similarities are preserved: if a query is close to a document in the original space, it remains relatively close in the -dimensional space. But this in itself is not sufficiently interesting, espe-cially given that the sparse query vector turns into a dense query vector in the low-dimensional space. This has a significant computational cost, when compared with the cost of processing in its native form.

LSI can be viewed as soft clustering by interpreting each dimension of the reduced space as a cluster and the value that a document has on that dimension as its fractional membership in that cluster.

4.5 Automatic Topic Extraction from Web Documents

With the rapid growth of the Web and the popularity of search engines, the continuously increasing amount of text available is overwhelming. A Web user, who wants to conduct an in-depth study on some topics, though with the capability to access millions of Web documents relevant to his/her interest, is not satisfied with simple keyword search. To allow effective extraction of valuable knowledge from a large amount of Web documents, a more structured method of interacting with a collection of Web documents is required: exploring the Web pages based on topics and navigating to other similar Web pages to learn more about the topic.

The scenario of in-depth learning on a specific topic from the Web is just one example of applications that need to automatically infer the underlying topics within a given collection Web documents. Automatic topic extraction can also be useful to applications such as intel-ligent Web crawling, topical pattern analysis, opinion mining, search results summarization, and Web spam filtering. Statistical topic models are generative, probabilistic models for ex-tracting latent topics within a text corpus based on hierarchical Bayesian analysis. Examples of statiscal topic models are PLSA [118] and LDA [35]. With the growing amount of text available as hyperlinked Web documents, many researchers have proposed topic models for processing both text and links, e.g. [64], [85], [75], [188], [104], [235].

In the remaining of this section, we first describe two widely used statistical topic models for plain text: PLSA and LDA. Then, we will explain topic models for processing Web docu-ments proposed in the literature. Finally, we discuss methods for inference and estimation (the algorithm for extracting topics).

4.5.1 Topic Models

Topic models (e.g. PLSA [118] and LDA [35]) are generative and probabilistic models that rely on hierarchical Bayesian analysis to uncover the semantic structure from a document col-lection. The key idea of these models is to represent a document as a mixture of topics and a topic as a distribution of words. As a generative model, the topic model specifies a scheme for generating documents. A new document can be generated as follows. First, a distribution over topics is chosen. Then, for each word in the new document, a topic is chosen randomly according to the distribution over topics and a word is drawn from that topic. The generative process of the topic models as described here is based on the bag-of-words assumption (no as-sumptions on the ordering of words). Having discussed the general concept of topic modeling, in the following subsections, we will explain two well known statistical topic models: PLSA (or an aspect model) and LDA. Table 4.1 gives the notations used in our discussion and their descriptions.

Table 4.1. Notations and Descriptions

Notation	Descriptions
D	a set of documents in corpus
$\boldsymbol{D}$	number of documents
d	a document
d'	a document
N_d	number of terms in a document d
L_d	number of outlinks in a document d
W	a vocabulary (i.e. a set of terms)
$\boldsymbol{W}$	number of terms
ω	a word within a document
Z	a set of latent topics within documents
z_k	a latent variable representing a topic
$\boldsymbol{K}$	number of latent topics
β	a random variable for $P(\omega \mid z)$
Ω	a random variable for $P(d \mid z)$
θ	a random variable for the joint distribution of a topic mixture
η, α	hyperparameters
$Mult(\cdot \mid \theta_d)$	Multinomial distribution with parameter θ_d
$Mult(\cdot \mid \beta_{z_i})$	Multinomial distribution with parameter β_{z_i}

PLSA: Probabilistic Latent Semantic Analysis

[118] proposed a statistical technique for the analysis of two-mode and co-occurrence of data, called *probabilistic latent semantic analysis* or the *aspect model*. The PLSA model defines a proper generative model of the data. Let the occurrence of a term ω in a document d be an event in the PLSA model and z denote a latent variable associated with each event in the model (i.e. the latent topic). The generative process of the PLSA model can be described as follows.

1. Choose a document over a distribution $P(d)$.
2. Choose a latent topic z with probability $P(z \mid d)$.
3. Choose a term ω according to $P(\omega \mid z)$.

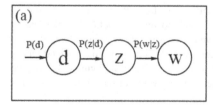
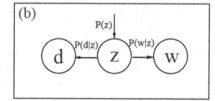

Fig. 4.2. Graphical model representation of the PLSA model [118].

The graphical model for this generative process is shown in Figure 4.2(a). The PLSA model postulates that a document d and a term w are conditionally independent given an unobserved topic z, i.e. the probability of an event $P(\omega \mid d)$ is defined as:

$$P(\omega, d) = P(d) \sum_z P(\omega \mid z)P(z \mid d).$$ (4.8)

In[118], the parameters of the PLSA model are estimated (i.e. a given document collection) using a standard procedure for maximum likelihood estimation in latent variable models i.e. the *Expectation aximization (EM) algorithm*[72]. The computation of EM alternates between the Expectation (E) step and the Maximization (M) step. During the E step, posterior probabilities of the latent variables z are computed as

$$P(z \mid d, \omega) = \frac{P(z)P(d \mid z)P(\omega \mid z)}{\sum_{z_k \in Z} P(z_k)P(d \mid z_k)P(\omega \mid z_k)},$$ (4.9)

The M step updates the parameters with the following formulae

$$P(\omega \mid z) \propto \sum_{d \in D} n(d, \omega)P(z \mid d, \omega),$$ (4.10)

$$P(d \mid z) \propto \sum_{\omega \in W} n(d, \omega)P(z \mid d, \omega),$$ (4.11)

$$P(z) \propto \sum_{d \in D} \sum_{\omega \in W} n(d, \omega)P(z \mid d, \omega).$$ (4.12)

The graphical model for the symmetric parameterization used in the model fitting process described aboved is shown in Figure 4.2(b). The PLSA model does not explicitly specify how the mixture weights of the topics $P(z)$ are generated, making it difficult to assign probability to a new as yet unseen document. Furthermore, the number of parameters that must be estimated in the PLSA model grows linearly with the number of training documents, suggesting that the model has the tendency to overfit the data. Empirical results in [118] showed that the model does suffer from overfitting. To prevent from overfitting, [118] refined the original PLSA model with parameters smoothing by a tempering heuristic. The refinement resulted in an inference algorithm, called *tempered EM*.

LDA: Latent Dirichlet Allocation

To alleviate the overfitting problem of the PLSA, [35] proposed a Bayesian model based approach called LDA (Latent Dirichlet Allocation). LDA is a three-level hierarchical Bayesian model in which each document in a collection is represented by a finite mixture over an underlying set of topics. LDA assumes a single multinomial random variable β for each topic. This random variable β defines the probability for a term given a topic $P(\omega \mid z)$ for all documents in the collection. A particular mixture of topics for each document is defined by the random variable θ. The generation of words for each document consists of two stages: first, selecting a hidden topic z from a multinomial distribution defined by θ; second, for the selected topic z, a term ω is drawn from the multinomial distribution with parameter β_z. Figure 4.3(a) depicts the generative process of the LDA model. The generative process of the LDA model can be described as follows.

1. For each topic $z = 1, ..., K$ choose W dimensional $\beta_z \sim Dirichlet(\eta)$
2. For each document $d = 1, ..., D$ choose K dimensional $\theta \sim Dirichlet(\alpha)$
   For each position $i = 1, ..., N_d$
     Choose a topic $z_i \sim Mult(\cdot \mid \theta_d)$
     Generate a term $\omega_i \sim Mult(\cdot \mid \beta_{z_i})$

The procedure for inference under the LDA involves the computation of the posterior distribution of the hidden variables given a document:

$$P(\theta,z \mid \omega,\alpha,\beta) = \frac{P(\theta,z,\omega \mid \alpha,\beta)}{P(\omega \mid \alpha,\beta)} \tag{4.13}$$

Unfortunately, this posterior distribution is intractable to compute for exact inference. [35] uses an approximate inference technique based on variational methods and an EM algortihm for empirical Bayes parameter estimation. A detailed discussion on the efficient procedures for inference and parameter estimation can be found in [35].

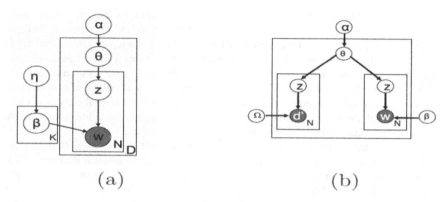

(a)   (b)

Fig. 4.3. Graphical model representation of (a) the LDA model (b) the Link-LDA model.

4.5.2 Topic Models for Web Documents

The statistical topic models, for example PLSA and LDA, exploit the pattern of word co-occurrence in documents to extract semantically meaningful clusters of words (i.e. topics). These models expresses the semantic properties of words and documents in terms of probability distributions, which enable us to represent and process the documents in the lower-dimensional space. With the continuously increasing amount of Web documents, there has been growing interest in extending these models to process link information associated with a collection of the Web documents. In this section, we will introduce methods for combining link information into the standard topic models that have been proposed in the literature.

Cohn and Hofmann [64] extended the PLSA model to consider link information in the generative process (henceforth, we will refer to this extended model as Link-PLSA). They proposed a mixture model to *simultaneously* extract the "topic" factors from the co-occurrence matrix of words and links. Within this framework, links are viewed as additional observations and are treated like additional words in the set of words (or the vocaburary). However, the weights assigned to the links during parameter estimation will differ from the weights assigned to the words. In [64] the authors empirically showed that the document representation obtained from their model improves the performance of a document classification task, compared to the document representation obtained from standard topic models for plain text. Erosheva et al. [85] modified the Link-PLSA model by using LDA instead of PLSA for content generation.

We will refer to this model as Link-LDA. The graphical model for the Link-LDA model is shown in Figure 4.3(b). The formal definition of the Link-LDA model can be described as:

1. For each document $d = 1, ..., \boldsymbol{D}$
   a) Choose K dimensional $\theta \sim Dirichlet(\alpha)$
   b) For each word ω_i, indexed by $i = 1, ..., N_d$
      Choose a topic $z_i \sim Mult(\cdot \mid \theta_d)$
      Generate a term $\omega_i \sim Mult(\cdot \mid \beta_{z_i})$
   c) For each link d'_i, indexed by $i = 1, ..., L_d$
      Choose a topic $z_i \sim Mult(\cdot \mid \theta_d)$
      Generate a citation $d'_i \sim Mult(\cdot \mid \Omega_{z_i})$

The Link-LDA and Link-PLSA models do not consider and exploit the topical relationship between the topics of the citing documents and the topics of the cited documents. Nallapati and Cohn [188] extended the Link-LDA model and proposed a new topic models called, Link-PLSA-LDA. The Link-PLSA-LDA combines PLSA and LDA into a single framework, and explicitly models the topical relationship between the citing and cited documents. In Link-PLSA-LDA, the hyperlink graph is converted to a bipartite graph consisting of a set of citing and cited documents. The generative process of the citing documents is similar to that of Link-LDA. However, the generative process of the cited documents is defined differently to allow the topical information flow from the citing document to the cited document.

Recently, Gruber et al. [104] has proposed a Latent Topic Hypertext Model (LTHM). The LTMH model enriches the Link-LDA model by considering links between documents. The LTHM allows the existence of links from every document to every document, including self-reference. A link is modeled as an entity originating from a specific word (or a collection of words) and pointing to a certain document. The probability of generating from a document d to a document d' depends on (1) the topics of the word from which the link is originated, (2) the in-degree of the target document d' (estimation of the importance of d'), and (3) the topic mixture of the target document d'.

4.5.3 Inference and Parameter Estimation

The topic models are generative probabilistic models that describe the process of generating documents. Given a set of Web documents, we can infer the topics by inverting the generative process of the chosen topic model using a standard statistical technique. Exact inference in hierarchical models (like PLSA, LDA, and their extensions) is intractable, because of the coupling of the latent topics and the mixing vectors β, θ. Several approximate inference techniques have been proposed in recent years. [118] used the EM algorithm to directly estimate the topic-word distribution and the topic distribution. The EM based approach suffered from the problems concerning local maxima of the likelihood function. D. M. Blei et al. [35] tried to overcome the difficulties of EM based approach with a convexity-based variational EM algorithm. Other approximate inference algorithms that have been suggested are Laplace approximation, Markov Chain Monte Carlo, and Expectation Propagation (see for example [130]).

4.6 Opinion Search and Opinion Spam

As introduced in [166], mining of opinions on the Web is not only technically challenging because of the need for natural language processing, but also very useful in practice. For example, businesses always want to find public or consumer opinions on their products and services. Potential customers also want to know the opinions of existing users before they use a service or purchase a product. Moreover, opinion mining can also provide valuable information for placing advertisements in Web pages. If in a page people express positive opinions or sentiments on a product, it may be a good idea to place an ad of the product. However, if people express negative opinions about the product, it is probably not wise to place an ad of the product. A better idea may be to place an ad of a competitor's product.

The Web has dramatically changed the way that people express their opinions. They can now post reviews of products at merchant sites and express their views on almost anything in Internet forums, discussion groups, blogs, etc., which are commonly called the user generated content or user generated media. This online word-of-mouth behavior represents new and measurable sources of information with many practical applications. Techniques are now being developed to exploit these sources to help businesses and individuals gain such information effectively and easily.

4.6.1 Opinion Search

Like the general Web search, one can also crawl the user-generated content on the Web and provide an opinion search service. The objective is to enable users to search for opinions on any object. Let us look at some typical opinion search queries:

(1) Search for opinions on a particular object or feature of an object, e.g., customer opinions on a digital camera or the picture quality of a digital camera, or public opinions on a political topic. Recall that the object can be a product, organization, topic, etc.
(2) Search for opinions of a person or organization (i.e., opinion holder) on a particular object or feature of the object. For example, one may search for Bill Clinton's opinion on abortion or a particular aspect of it. This type of search is particularly relevant to news documents, where individuals or organizations who express opinions are explicitly stated. In the user-generated content on the Web, the opinions are mostly expressed by authors of the postings.

For the first type of queries, the user may simply give the name of the object and/or some features of the object. For the second type of queries, the user may give the name of the opinion holder and also the name of the object. Clearly, it is not appropriate to simply apply keyword matching for either type of queries because a document containing the query words may not have opinions. For example, many discussion and blog posts do not contain opinions, but only questions and answers on some objects. Opinionated documents or sentences need to be identified before search is performed. Thus, the simplest form of opinion search can be keyword-based search applied to the identified opinionated documents/sentences.

As for ranking, traditional Web search engines rank Web pages based on authority and relevance scores. The basic premise is that the top ranked pages (ideally the first page) contain sufficient information to satisfy the user's information need. This may be fine for the second type of queries because the opinion holder usually has only one opinion on the search object, and the opinion is usually contained in a single document or page (in some cases, using a general search engine with an appropriate set of keywords may be sufficient to find answers for such queries). However, for the first type of opinion queries, the top ranked documents only represent the opinions of a few persons. Therefore, they need to reflect the natural distribution of positive and negative sentiments of the whole population. Moreover, in many cases, opinionated documents are very long (e.g., reviews). It is hard for the user to read many of them in order to obtain a complete picture of the prevailing sentiments. Some form of summary of opinions is desirable, which can be either a simple rating average of reviews and proportions of positive and negative opinions, or a sophisticated feature-based summary as we discussed earlier. To make it even easier for the user, two rankings may be produced, one for positive opinions and one for negative opinions.

Providing a feature-based summary for each search query is an ideal solution. An analogy can be drawn from traditional surveys or opinion polls. An opinionated document is analogous to a filled survey form. Once all or a sufficient number of survey forms are collected, some analysts will analyze them to produce a survey summary, which is usually in the form of a bar or pie chart. One seldom shows all the filled survey forms to users (e.g., the management team of an organization or the general public) and asks them to read everything in order to draw their own conclusions. However, automatically generating a feature-based summary for each search object (or query) is a very challenging problem.

Opinions also have a temporal dimension. For example, the opinions of people on a particular object, e.g., a product or a topic, may change over time. Displaying the changing trend of sentiments along the time axis can be very useful in many applications. Finally, like opinion search, comparison search will be useful as well. For example, when you want to register for a free email account, you most probably want to know which email system is best for you, e.g., hotmail, gmail or Yahoo! mail. Wouldn't it be nice if you can find comparisons of features of these email systems from existing users by issuing a search query "hotmail vs. gmail vs. yahoo mail"?

4.6.2 Opinion Spam

Web spam refers to the use of "illegitimate means" to boost the search rank position of some target Web pages. The reason for spamming is because of the economic and/or publicity value of the rank position of a page returned by a search engine. In the context of opinions on the Web, the problem is similar. It has become a common practice for people to find and to read opinions on the Web for many purposes. For example, if one wants to buy a product, one typically goes to a merchant or review site (e.g., amazon.com) to read some reviews of existing users of the product. If one sees many positive reviews of the product, she/he is very likely to buy the product. On the contrary, if one sees many negative reviews, he/she will most likely choose another product. Positive opinions can result in significant financial gains and/or fames for organizations and individuals. This, unfortunately, gives good incentives for opinion spam, which refers to human activities (e.g., write spam reviews) that try to deliberately mislead readers or automated opinion mining systems by giving undeserving positive opinions to some target objects in order to promote the objects and/or by giving unjust or false negative opinions on some other objects in order to damage their reputation. In this section, we use customer reviews of products as an example to study opinion spam on the Web. Most of the analyses are also applicable to opinions expressed in other forms of user-generated contents, e.g., forum postings, group discussions, and blogs.

So far, little study has been done on opinion spam detection. This subsection outlines some possible approaches. We note that each individual technique below may not be able to reliably detect spam reviews, but it can be treated as a spam indicator. A holistic approach that combines all evidences is likely to be effective. One possible combination method is to treat spam detection as a classification problem. All the individual methods simply compute spam evidences which can be put in a data set from which a spam classifier can be learned. For this approach to work, a set of reviews needs to be manually labeled for learning. The resulting classifier can be used to classify each new review as a spam review or not one.

As more and more people and organizations are using opinions on the Web for decision making, spammers have more and more incentives to express false sentiments in product reviews, discussions and blogs. To ensure the quality of information provided by an opinion mining and/or search system, spam detection is a critical task. Without effective detection, opinions on the Web may become useless. This section analyzed various aspects of opinion spam and outlined some possible detection methods. This may just be the beginning of a long journey of the "arms race" between spam and detection of spam.

Summary

In this chapter, we review the researches conducted in Web content mining. Starting from the vector space model, we elaborate the principle of Web search, which consists of crawling, archiving, indexing and searching processes. In order to deal with sparse and low overlapping problems of Web contents, we present some algorithms on feature enrichment and latent semantic analysis. Moreover we also discuss the research issues of automatic topic extraction from Web documents and opinion mining.

5

Web Linkage Mining

In the last chapter, we have addressed some research issues in web content mining. In addition to textual representation embedded in web data, linkage feature is another important aspect we are often interested in. Web linkage conveys the information how various pages are associated together and formed the huge Web. Web linkage mining is, therefore, to reveal the underlying structures hidden in the hyperlinks and to utilize them for more web applications such as search. In this chapter, we will talk about some well known algorithms and their applications.

5.1 Web Search and Hyperlink

Traditional information retrieval systems and the first generation of search engines retrieved relevant documents for the users based primarily on the content similarity of the input query and the indexed pages. During the late 1990s, it became clearly that the content based methods alone were no longer sufficient for Web search due to two reasons. Firstly, the abundance of information available on the Web causes a serious problem for search ranking. Given a search query, the number of relevant pages can be very large. For example, the number of relevant pages for the query social network estimated by the Google search engine is about 33.4 million pages. To satisfy the users, search engines must choose only 30-40 high quality related pages and rank them near the top of search results. Secondly, the content based methods are easily spammed e.g. by adding some important words to a Web page.

To solve these problems, researchers have resorted to hyperlinks. Unlike text documents, Web pages are connected together with hyperlinks. The hyperlinks embed important information regarding the relationships between Web pages. Some hyperlinks are used to organize information within the websites. Other hyperlinks are used to convey authority to the pages being pointed to. Therefore, Web pages that are being pointed to by many other pages are likely to be authoritative information sources. This implicit conveyance of authority is an important key that can be used to improve the efficiency of Web search ranking.

In 1998, two most important hyperlink based search algorithms were designed: PageRank [196, 43] and HITS [137]. Both PageRank and HITS were originated from social network analysis [250]. They exploit the hyperlink structure of the Web to rank pages according to their degree of prestige or authority. We will introduce these algorithms in this section.

G. Xu et al., *Web Mining and Social Networking*,
DOI 10.1007/978-1-4419-7735-9_5, © Springer Science+Business Media, LLC 2011

5.2 Co-citation and Bibliographic Coupling

Citation analysis is an area of bibliometric research, which studies citations to establish the relationship between authors and their work. When a paper cites another paper, a relationship (or link) is establish between the papers. Citation analysis uses these relationships (links) to perform various types of analysis. We will introduce two specific types of citation analysis related to the HITS algorithm, co-citation and bibliographic coupling.

5.2.1 Co-citation

Co-citation is used to measure the similarity of two documents in clustering. If paper i and j are cited together by many papers, it means that i and j have a strong relationship or similarity. The more papers they are cited together, the stronger their relationship is. Figure 5.1 below shows this main idea.

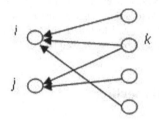

Fig. 5.1. Paper i and j are co-cited by k

Let L be the citation matrix. Each cell of the matrix is defined as follows: $L_{ij} = 1$ if paper i cites paper j, and 0 otherwise. Co-citation (denoted by C_{ij}) is defined as the number of papers that co-cite i and j, and is computed with

$$C_{ij} = \sum_{k=1,...n} L_{ki}L_{kj} = \left(L^T L\right)_{ij} \qquad (5.1)$$

Where, n is the total number of papers. A square matrix C can be formed with C_{ij}, and it is called the co-citation matrix.

5.2.2 Bibliographic Coupling

Bibliographic coupling is also a similarity measure of two papers in clustering. We can look at the bibliographic coupling as the mirror image of co-citation. The main idea here is that if paper i and paper j both cite paper$k$, they may be said to be related, even though they do not cite each other directly (see Fig. 5.2 below).

B_{ij} is the number of papers that are cited by both papers i and paper j:

$$B_{ij} = \sum_{k=1,...n} L_{ik}L_{jk} = \left(LL^T\right)_{ij} \qquad (5.2)$$

Where, n is the total number of papers. A square matrix B can be formed with B_{ij}, and it is called the bibliographic coupling matrix.

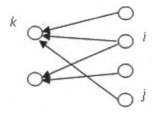

Fig. 5.2. Paper i and j cite paper k

5.3 PageRank and HITS Algorithms

5.3.1 PageRank

In 1998, Sergey Brin and Larry Page invented PageRank and presented it at the Seventh International World Wide Web Conference (WWW7). The PageRank is a measure of pages quality used in the Google search engine. PageRank utilizes hyperlinking as an indicator of the quality of a Web page. In essence, PageRank interprets a hyperlink from page x to page y as a conveyance of prestige, by page x, for page y. However, PageRank does not just consider the sheer number of links that a page receives. It also takes into account the importance or quality of the page that conveys the prestige. Hyperlinks from pages that are themselves important weigh high and help to make other pages more important. This idea is based on the concept of rank prestige in social network analysis [250].

Algorithm: PageRank
PageRank [196, 43] is a search query independent ranking algorithm for Web pages. It is based on the measure of rank prestige in social network analysis. A PageRank value is calculated for each indexed page off-line. The main concepts underlying the PageRank algorithm can be described as follows.

1. A hyperlink from a page pointing to another page is an implicit conveyance of authority to the target page. Thus, a Web page is important if it receives a lot of in-links.
2. A hyperlink from a high prestige page is more important than a hyperlink from a low prestige page. Thus, a Web page is important if it is pointed to by other important pages.

To formulate the above concepts, we represent the Web as a directed graph G = (V, E), where V is the set of vertices or nodes, i.e. the set of all pages in the Web, and E is the set of directed edges between a pair of nodes, i.e. hyperlinks. Let the total number of pages on the Web be n ($n = |V|$). The PageRank score of the page i, P(i), is defined by:

$$P(i) = (1-d) + d \sum_{(j,i) \in E} P(j) / outdegree(j) \tag{5.3}$$

where d is a damping factor usually set between 0.8 and 0.9; $outdegree(q)$ is the number of hyperlinks on page q.

Alternately, the PageRank can be defined by the stationary distribution of the following infinite, random walk $p_1, p_2, p_3, \ldots$, where each p_i is a node in G: The walk starts at each node with equal probability. To determine node p_{i+1} a biased coin is flipped: With probability 1-d node p_{i+1} is chosen uniformly at random from all nodes in G, with probability d it is chosen uniformly from all nodes q such that (p_i, q) exists in the graph G.

Equation 5.1 can be rewritten in a matrix notation. Let P be a n-dimensional column vector of PageRank values: $P = (P(1), P(2), \cdots, P(n))^T$. Let A be the adjacency matrix of G with

$$A_{ij} = \begin{cases} 1/out\,deg\,ree\,(i)\,, if\,(i,j) \in E \\ 0, otherwise \end{cases} \qquad (5.4)$$

We can write the system of n equations with

$$P = (1-d)e + dA^T P \qquad (5.5)$$

where, e is a column vector of all 1's.

This is the characteristic equation of the eigensystem, where the solution to P is an eigenvector with the corresponding eigenvalue of 1. Since this is a recursive definition, an iterative algorithm is used to solve it. It turns out that if the adjacency matrix A is a stochastic (transition) matrix, irreducible and aperiodic, then 1 is the largest eigenvalue and the PageRank vector P is the principal eigenvector. A well known power iteration method [103] can be used to find P. The power iteration algorithm for PageRank is given in Fig.5.3 below. The algorithm can start with any initial assignments of PageRank values. The iteration ends when the PageRank values do not change much or converge such as when the 1-norm of the residual vector is less than a threshold value ε. Note that, the 1-norm for a vector is simply the sum of all the components. For a detailed discussion of the derivation of PageRank, interested readers can refer to [166, 151], and [150].

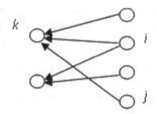

Fig. 5.3. The power iteration method for PageRank

The main advantage of PageRank is its ability to combat spam. Since it is not easy for the page owner to add in-links into his/her pages from other important pages, it is therefore not easy to deliberately boost the PageRank. Nevertheless, there are reported ways to boost PageRank. Identifying and combating web spam is an important research issue in Web search. Another strong point of PageRank is that it is a global rank measure and is query independent. In Google, the Web graph induced from the crawled pages is first used to compute PageRank scores of all pages, and the computed PageRank scores are kept for later process. When a search query is submitted, a text index is first consulted to select possible response pages. Then an undisclosed ranking scheme that combines PageRank with textual match is used to produce a final rank list of response URLs. This makes Google much comparably faster than conventional text-based search engines.

The main shortcoming of PageRank is also caused by the query-independence, global nature of PageRank. PageRank could not distinguish between pages that are authoritative in general and pages that are authoritative on the query topic. Another shortcoming is that PageRank does not consider timeliness of authoritative sources.

5.3.2 HITS

HITS stands for Hypertext Induced Topic Search [137]. HITS is a search query dependent ranking algorithm. When the user issues a search query, HITS first expands the list of relevant pages returned by a search engine and then produces two rankings of the expanded set of pages, authority ranking and hub ranking.

An authority is a page with many inlinks. The idea is that the page may have good or authoritative content on some topic and thus many people trust it and link to it. A hub is a page with many outlinks. The hub page serves as an organizer of the information on a particular topic and points to many good authority pages on the topic. When a user comes to this hub page, he/she will find many useful links which take him/her to good content pages on the topic.

The key idea of HITS is that a good hub points to many good authorities and a good authority is pointed to by many good hubs. Thus, authorities and hubs form a mutual reinforcement relationship. The mutual reinforcement relationship usually manifests itself as a set of densely linked authorities and hubs (a bipartite subgraph). Figure 2.8 shows an example of hubs and authorities.

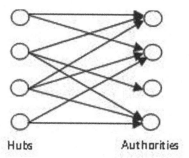

Hubs   Authorities

Fig. 5.4. A densely linked set of authorities and hubs

Algorithm: HITS
The HITS algorithm can be divided into two phases: (1) construction of a focused WWW subgraph, and (2) computation of hubs and authorities.

Given a broad-topic search query q, HITS first constructs a focused WWW subgraph which contains many of the strongest authorities. HITS achieves this by first using search engines to obtain the root set W of relevant pages with high rank score. Then, the root set W is expanded by including any page pointed to by a page in W and any page that points to a page in W. This gives a larger set called the base set S. HITS then works on the second phase: computing an authority score and a hub score for every page in S.

Let the number of pages in S be n. We use $G = (V, E)$ to denote the hyperlink graph induced from S. V is the set of pages (or nodes) and E is the set of directed edges (or links). Then, L is used to denote the adjacency matrix of the graph.

$$L_{ij} = \begin{cases} 1, \text{if}\,(i, j) \in E \\ 0, \text{otherwise} \end{cases} \tag{5.6}$$

Let the authority score of the page i be $a(i)$, and the hub score of the page i be $h(i)$. Let us define a column vector $h = (h(1), \cdots, h(n))^T$ be the vector of hub scores, and a column vector

$a = (a(1), \cdots, a(n))^T$ be the vector of authority scores. The mutual reinforcement relationship of the authority and hub scores can be represented as follows.

$$a = L^T h \tag{5.7}$$

$$h = La \tag{5.8}$$

The authority and hub scores can be computed using the power iteration method. Starting with $a_0 = h_0 = (1, 1, \cdots, 1)$, if we use a_k and h_k to denote authority and hub scores at the k-th iteration, the final solutions for the iteration processes obtained by substitutions are

$$a_k = L^T L a_{k-1} \tag{5.9}$$

$$h_k = LL^T h_{k-1} \tag{5.10}$$

The power iteration algorithm for HITS is given in Fig.5.5. The pages with large authority and hub scores are better authorities and hubs respectively. HITS will select some top ranked pages as authorities and hubs, and return them to the user.

HITS-Iterate(G)
$a_0 = h_0 = (1, 1, ..., 1);$
$k = 1$
Repeat
    $a_k = L^T L a_{k-1};$
    $h_k = LL^T h_{k-1};$
    $a_k = a_k / \| a_k \|_1;$ // normalization
    $h_k = h_k / \| h_k \|_1;$ // normalization
    $k = k + 1;$
until $\| a_k - a_{k-1} \|_1 < \varepsilon_a$ and $\| h_k - h_{k-1} \|_1 < \varepsilon_h;$
return a_k and h_k

Fig. 5.5. The power iteration method for HITS

Although HITS will always converge, there is a problem with uniqueness of converged authority and hub vectors. It is shown that for certain types of graphs, different initializations to the power method produce different final authority and hub vectors [90]. Moreover, some results can be inconsistent or wrong. The heart of the problem is that there are repeated dominant (principal) eigenvalues, which are caused by the problem that $L^T L$ and LL^T are reducible [150]. The PageRank solution has the same problem, and it was solved by adding virtual links from a node to every other nodes in the graph (corresponding to the $(1Cd)$ term into the equation). A similar modification may be applied to HITS.

Authority and hub pages have their matches in the bibliometric citation. An authority page is like an influential paper which is cited by many subsequent papers. A hub page is like a survey paper which cites many other papers (including those influential papers). It can be shown easily that the authority matrix $(L^T L)$ of HITS is in fact corresponding to the co-citation matrix, while the hub matrix (LL^T) of HITS is the bibliographic coupling in the Web context [166].

The major strength of HITS is the ability to rank pages according to the query topic, which may be able to provide more relevant authority and hub pages. Like PageRank, the ranking scores may also be combined with other content based ranking scores. The major weaknesses of the HITS algorithm are

- Lack of the anti-spam capability. It is quite easy to boost the hub score of a page by adding outlinks from ones own page to point to many good authorities. Because hub and authority scores are interdependent, it in turn also increases the authority score of the page.
- Topic drift. The expansion of the root set may include many irrelevant, noise pages into the seed set.
- Query time evaluation. Getting the root set, expanding it, and then performing the power iteration method are all time consuming operations. Many researchers have tried to remedy the above problems. Interested reader can refer to [31, 152, 55, 51, 47].

In addition to search result ranking, hyperlinks are also useful for discovering Web communities. A Web community is a set of densely linked pages representing a group of people or organizations with a common interest. We will introduce some current algorithms for finding communities in the following section.

5.4 Web Community Discovery

A web community is a set of web pages that provide resources on a specific topic. Intuitively, a community is simply a group of entities (e.g., people or organizations) that shares a common interest or is involved in an activity or event. An example of the PC-vendors web community is shown in Fig.5.6. Kumar et al. [146] gave three reasons why one might be interested in discovering these communities.

1. Communities provide valuable and up-to-date information resources for a user.
2. Communities represent the sociology of the Web, so we can learn and understand the Web evolution by studying them.
3. Communities enable target advertising at a very precise level.

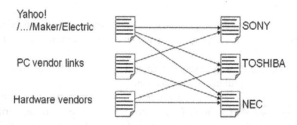

Fig. 5.6. A web community of PC vendors

Web communities can be characterized as a phenomenon manifested by both link proximity and content coherence, but there has been significant success in identifying communities based on the link structure alone. There are several algorithms for finding web communities. Here, we will briefly discuss three community finding algorithms. The first one, inspired by HITS, extracts small complete bipartite subgraphs as the cores of web communities [146]. The second approach is inspired by notions of a maximum flow model: it finds a densely connected subgraph isolated from the remainder of the Web by a sparse cut [93]. The third approach [243] is an algorithm for creating a community chart: given a set of seed pages, it not only identifies individual communities in the graph, but also derives their relationships and connect related communities together.

5.4.1 Bipartite Cores as Communities

Although broad topics evolve only slowly, more specific topics may be quite ephemeral on the Web. While well established communities are represented by large bipartite core, these emerging topics are usually represented by a small bipartite core. HITS finds dense bipartite graph communities based on broad topic queries using eigenvector computation. However, it is too inefficient to iterate all such communities in the Web graph with eigenvector computation. Kumar et al. [146] proposed a technique to hunt for these emerging communities from a large Web graph, which can be described as follows.

First, a bipartite core is defined as a complete bipartite sub-graph which can be partitioned into two subsets denoted as F and C. A complete bipartite sub-graph on node sets F ($|F| = i$) and C ($|C| = j$) contains all possible directed edges from the vertices of F to the vertices of C. Intuitively, the set F corresponds to pages created by members of the community, pointing to what they believe are valuable pages for that community. For this reason, we will refer to the set F as a set of fans, and the set C as centers. Fans are like hubs, and centers are like authorities. Fig.5.7 below shows an example of a $(4,3)$ bipartite core (4 fans and 3 centers).

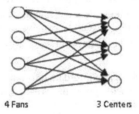

4 Fans   3 Centers

Fig. 5.7. A $(4,3)$ bipartite core

Given a large Web crawl data represented as a directed graph, the procedure as proposed in [146] consists of two major steps: pruning and core generation, which can be summarized as follows.

Step 1: Pruning. Unqualified web pages are removed with many types of pruning, e.g. pruning by in-degree, and iterative pruning of fans and centers.

Step 2: Generating all (i,j) cores. After pruning, the remaining pages will be used to find cores. First, fixing j, we start with all $(1,j)$ cores which is the set of all vertices with out-degree at least j. Then, all $(2,j)$ can be constructed by checking every fan which also points to any center in a $(1,j)$ core. All $(3,j)$ cores can be constructed by checking every fan which points to any center in a $(2,j)$ core, and so on. This idea is similar to the concept of Apriori algorithm for association rule mining [6] as every proper subset of the fans in any (i,j) core forms a core of smaller size.

In [146], a large number of emerging communities have been found from a large Web crawl data. Note that, this method does not find all members pages in the communities, and it also does not find the topics of the communities, their hierarchical organizations, or relationships between communities.

5.4.2 Network Flow/Cut-based Notions of Communities

Bipartite cores based communities are usually very small and do not represent full communities. Flake et al. [93] defined a more general community as a subgraph whose internal link density exceeds the density of connection to nodes outside it by some margin.

Formally, a community is defined as a subset C of V $C \subset V$ such that each $c \in V$ has at least as many neighbors in C as in VCC. This is a NP-complete graph partitioning problem. Hence, we need to approximate and recast it into a less stringent definition, based on the network flow model from operations research.

The max-flow/min-cut problem [66] is posed as follows. We are given a graph $G = (V, E)$ with a source node $s \in V$ and a target node $t \in V$. Each edge (u, v) is like a water pipe with a positive integer maximum flow capacity $c(u, v)$. The max-flow algorithm finds the maximum rate of flow from s to t without exceeding the capacity constraints on any edge. It is known that this maximum flow is the same as a minimum-capacity cut (min-cut) separating s and t.

Flake et al. [93] applied the above concept to the Web context as follows. Suppose we are given the Web graph $G = (V, E)$ with a node subset $S \subset V$ identified as seed URLs, which are examples of the community the user wishes to discover. An artificial source s will be created and connected to all seed nodes $u \in S$, setting $c(s, u) = \infty$. Then, we connect all $v \in V - S - \{s, t\}$ to an artificial target t with $c(v, t) = 1$. Each original edge is made undirected and heuristically set the capacity to k (usually set to $|S|$). The $s \rightarrow t$ max-flow algorithm is applied on the resulting graph. All nodes in the s-side of the min-cut are defined as members of the community C.

In reality, we do not have the whole Web graph and must collect the necessary portions by crawling. The crawler begins with the seed set S and finds all in- and out-neighbors of the seed nodes to some fixed depth. The crawled nodes together with the seed set S are then used to set up the max-flow problem described above. And the process can continue until some conditions are satisfied. This crawling process can be thought of as a different form of focused crawling that is driven not by textual content but by consideration based solely on hyperlink.

Compared with the bipartite cores based approach, the max-flow based community discovery can extract larger, more complete communities. However, it cannot find the theme, the hierarchy, and the relationships of Web communities.

5.4.3 Web Community Chart

The two community finding algorithms described earlier can only identify groups of pages that belong to web communities. They cannot derive or infer the relationships between extracted communities. M. Toyoda and M. Kitsuregawa [243] have proposed a technique for constructing a web community chart that provides not only a set of web communities but also the relationships between them.

Their technique is based on a link-based related page algorithm that gives related pages to a given input page. The main idea is to apply a related page algorithm to a number of pages, and investigate how each page derives other pages as related pages. If a page s derives a page t as a related page and the page t also derives s as a related page, then we say that there is a symmetric derivation relationship between s and t. For example, a fan page i of a baseball team derives other fan pages as related pages. And, when we apply the related page algorithm to another fan page j, the page j also derives the original fan page i as its related page. The symmetric derivation relationship between two pages often means that they are both pointed to by similar set of hubs.

Next, consider the case that a page s derives a page t as a related page but the page t does not derive s as a related page. This means that t is pointed to by many different hubs. For example, a fan page of a baseball team often derives an official page of the team as one of its related pages. However, when we apply the related page algorithm to the team official page, it derives official pages of other teams as related pages instead of the fan page. This is due to the fact that the team official page is often linked together with official pages of other teams in a number of more generic hubs and the number of such hubs is greater than the number of hubs for the fans. In this case, we say that the official page is related to the fan community but the page itself belongs to the baseball team community. This kind of derivation relationship is used to find related communities.

To summarize, identification of web communities and deducing of the relationships between them are done based on the derivation relationship between seed pages and the corresponding related pages. A community is defined as a set of pages strongly connected by the symmetric derivation relationship, and two communities are related when a member of one community derives a member of another community.

Since the related page algorithm is at the heart of the method for creating a web community chart [243]. The precision with popular pages of the algorithm is especially desirable. M. Toyoda and M. Kitsuregawa [243] proposed CompanionC which is a modified version of a well known related page algorithm, Companion [70]. The user study based evaluation result showed that CompanionC gives the highest average precision amongst other related page algorithms (HITS and Companion). The Companion- algorithm can be described as follows.

Related page algorithm: Companion-

Companion- takes a seed page as an input, and outputs related pages to the seed. First, it builds a vicinity graph for a given seed, which is a subgraph of the web around the seed. A vicinity graph is a directed graph, $G(V,E)$, where nodes in V represent web pages, and edges in E represent links between these pages. V consists of the seed, a set of nodes pointing to the seed (B), and a set of nodes pointed to by nodes in B (BF). When following outgoing links from each node in B, the order of links in the node is considered. Not all the links are followed but only R links immediately preceding and succeeding the link pointing to the seed. This is based on an observation that links to related pages are clustered in a small portion of a page. Usually, the value 10 as R gives a stable result.

After obtaining the vicinity graph G, the Companion- algorithm will compute the authority scores for every node in G. The computation process consists of two major steps: (1) assigning authority weight and hub weight, and (2) calculating hub and authority scores.

(1) assigning authority weight and hub weight

To decrease the influence of links from a single large server, Companion- assigns two kinds of weights, an authority weight and a hub weight to each edge in G. The authority weight is used for calculating an authority score of each node; and the hub weight is used for calculating a hub score of each node. The following weighting method, proposed in [45], is used: (1) if two nodes of an edge are in the same server, the edge has the value 0 for both weights; (2) if a node has n incoming edges from the same server, the authority weight of each edge is 1/n; and (3) If a node has m outgoing edges to the same server, the hub weight of each edge is 1/m.

(2) calculating hub and authority scores

Let $h(n)$ be a hub score and $a(n)$ be an authority score for each node n in V. The following is the process of the calculation. Here, we use $aw(n,m)$ and $hw(n,m)$ to represent the authority weight and the hub weight of an edge from n to m, respectively.

Step 1. Initialize $h(n)$ and $a(n)$ of each node n to 1.

Step 2. Repeat the following calculation until $h(n)$ and $a(n)$
converge for each node n.

For all node n in V, $h(n) \leftarrow \sum_{(n,m)\in E} a(m) \times hw(n,m)$

For all node n in V, $a(n) \leftarrow \sum_{(m,n)\in E} h(m) \times aw(m,n)$

Normalize $h(n)$, so that the sum of squares equals to 1.

Normalize $a(n)$, so that the sum of squares equals to 1.

Step 3. Return nodes with the N highest authority scores.

Web community chart construction algorithm

Given a seed set, a web community chart is built as follows. First, we extend the seed set by applying Companion- to each page in the seed and gathering results. Then, we classify seeds in the extended seed set into communities using symmetric derivation relationship. After that the related communities are connected by edges. The procedure is given below.

(1) Extending the seed set

Since the number of the input seeds may be too small to find sufficient symmetric relationships. The extended set is generated by applying Companion- to each seed separately. For each result, we select the top N authorities, and aggregate them into the extended seed set.

(2) Building the Authority Derivation Graph

An authority derivation graph (ADG) is a directed graph that shows derivation relationships between seeds. Each node represents a seed page in the extending seed set, and each directed edge from a node s to another node t represents the fact that s derives t as one of the top N authorities using the Companion- algorithm. (In [243], N is set to 10).

(3) Extracting the Symmetric Derivation Graph

A symmetric derivation graph (SDG) is a directed graph that shows mutual derivation relationship between seeds. Nodes in the SDG correspond to the nodes in the ADG graph. There exists a directed edge from node s to node t if s and t are mutually connected in ADG.

(4) Identifying web communities

The connected components in the SDG graph obtained in the previous steps may consist of nodes from various categories, so it is necessary to partition the graph further to get more consistent web communities. The partition is done based on a node triangle using following process.

1. Extract triangles of nodes from SDG, and regard a subgraph with triangles connected by edges as a core.

2. Add each node to a core, if the node has incoming edges connected to the core.

3. Eliminate partitions from SDG

4. Extract the remaining connected component in SDG as a partition

(5) Creating the web community chart

Finally, we construct a web community chart which is a directed graph with nodes corresponding to communities and weighted directed edges connect the related communities. The community chart is constructed by including the communities identified in the previous step as nodes. The edges in the chart is created using information from the ADG. A directed edge from a community c to another community d with a weight w is created when there exist w directed edges in ADG from nodes in c to nodes in d. Figure 2.12 shows an example of a part of the resulting web community chart [243].

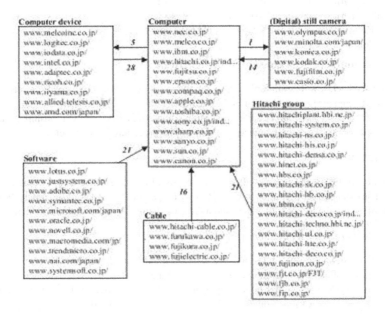

Fig. 5.8. A part of the web community chart

5.5 Web Graph Measurement and Modeling

The information available on the Internet is associated together by hyperlinks between pairs of web pages, forming a large graph of hyperlinks or the Web graph. The Web graph shares various graphical properties with other kinds of complex networks e.g. a citation network, a power grid network, etc. There are several previous works on the statistical and empirical studies of the Web graph. These studies consistently reported emerging properties of the Web graph at varying scales. Several portions of the Web graph have been reported to have a power-law connectivity and a macroscopic structure that are different from the properties of a random graph. Designers of Web crawler and other Web algorithmic tools must be aware of these characteristics. In this section, we will first review necessary graph terminologies. Then, we will introduce concepts of power-law distributions, the power-law connectivity of the Web graph. Finally, we will describe a bow-tie structure which is usually used in the literature to depict the large-scale overall structure of the Web graph.

5.5.1 Graph Terminologies

A directed graph $G(V,E)$ consists of a set V of nodes and a set E of ordered pairs of nodes, called edges. A Web graph [44] is a directed graph induced from a set of web pages where each node represents a web page and each directed edge represents a hyperlink from a source web page to a destination web page. A Host graph [31] is a weighted directed graph where each node represents a web host and each directed edge represents the hyperlinks from web pages on the source host to web pages on the destination host. The weight of the edge is equal to the number of such hyperlinks.

- The **in-degree** of a node is the number of incoming edges incident to it.
- The **out-degree** of a node is the number of outgoing edges incident to it.
- A **path** from node u to node v is a sequence of nodes such that from each of its node, there exists an edge to the next node in the sequence.
- A **connected component** of an undirected graph is a set of nodes such that for any pair of nodes u and v there exists a path from u to v.
- A **strongly connected component** (SCC) of a directed graph G is a set of nodes S such that for every pair of nodes $u, v \in S$ there exists a path from u to v and from v to u.
- A **weakly connected component** (WCC) of a directed graph G is a set of nodes W, where W is a connected component of the undirected graph obtained by ignoring the directions of all edges in G.

5.5.2 Power-law Distribution

A discrete power-law distribution is a distribution of the form:

$$\Pr(X = k) = Ck^{-v}; \text{for} k = 1, 2, \cdots \tag{5.11}$$

Where v is a coefficient (or a power-law exponent), X is a random variable, and C is a constant.

A power-law distribution can be checked by plotting the data in a log-log plot. The signature of the power-law distribution in a log-log plot is a line with slope corresponding to the power-law exponent α. The power-law distribution is ubiquitous and it has been observed in many complex networks such as social networks, transportation networks, biological networks, etc. [20]. A notable characteristic of the power-law distribution is the fact that the power-law distribution decays polynomially for large values of independent variable X. As a result, in contrast to other standard distributions such as exponential and Gaussian, in a power-law distribution the average behavior is not the most typical.

5.5.3 Power-law Connectivity of the Web Graph

A power-law connectivity was observed in various scales of the Web graphs [12, 22, 44]. The study results in [12] show that the distribution of links on the World Wide Web follows the power-law, with power-law exponent of 2.1 and 2.45 for the in-degree and the out-degree distribution respectively. [44] reported on the power-law connectivity of the Web graph having exponent of 2.09 and 2.72 for the in-degree and the out-degree distribution respectively. The power-law distribution for the connectivity of the Web graph is very different from the distribution found in traditional uniform random graphs. In a random uniform graph with random independent edges of fixed probability p, where p is small, the number of nodes with k connectivity has a Poisson distribution and decay exponentially fast to zero as k increases towards its maximum value $n-1$ (n = the number of nodes in the random graph). Thus the power-law distribution is a representative emerging regularity in a large graph created by several distributed independent agents.

5.5.4 Bow-tie Structure of the Web Graph

Another special property of the Web graph is its bow-tie structure. The authors in [44] conducted a series of experiments including analyses on WCC, SCC, and random start BFS using large-scale Web graphs induced from two AltaVista crawls, each with over 200 million nodes and 1.5 billion links. Based on the results of these experiments, The authors in [44] also inferred and depicted macroscopic structure of the Web graph as a *bow-tie* structure. Fig.5.9 shows an illustration of the bow-tie structure as defined in [44].

Using Broder et al.'s terminology in [44], the bow-tie structure consists of

- SCC is the core of the structure, corresponding to the largest strongly connected component whose pages can reach each other via directed paths. Most of the well known websites are in this core component.
- IN consists of upstream pages that can reach the SCC via a directed path of hyperlinks, but cannot be reached from the SCC in a similar way.
- OUT consists of downstream pages that can be reached from the SCC via a directed path of hyperlinks, but it cannot reach the SCC in a similar way.
- TENDRILS consists of pages that can only be reached from the IN component (TENDRIL-IN) and those that can only reach to the OUT component (TENDRIL-OUT).
- DISCONNECTED consists of pages outside the largest weakly connected component (WCC) in the Web graph.
- TUBES are directed paths from a page in the TENDRIL-IN component to a page in the OUT component.

Results from [44] reveal that each of the four components of the Web graph for the AltaVista crawl datasets has approximately the same size (i.e. each contains about 50 million pages). Moreover, it is found that more than 90% of nodes reside in the largest WCC. Because there is a disconnected component in the bow-tie structure, it is clear that there are sizable portions of the Web that cannot be reached from other portions.

5.6 Using Link Information for Web Page Classification

Web pages, unlike standard text collections, can contain both multimedia (images, sounds, flash, etc.) and connections to other documents (through hyperlinks). Hyperlinks are increasingly being used to improve the ability to organize, search, and analyze the web. Hyperlinks (or citations) are being actively used to classify target web pages. The basic assumption made by citation or link analysis is that a link is often created because of a subjective connection between the original document and the cited, or linked document.

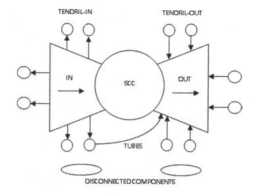

Fig. 5.9. The bow-tie structure

For example, if I am making a web page about my hobbies, and I like playing scrabble, I might link to an online scrabble game, or to the home page of Hasbro. The belief is that these connections convey meaning or judgments made by the creator of the link or citation. In this section, we introduce two ways of utilizing link information for Web page classification. One uses inbound anchortext and surrounding words to classify pages; the other extends the concept of linkages from explicit hyperlinks to implicit links built between Web pages.

5.6.1 Using Web Structure for Classifying and Describing Web Pages

As introduced in [101], anchortext, since it is chosen by people who are interested in the page, may better summarize the contents of the page C such as indicating that Yahoo! is a web directory. They describe their technique for creating "virtual documents" from the anchortext and inbound extended anchortext(the words and phrases occurring near a link to a target page). In other words, a virtual document can be regarded as a collection of anchortexts or extended anchortexts from links pointing to the target document, as shown in Figure 5.10.

Extended anchortext is defined as the set of rendered words occurring up to 25 words before and after an associated link. The virtual document are limited to 20 inbound links, always excluding any Yahoo! pages, to prevent the Yahoo! descriptions or category words from biasing the results.

To generate each virtual document, Eric J. Glover et al. queried the Google search engine for backlinks pointing into the target document. Each backlink was then downloaded, the anchortext, and words before and after each anchortext were extracted. They generated two virtual documents for each URL. One consists of only the anchortexts and the other consists of the extended anchortexts, up to 25 words on each side of the link, (both limited to the first 20 non-Yahoo! links). Although we allowed up to 20 total inbound links, only about 25% actually had 20 (or more). About 30% of the virtual documents were formed with three or fewer inbound links. If a page had no inbound links, it was not considered for this experiment. Most URLs extracted from Yahoo! pages had at least one valid-non Yahoo! link.

For this experiment, the authors in [101] considered all words and two or three word phrases as possible features. They used no stopwords, and ignored all punctuation and HTML structure (except for the Title field of the full-text documents). Each document (or virtual

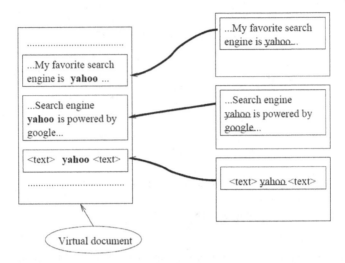

Fig. 5.10. A virtual document is comprised of anchortexts and nearby words from pages that link to the target document

document) was converted into a set of features that occurred and then appropriate histograms were updated.

For example, if a document has the sentence: "My favorite game is scrabble", the following features are generated: my, my favorite, my favorite game, favorite, favorite game, favorite game is, etc. From the generated features an appropriate histogram is updated. There is one histogram for the positive set and one for the negative set.

Categorizing web pages is a well researched problem. An SVM classifier [248] are used because it is resistant to overfitting, can handle large dimensionality, and has been shown to be highly effective when compared to other methods for text classification. When using a linear kernel function, the final output is a weighted feature vector with a bias term. The returned weighted vector can be used to quickly classify a test document by simply taking the dot product of the features.

In [101], authors compare three different methods for classifying a web page: full-text, anchortext only, and extended anchortext only. Their experiment results show that anchortext alone is comparable for classification purposes with the full-text. Several papers agree that features on linking documents, in addition to the anchortext (but less than the whole page) can provide significant improvements. This work is consistent with these results, showing significant improvement in classification accuracy when using the extended anchortext instead of the document fulltext. For comparison, this method is applied to full-texts for the categories of courses and faculty from the WebKB dataset.

The combination method is also highly effective for improving positive-class accuracy, but reduces negative class accuracy. The automatic combination also provided substantial improvement over the extended anchortext or the full-text alone for positive accuracy, but caused a slight reduction in negative class accuracy as compared to the extended anchortext case. More details are in [101].

Other works have utilized in-bound anchortext to help classify target web pages. For example, Blum and Mitchell [37] compared two classifiers for several computer science web pages (from the WebKB dataset), one for full-text, and one for the words on the links point-ing to the target pages (inbound anchortext). From their results, anchortext words alone were slightly less powerful than the full-text alone, and the combination was better. Other work, in-cluding work by Fürnkranz [94], expanded this notion to include words beyond the anchortext that occur near (in the same paragraph) and nearby headings. Fürnkranz noted a significant improvement in classification accuracy when using the link-based method as opposed to the fulltext alone, although adding the entire text of "neighbor documents" seemed to harm the ability to classify pages [54].

5.6.2 Using Implicit and Explicit Links for Web Page Classification

. The hyperlinks sometimes may not reflect true relationships in content between Web pages, and the hyperlinks themselves may be sparse. A technical Web page may link to a commercial page describing a beauty product. In such situations, it is unreliable to employ hyperlinks for classification [80] where authors observe that hyperlinks provide only one kind of linkages be-tween Web pages. By properly utilizing the Web query logs, we can discover other important linkages that are just as important. In addition, Xue et al. [260] proposed a novel categoriza-tion algorithm named IRC (Iterative Reinforcement Categorization algorithm) to categorize the interrelated Web objects by iteratively reinforcing individual classification results via rela-tionships across different data types extracted from query logs.

They define two kinds of implicit links that can be extracted from a query log and three kinds of explicit links using the traditional hyperlink concepts. They further define two differ-ent approaches in making use of these links. The first one is to classify a target page according to the labels of the neighbors of that page. They show that using this algorithm for classifica-tion, the implicit links are more reliable in classification. The best result of using implicit links is about 20.6% higher than the best result through the explicit links in terms of the Micro-F1 measure. The second classification method they use is to construct a virtual document based on different kinds of links, and then conduct classification on the virtual documents. The ex-periments on the Web pages crawled from the Open Directory Project (ODP) and the query logs collected by MSN show that using the implicit links can achieve 10.5% improvement compared to the explicit links in terms of Macro-F1.

Consider a typical scenario when a Web user finds information by a search engine. A user issues a query which may be a well-formed natural language question or one or more keywords or phrases to a search engine. The search engine replies with a list of Web pages to the user together with a summary of each page. The summary, together with other clues such as the URL and title, can give the user a general idea of the contents of the page. Based on this information, the Web user clicks on some Web pages that appear to be most relevant to the query. The query log records the process, by keeping an entry in query log for every session in which the Web user submits a query and clicks on some returned pages. An example of such a quadruple is as follows:

$$Entry := < U, Q, D_q, T > \qquad (5.12)$$

where U denotes the web user who submits the query. The user is often represented by the IP address from which the user accesses the Internet. Q denotes the query the Web user submits to the search engine. D_q represents the returned Web pages clicked by the user. T represents the time when such an entry occurs. In this work, we only focus on using the query logs for Web page classification. Thus, they omit T and consider an entry as $< U, Q, D_q >$. In fact, the entry could be further simplified as $< Q, D_q >$ by omitting U. However, often times when the same query is issued by two different users, it may mean different things. Such ambiguities between users make the pages that are constrained by Q alone to be more heterogeneous in content than the pages that are constrained by both U and Q.

Based on a query log, two kinds of implicit link relations are defined according to two different constraints:

1. L_I1: d_i and d_j appear in the same entries constrained by U and Q in the query log. That is d_i and d_j are clicked by the same user issuing the same query;
2. L_I2: d_i and d_j appear in the same entries constrained by the query Q only. That is d_i and d_j are clicked according to the same query, but the query may be issued by different users. It is clear that the constraint for L_I2 is not as strict as that for L_I1. Thus, more links of L_I2 can be found than L_I1, however they may be more noisy.

Similar to the implicit links, three kinds of explicit links are defined based on the hyperlinks among the Web pages according to the following three different conditions:

$$L_E(i,j) = \begin{cases} 1 & Cond_E \\ 0 & Other \end{cases} \tag{5.13}$$

1. $Cond_E1$: there exist hyperlinks from d_j to d_i (In-Link to d_i from d_j);
2. $Cond_E2$: there exist hyperlinks from d_i to d_j (Out- Link from d_i to d_j);
3. $Cond_E3$: either $Cond_E1$ or $Cond_E2$ holds.

These three types of explicit links under the above conditions are denoted as LE1, LE2, LE3 respectively. In the above definitions, the inlink and out-link are distinguished because, given the target Web page, the in-link is the hyperlink created by other Web page editors who refer to the target Web page. In contrast, the out-link is created by the editor of the source Web page. They may be different when used to describe the target Web page. From the above definitions, D.Shen et al. [80]said that the implicit links give the relationships between Web pages from the view of Web users. However, the explicit links reflect the relationships among Web pages from the view of Web-page editors.

To utilize these link information for classification, D.Shen et al. [80] propose two approach. One is to predict the label of the target Web page by the labels of its neighbors through majority voting.This algorithm is similar to k-Nearst Neighbor (KNN). However, k is not a constant as in KNN and it is decided by the set of the neighbors of the target page.

The other enhances classification performance through the links by constructing virtual documents. Given a document, the virtual document is constructed by borrowing some extra text from its neighbors. Although originally the concept of the virtual document is pioneered by [101], the notion are extended by including different links. After constructing the virtual document through links, any traditional text classification algorithm could be employed to classify the web pages. In [80], they take Naive Bayesian classifier and Support Vector Machine as the classifiers. The experimental results show that implicit links can improve the classification performance obviously as compared to the explicit links based methods. More details are in [80].

Summary

In this chapter, we have reported some interesting research topics in the context of web linkage mining. The principal technologies used in linkage analysis have been substantially addressed and the real applications have been covered as well. We start with the theory of co-citation and bibliographic couple, followed by two most famous linkage mining algorithms, i.e. PageRank and HITS. The detailed algorithmic discussions provide readers a conceptual understanding on how current commercial search engines work. In the next section, we will introduce one of the main extensions of web linkage mining - web community discovery. The related algorithms and techniques have been elaborated. In this chapter, we have also talked about the web graph modeling theory and its applications in web page classification.

6

Web Usage Mining

In previous chapters, we have discussed the techniques with respect to Web content and Web linkage mining. These mining processes are mainly performed on the Web page itself, either from the perspective of textual content or from the perspective of linking property. Since Web is an interaction media between Web users and Web pages, the role of users' action to the Web needs to be fully concerned during Web mining. Mining user navigational behavior, i.e. Web usage mining, is able to capture the underlying correlations between users and pages during browsing, in turn, providing complementary assistance for advanced Web applications, such as adaptive Web design and Web recommendation. In this chapter, we will concentrate the discussion on this aspect. We start with the theoretical background of Web usage in terms of data model and algorithmic issues, then present a number of Web usage mining solutions along with the experimental studies. Finally, we present a number of applications in Web usage mining.

6.1 Modeling Web User Interests using Clustering

Web clustering is one of the mostly used techniques in the context of Web mining, which is to aggregate similar Web objects, such as Web page or user session, into a number of object groups via measuring their mutual vector distance. Basically, clustering can be performed upon these two types of Web objects, which results in clustering Web users or Web pages, respectively. The resulting Web user session groups are considered as representatives of user navigational behavior patterns, while Web page clusters are used for generating task-oriented functionality aggregations of Web organization. Moreover, the mined usage knowledge in terms of Web usage pattern and page aggregate property can be utilized to improve Web site structure design such as adaptive Web design and Web personalization. In this section, we present two studies on clustering Web users.

6.1.1 Measuring Similarity of Interest for Clustering Web Users

Capturing the characteristics of Web users is an important task for the Web site designers. By mining Web users' historical access patterns, not only the information about how the Web is being used, but also some demographics and behavioral characteristics of Web users could

G. Xu et al., *Web Mining and Social Networking,*
DOI 10.1007/978-1-4419-7735-9_6, © Springer Science+Business Media, LLC 2011

be determined [56]. The navigation path of the Web-users, if available to the server, carries valuable information about the user interests.

The purpose of finding similar interests among the Web-users is to discover knowledge from the user profile. If a Web site is well designed, there will be strong correlation among the similarity of the navigation paths and similarity among the user interests. Therefore, clustering of the former could be used to cluster the latter.

The definition of the similarity is application dependent. The similarity function can be based on visiting the same or similar pages, or the frequency of access to a page [77, 140], or even on the visiting orders of links (i.e., clients' navigation paths). In the latter case, two users that access the same pages can be mapped into different groups of interest similarities if they access pages in distinct visiting orders. In [256], Xiao et al. propose several similarity measures to capture the users' interests. A matrix-based algorithm is then developed to cluster Web users such that the users in the same cluster are closely related with respect to the similarity measure.

Problem Definitions

The structure of an Internet server site S could be abstracted as a directed graph called connectivity graph: The node set of the graph consists of all Web pages of the site. The hypertext links between pages can be taken as directed edges of the graph as each link has a starting page and an ending page. For some of the links starting points or end points could be some pages outside the site. It is imagined that the connectivity graph could be quite complicated. For simplicity, the concerns here is limited on the part of clients' navigation path inside a particular site. From the Internet browsing logs, the following information about a Web user could be gathered: the frequency of a hyper-page usage, the lists of links she]he selected, the elapsed time between two links, and the order of pages accessed by individual Web users.

Similarity Measures

Suppose that, for a given Web site S, there are m users $U = \{u_1, u_2, ..., u_m\}$ who accessed n different Web pages $P = p_1, p_2, ..., p_n$ in some time interval. For each page p_i, and each user u_j, it is associated with a usage value, denoted as $use(p_i, u_j)$, and defined as

$$use\left(p_i, u_j\right) = \begin{cases} 1 & \text{if } p_i \text{ is accessed by } u_j \\ 0 & \text{Otherwise} \end{cases}$$

The **use** vector can be obtained by retrieving the access logs of the site. If two users accessed the same pages, they might have some similar interests in the sense that they are interested in the same information (e.g., news, electrical products etc). The number of common pages they accessed can measure this similarity. The measure is defined by

$$Sim1\left(u_i, u_j\right) = \frac{\sum_k \left(use\left(p_k, u_i\right) * use\left(p_k, u_j\right)\right)}{\sqrt{\sum_k use\left(p_k, u_i\right) * \sum_k use\left(p_k, u_j\right)}} \tag{6.1}$$

where $\sum_k use\left(p_k, u_i\right)$ is the total number of pages that were accessed by user u_i, and the product of $\sum_k use\left(p_k, u_i\right) * \sum_k use\left(p_k, u_j\right)$ is the number of common pages accessed by both user u_i, and u_j. If two users access the exact same pages, their similarity will be 1. The similarity measure defined in this way is called *Usage Based* (UB) measure.

Generally, the similarity between two users can be measured by counting the number of times they access the common pages at all sites. In this case, the measure is defined by

$$Sim2\left(u_i, u_j\right) = \frac{\sum_k \sum_s \left(acc_s\left(p_k, u_i\right) * acc_s\left(p_k, u_j\right)\right)}{\sqrt{\sum_k use\left(p_k, u_i\right) * \sum_k use\left(p_k, u_j\right)}} \tag{6.2}$$

where $acc_s\left(p_k, u_i\right)$ is the total number of times that user u_i accesses the page P_k at site S. This measure is called *Frequency Based* (FB) measure.

The similarity between two users can be measured more precisely by taking into account the actual time the users spent on viewing each Web page. Let $t\left(p_k, u_j\right)$ be the time the user u_j spent on viewing page p_k (assume that $t\left(p_k, u_j\right) = 0$ if u_j did not access page p_k). In this case, the similarity between users can be expressed by

$$Sim3\left(u_i, u_j\right) = \frac{\sum_k \left(t\left(p_k, u_i\right) * t\left(p_k, u_j\right)\right)}{\sqrt{\sum_k \left(t\left(p_k, u_i\right)\right)^2 * \sum_k \left(t\left(p_k, u_j\right)\right)^2}} \tag{6.3}$$

where $\sum_k \left(t\left(p_k, u_i\right)\right)^2$ is the square sum of the time user u_i spent on viewing pages at the site, and $\sum_k \left(t\left(p_k, u_i\right) * t\left(p_k, u_j\right)\right)$ is the inner-product over time spent on viewing the common pages by users u_i and u_j. Even if two users access exact the same pages, their similarity might be less than 1 in this case, if they view a page in different amount of time. This measure is called *Viewing-Time Based* (VTB) measure.

In some applications, the accessing order of pages by a user is more important than that of the time on viewing each page. In this case, two users are considered to have the same interests only when they access a sequence of Web pages in the exact same order. The similarity between users, in such a situation, can be measured by checking the access orders of Web pages in their navigation paths. Let $Q = q_1, q_2, ..., q_r$ be a navigation path, where q_i, $1 \leq i \leq r$, stands for the page accessed in order. We call Q an r-hop path. Define Q_l as the set of all possible l-hop subpaths $(1 \leq r)$ of Q, i.e., $Q_l = \{q_i, q_{i+1}, ..., q_{i+l-1} | i = 1, 2, ..., r - l + 1\}$. It is obvious that Q_l contains all pages in Q. We call $f(Q) = \bigcup_{l=1}^r Q_l$ the feature space of path Q. Note that a cyclic path may include some of its subpaths more than once, and $Q \subseteq f(Q)$.

Now let Q^i and Q^j be the navigation paths accessed by user u_i, and u_j, respectively. The similarity between users u_i, and u_j can be defined using the natural angle between paths Q^i and Q^j (i.e., $\cos\left(Q^i, Q^j\right)$), which is defined as:

$$Sim4\left(u_i, u_j\right) = \frac{\langle Q^i, Q^j \rangle_l}{\sqrt{\langle Q^i, Q^i \rangle_l \langle Q^j, Q^j \rangle_l}} \tag{6.4}$$

where $l = min(length(Q^i), length(Q^j))$, and $\langle Q^i, Q^j \rangle_l$ is the inner product over the feature spaces of paths Q^i and Q^j, which is defined as $\langle Q^i, Q^j \rangle_l = \sum_{k=1}^l \sum_{q \in Q_k^i \cap Q_k^j} length(q) * length(q)$

Based on the above definitions, the similarity between two users will be 1 if they access a sequence of pages in the exact same access order, and 0 if they access no common pages at all. Note that $\langle Q^i, Q^j \rangle_l$ is the same for all $l \leq min(length(Q^i), length(Q^j))$. We call (6.4) the *Visiting-Order Based* (VOB) measure.

An Example

Below an example is given to illustrate how the different similarity measures are calculated. It is a simplified example derived from [223]. The navigation paths (shown in Fig.6.1) are reproduced as follows. The names (in italic) in the paths are the title of Web pages. The names of the links (underlined, followed by the corresponding link times) are the click-able hypertext, corresponding to links in the connectivity graph. The computation of similarity among Web

1) Main Movies: 20sec *Movies* News : 15sec *NewsBox*: 43sec *Box-Office* Evita: 52sec *News* Argentina:31 sec *Evito*: 44sec

2) Music Box: 11sec *Box-Office* Crucible: 12sec *Crucible* Book 13sec *Books: 19sec*

3) Main Movies: 33sec *Movies* Box: 21sec *Boxoffice* Evita: 44sec *News* Box: 53sec *Box-office* Evita: 61sec *Evito : 31sec*

4) Main Movies: 19sec *Movies* News : 21sec *News box*: 38sec *Box-Office* Evita:61sec *News* Evita:24sec *Evito* News : 31sec *News* Argentina: 19sec *Evito: 39sec*

5) Movies Box: 32sec *Box-Office* News : 17sec *News* Jordan: 64sec *Box-Office* Evita: 19sec *Evito : 50sec*

6) Main Box: 17sec *Box-Office* Evita: 33sec *News* Box: 41sec *Box-Office* Evita: 54sec *Evito* News : 56sec *News:47sec*

Fig. 6.1. A usage snapshot example

users' results in an $m \times m$ matrix, called users' similarity matrix (*SM*). Assuming that the six navigation paths be the access traces of six users identified by $u_1, u_2, ..., u_6$. By using eq.6.1-6.4, we obtain the following similarity measures

$$SM1 = \begin{bmatrix} 1 & .224 & 1 & 1 & .894 & .894 \\ .224 & 1 & .224 & .224 & .25 & .25 \\ 1 & .224 & 1 & 1 & .894 & .894 \\ 1 & .224 & 1 & 1 & .894 & .894 \\ .894 & .25 & .894 & .894 & 1 & .75 \\ .894 & .25 & .894 & .894 & .75 & 1 \end{bmatrix}, SM2 = \begin{bmatrix} 1 & .177 & .875 & .972 & .802 & .894 \\ .177 & 1 & .354 & .125 & .378 & .316 \\ .875 & .354 & 1 & .795 & .953 & .894 \\ .972 & .125 & .795 & 1 & .756 & .87 \\ .802 & .378 & .953 & .756 & 1 & .837 \\ .894 & .316 & .894 & .87 & .837 & 1 \end{bmatrix}$$

$$SM3 = \begin{bmatrix} 1 & .224 & .885 & .988 & .949 & .976 \\ .224 & 1 & .35 & .205 & .162 & .27 \\ .885 & .35 & 1 & .863 & .779 & .92 \\ .988 & .205 & .863 & 1 & .968 & .964 \\ .949 & .164 & .779 & .968 & 1 & .895 \\ .976 & .27 & .92 & .964 & .895 & 1 \end{bmatrix}, SM4 = \begin{bmatrix} 1 & .01 & .096 & .618 & .096 & .08 \\ .01 & 1 & .02 & .006 & .027 & .02 \\ .096 & .02 & 1 & .063 & .027 & .271 \\ .618 & .006 & .063 & 1 & .066 & .069 \\ .096 & .027 & .735 & .066 & 1 & .362 \\ .08 & .02 & .271 & .069 & .362 & 1 \end{bmatrix}$$

A Clustering Algorithm

Data Preprocessing

Data preprocessing is necessary, as the interest items need to be extracted from the access log files. A Web page may be considered as an interest item, or a group of them may be taken into a "semantic" interest item set.

The data in the SM matrix also need to be preprocessed. In most cases, we are interested in those users among them higher similar interests are shown with respect to a particular similarity measure. For this purpose, a similarity threshold, λ, is determined to split the user clusters. Users with similarity measure greater than or equal to λ are considered in a same cluster. For instance, if $\lambda = 0.9$, $SM2$ becomes the following $SM5$ after preprocessing.

$$SM5 = \begin{bmatrix} 1 & 0 & 0 & .972 & 0 & 0 \\ 0 & 1 & 0 & 0 & 0 & 0 \\ 0 & 0 & 1 & 0 & .935 & 0 \\ .972 & 0 & 0 & 1 & 0 & 0 \\ 0 & 0 & .935 & 0 & 1 & 0 \\ 0 & 0 & 0 & 0 & 0 & 1 \end{bmatrix}$$

$SM(i,j)$ represents the similarity measure between users u_i and u_j ($1 \le i,j \le m$). The greater the value of $SM(i,j)$, the closer the two users u_i and u_j is related. Note that SM is a symmetric matrix and elements along the main diagonal are all the same (i.e., $SM(i,i) = 1$, for all $1 \le i \le m$). Thus only those elements in the upper triangular matrix need to be stored in implementation.

Clustering Web-users into groups is equivalent to decomposing their SM matrix into submatrices. The goal of clustering users is achieved by two steps: (1) permute rows and columns of the matrix such that those "closely related" elements are located closely in the matrix; and (2) find the dividing point that decomposes the matrix into sub-matrices. The next two subsections discuss the two steps in details.

Permutation of the matrix

In order to locate those closely related users in the matrix, the authors use affinity to measure how close two users are related in the SM matrix, which is defined as: $A(i,j) = \sum_{p=1}^{m} SM(i,p) * SM(p,j)$. For users u_i, $u_j \in U$, they contribute to the affinity $A(i,j)$ if $SM(i,j) \ne 0$, or if there exists $p, 1 \le p \le m$, such that $SM(i,p) \ne 0$ and $SM(p,j) \ne 0$. Two users with higher affinity should have a higher chance to be put in the same cluster.

To measure how closely those users with high affinity are located together in the matrix, we define the global affinity of a matrix as:

$$GA(SM) = \sum_{i=1}^{m} A(i,i-1) + A(i,i+1) \tag{6.5}$$

$A(i,i-1)$ is the affinity of u_i with its preceding user, and $A(i,i+1)$ is the affinity of u_i, with its succeeding user, in the matrix. For u_1, and u_k, th authors assume that $A(0,1) = A(1,0) = A(m+1,m) = A(m,re+1) = 0$. $GA(SM)$ represents the global affinity of each user in the matrix with its neighboring users. The higher the $GA(SM)$ is, the closer the elements of greater values get together, which is the case where the users with higher similar interests are located together in the matrix.

In order to get a higher global affinity, we permute the rows and columns of the matrix. The permutation procedure starts from the first column. It compares the GAs by swapping the positions of every pair of columns. If the GA becomes higher after swapping, the two columns swap their positions (the rows should be swapped accordingly to maintain the same relative positions as columns); otherwise the positions of the two columns remain unchanged.

When the permutation is complete, the global affinity of the matrix is maximized. That is, those closely related users are located closely to each other in the matrix.

Decomposition of the Matrix

After the global affinity of the matrix is maximized, it needs to partition the matrix so that the users in one sub-matrix will be in the same cluster. By choosing a dividing point, X, along the main diagonal of the matrix, SM is divided into four sub-matrices $SM_{1,1}$ (the upper-left part of SM from X), $SM_{1,2}$ (upper-right), $SM_{2,1}$ (left-bottom) and $SM_{2,2}$ (right-bottom). Note that $SM_{1,2} = SM_{2,1}^{T}$ because of the symmetry of SM.

The dividing point should be properly chosen so that users of high affinity are in the same submatrix. To decide this dividing point, we define the weight of a sub-matrix $SM_{p,q}$, $(l \leq p, q \leq 2)$, as:

$$W_{SM_{p,q}} = \sum_{i=(p-1)*r+1}^{r+(m-1)*(p-1)} \sum_{j=(q-1)*r+1}^{r+(m-r)*(q-1)} SM(i,j) \tag{6.6}$$

here r stands for the row (and column) number of the dividing point. A non-zero element in $SM_{1,1}$ (or $SM_{2,2}$) indicates that the corresponding users within the cluster of $SM_{1,2}$ (or $SM_{2,1}$) accessed the same pages with a similarity value of the element. A non-zero element in $SM_{1,2}$ (or $SM_{2,1}$) indicates that the corresponding users between two clusters of $SM_{1,2}$ (or $SM_{2,1}$) accessed the same pages with a similarity value of the element. Since the strategy is to cluster the Web users with higher similarity, the dividing point should be chosen such that the following function is maximized:

$$C_X = W_{SM_{1,1}} * W_{SM_{2,2}} - W_{SM_{1,2}} * W_{SM_{2,1}} \tag{6.7}$$

The maximum C_X can be achieved where the sum of similarities between users inside clusters is maximized, and the sum of similarities between users across clusters is minimized.

Once a dividing point is found, the submatrices $SM_{1,1}$ and $SM_{2,2}$ correspond to two clusters of Web users of U. Each of the two submatrices can be further clustered using the same clustering strategy. This clustering will be recursively called until no further clusters could be found, which is the case where the dividing point X locates in the first or the last column of the matrix.

The matrix based clustering algorithm is depicted in Algorithm 6.1, where $|SM|$ stands for the number of rows (or columns) of the square matrix SM.

Algorithm 6.1: Cluster(SM)

Input: the similarity matrix SM;
Output: clusters of Web users of $U = U_1 U_2, ...$;
begin
    $U_1 = U_2 = \cdots = \varphi$; $m = |SM|$;
    permute SM such that (6.6) is maximized;
    find the dividing point of SM such that
        objective (6.7) is maximized;
    if $(X == l)$ or $(X == m)$
        convert SM into the next U_i;
    else begin
        cluster $(SM_{1,1})$;
        cluster $(SM_{2,2})$;
    end
end

6.1.2 Clustering Web Users using Latent Semantic Indexing

Latent Semantic Indexing (LSI) is a statistical method, which is to reconstruct the co-occurrence observation space into a dimension-reduced latent space that keeps the maximum approximation of the original space by using mathematical transformation procedures such as Single Value Decomposition (SVD) [71]. With the reduced dimensionality of the transformed data expression, the computational cost is significantly decreased accordingly, and the problem of sparsity of data is also well handled as well. Besides, LSI based techniques are capable of capturing semantic knowledge from the observation data, while the conventional statistical analysis approaches such as clustering or classification lacks in finding underlying association among the observed co-occurrence. In the last decades, LSI is extensively adopted in the applications of information retrieval, image processing, Web research and data mining, and a great deal of successes have been achieved. In this section, we aim to introduce a study of integrating LSI analysis with Web clustering process, to discover Web user session aggregates with better clustering quality [273].

Latent Semantic Indexing Algorithm

In this section, we first introduce the Web usage data model, and review LSI algorithm and its related mathematical background.

Web Usage Data Model

The Web usage data is originally collected and stored in Web sever logs of website, and is pre-processed for data analysis after performing data cleaning, pageview identification, and user identification. Such kinds of data preparations are conducted to construct the co-occurrence observation. In this section, we mainly look at the refined usage data instead of raw data. More details regarding data preparation steps could be found in [65].

We first introduce a concept of session-pageview matrix for Web usage mining. In the context of Web usage mining, we construct two sets of Web objects, Web session set $S = \{s_1, s_2, \ldots s_m\}$ and Web page set $P = \{p_1, p_2, \ldots p_n\}$.

Furthermore, each user session is considered as a sequence of page-weight pairs. say $s_i = \{(p_1, a_{i1}), (p_2, a_{i2}), \ldots (p_n, a_{in})\}$. For simplicity reason of expression, each user session can be re-written as a sequence of weights over the page space, i.e. $s_i = \{a_{i1}, a_{i2}, \ldots a_{in}\}$, where a_{ij} denotes the weight for page p_j in s_i user session. As a result, the whole user session data can be formed as a Web usage data matrix represented by a session-pageview matrix (Figure 6.2 illustrates the schematic structure of the session-pageview matrix). The entry value in

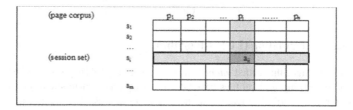

Fig. 6.2. The schematic structure of session-pageview matrix

the session-pageview matrix, a_{ij} is usually determined by the number of hits or the amount time spent by a specific user on the corresponding page. Generally, in order to eliminate the influence caused by the relative amount difference of visiting time duration or hit number, the normalization manipulation across pageview space in same user session is performed. Figure 6.3 illustrates two snapshots of Web log records extracted from a Web access log, in which each field is separated by a space. Particularly, note that the first and fourth fields are identified as the visitor IP address and the requested URL respectively, and utilized to assist usage data collection. Thus, the first field can be identified as user session ID and the fourth attribute is treated as the page ID.

202.161.108.167 - - [01/Feb/2003:00:00:03 +1100] "GET/timetables/city/2003s1/cc 4logo.gif HTTP/1.1" 206 14102   "http://www.cs.rmit.edu.au/timetables/city/2003s1/ cover.html "Mozilla/4.0 (compatible; MSIE 5.5; Windows 98)"

213.183.13.65 - - [01/Feb/2003:00:00:16 +1100] "GET/~winikoff/palm/dev.html HTT P/1.1" 302 244 "http://www.google.de/search?q=sources+onboard+c+examples&ie=UTF- 8&oe=UTF-8&hl=de&meta=" Scooter/3.3"

Fig. 6.3. A snapshot of Web access log

Representation of User Session in Latent Semantic Space

Employing LSI algorithm on the usage data, we may rewrite user sessions with the obtained approximation matrix U_k, Σk and V_k by mapping them into another reduced k-dimensional latent semantic space. For a given session s_i, it is originally represented as a coordinate vector with respect to pages, $s_i = \{a_{i1}, a_{i2}, \ldots, a_{in}\}$. The projection of the coordinate vector s_i in the k-dimensional latent semantic subspace is re-parameterized as

$$s_i' = s_i V_k \sum k = (t_{i1}, t_{i2}, \ldots, t_{ik}) \tag{6.8}$$

where $s_i' = s_i V_k \Sigma k = (t_{i1}, t_{i2}, \ldots, t_{ik})$.

It is believed that the transformed s_i' carries the concise but more meaningful associations with the latent semantic space [120]. We then exploit the traditional cosine function to capture the common interests shared by user sessions, i.e. for two session vectors $x = (x_1, x_2, \ldots, x_k)$ and $y = (y_1, y_2, \ldots, y_k)$ in a k-dimensional space, the similarity between them is defined as $sim(x, y) = (x \cdot y) / (\|x\|_2 \|y\|_2)$, where $x \cdot y = \sum_{i=1}^{k} x_i y_i$, $\|x\|_2 = \sqrt{\sum_{i=1}^{k} x_i^2}$. In this manner, the similarity between two transformed user sessions is defined as:

$$sim(s_i', s_j') = \left(s_i' \cdot s_j'\right) / \left\|s_i'\right\|_2 \left\|s_j'\right\|_2 \tag{6.9}$$

Latent Usage Information (LUI) Algorithm

In this section, an algorithm called *latent Usage Information* (LUI) is given for clustering Web sessions and generating user profiles based on the discovered semantic clusters of sessions. This algorithm is comprised of two steps, the first step is a clustering algorithm, which is to cluster the converted latent usage data into a number of session groups; and the next step is about generating a set of user profiles, which are derived from calculating the centroids of the discovered session clusters.

Here a modified k-means clustering algorithm, named MK-means clustering, is devised to partition user sessions based on the transformed usage data matrix over the latent k-dimensional space. The algorithm is described as follows:

Algorithm 6.2: MK-means clustering

Input: A converted usage matrix SP and a similarity threshold ε

Output: A set of user session clusters $SCL = \{SCL_i\}$ and corresponding centroids $Cid = \{Cid_i\}$

Step 1: Choose the first user session s'_i as the initial cluster SCL_1 and the centroid of this cluster, i.e. $SCL_1 = \{s'_i\}$ and $Cid_1 = s'_i$.

Step 2: For each session s'_i, calculate the similarity between s'_i and the centroids of other existing cluster $sim(s'_i, Cid_j)$.

Step 3: if $sim(s'_i, Cid_k) = \max_j(sim(s'_i, Cid_j)) > \varepsilon$, then allocate s'_i into SCL_k and recalculate the centroid of cluster SCL_k as $Cid_k = 1/|C_k| \sum_{j \in C_k} s'_j$;

Otherwise, let s'_i itself construct a new cluster and be the centroid of this cluster.

Step 4: Repeat step 2 to 4 until all user sessions are processed and all centroids do not update any more.

After obtaining the user session clusters, the centroid of each cluster is calculated and the pages with less significant weights are filtered out, based on which the final user profiles are produced. Below Algorithm 6.3 depicts the detailed procedures.

Algorithm 6.3: Building user profile based on LUI

Input: A set of user session cluster $SCL = \{SCL_k\}$

Output: A set of user profile $SCL = \{SCL_k\}$

Step 1: For each page p in the cluster SCL_k, we compute the mean weight value of page

$$wt(p, SCL_k) = 1/|SCL_k| \sum_{s \in SCL_k} w(p, s) \qquad (6.10)$$

where $w(p,s)$ is the weight of page p in the session $w(p,s)$, and $|SCL_k|$ denotes the session number in the cluster SCL_k.

Step 2: For each cluster, furthermore, we calculate its mean vector (i.e. centroid) as

$$mv_C = \{< p, wt(p, SCL_k) > | p \in P\} \qquad (6.11)$$

Step 3: For each page within the cluster, if the value is less than the threshold μ, the corresponding page will be filtered out, otherwise keep it left.

Step 4: Sort the pages with their weights in a descending order and output the mean vector as the user profile.

$$up_k = \{< p_{1k}, wt(p_{1k}, SCL_k) >, < p_{2k}, wt(p_{2k}, SCL_k) >, \cdots, < p_{tk}, wt(p_{tk}, SCL_k)\} \quad (6.12)$$

where $wt(p_{1k}, SCL_k) > wt(p_{2k}, SCL_k) > \cdots > wt(p_{tk}, SCL_k) > \mu$.

Step 5: Repeat step 1 to 4 until all session clusters are processed, output the user profiles.

6.2 Web Usage Mining using Probabilistic Latent Semantic Analysis

In previous section, we partially discuss the topic of using latent semantic analysis in Web usage mining. The capability of the mentioned approach, i.e. latent semantic indexing, however, is limited, though it is able to map the original user sessions onto a more latent semantic space but without revealing the semantic space itself. In contrast, another variant of LSI, *Probabilistic Latent Semantic Analysis* (PLSA) is a promising paradigm which can not only reveal underlying correlation hidden in Web co-occurrence observation, but also identify the latent task factor associated with usage knowledge.

In this section Probabilistic Latent Semantic Analysis (PLSA) model is introduced into Web usage mining, to generate Web user groups and Web page clusters based on latent usage analysis [257, 127].

6.2.1 Probabilistic Latent Semantic Analysis Model

The PLSA model has been firstly presented and successfully applied in text mining by [118]. In contrast to the standard LSI algorithm, which utilizes the Frobenius norm as an optimization criterion, PLSA model is based on a maximum likelihood principle, which is derived from the uncertainty theory in statistics.

Basically, the PLSA model is based on a statistic model called aspect model, which can be utilized to identify the hidden semantic relationships among general co-occurrence activities. Theoretically, we can conceptually view the user sessions over Web pages space as co-occurrence activities in the context of Web usage mining, to infer the latent usage pattern. Given the aspect model over user access pattern in the context of Web usage mining, it is first assumed that there is a latent factor space $Z = (z_1, z_2, \cdots z_k)$, and each co-occurrence observation data (s_i, p_j) (i.e. the visit of page p_j in user session s_i) is associated with the factor $z_k \in Z$ by a varying degree to z_k. According to the viewpoint of the aspect model, it can be inferred that there do exist different relationships among Web users or pages corresponding to different factors. Furthermore, the different factors can be considered to represent the corresponding user access pattern. For example, during a Web usage mining process on an e-commerce website, we can define that there exist k latent factors associated with k kinds of navigational behavior patterns, such as z_1 factor standing for having interests in sports-specific product category, z_2 for sale product interest and z_3 for browsing through a variety of product pages in different categories and z_4 *cdots* etc. In this manner, each co-occurrence observation data (s_i, p_j) may convey user navigational interest by mapping the observation data into the k-dimensional latent factor space. The degree, to which such relationships are "explained" by each factors, is derived by a conditional probability distribution associated with the Web usage data. Thus, the goal of employing PLSA model, therefore, is to determine the conditional probability distribution, in turn, to reveal the intrinsic relationships among Web users or pages based on a probability inference approach. In one word, the PLSA model is to model and infer user navigational behavior in a latent semantic space, and identify the latent factor associated. Before we propose the PLSA based algorithm for Web usage mining, it is necessary to introduce the mathematical background of the PLSA model, and the algorithm which is used to estimate the conditional probability distribution. Firstly, let's introduce the following probability definitions:

- $P(s_i)$ denotes the probability that a particular user session s_i will be observed in the occurrences data,

- $P(z_k|s_i)$ denotes a user session-specific probability distribution on the latent class factor z_k,
- $P(p_j|z_k)$ denotes the class-conditional probability distribution of pages over a specific latent variable z_k.

Based on these definitions, the probabilistic latent semantic model can be expressed in the following way:

- Select a user session s_i with a probability $P(s_i)$,
- Pick a hidden factor z_k with a probability $P(z_k|s_i)$,
- Generate a page p_j with probability $P(p_j|z_k)$;

As a result, we can obtain an occurrence probability of an observed pair (s_i, p_j) by adopting the latent factor variable z_k. Translating this process into a probability model results in the expression:

$$P(s_i, p_j) = P(s_i) \cdot P(p_j|s_i) \tag{6.13}$$

where $P(p_j|s_i) = \sum_{z \in Z} P(p_j|z) \cdot P(z|s_i)$.

By applying the Bayesian formula, a re-parameterized version will be transformed based on above equations as

$$P(s_i, p_j) = \sum_{z \in Z} P(z) P(s_i|z) P(p_j|z) \tag{6.14}$$

Following the likelihood principle, we can determine the total likelihood of the observation as

$$Li = \sum_{s_i \in S, p_j \in P} m(s_i, p_j) \cdot \log P(s_i, p_j) \tag{6.15}$$

where $m(s_i, p_j)$ corresponds to the entry of the session-pageview matrix associated with session s_i and pageview p_j, which is discussed in the previous section.

In order to maximize the total likelihood, it needs to repeatedly generate the conditional probabilities of $P(z)$, $P(s_i|z)$ and $P(p_j|z)$ by utilizing the usage observation data. Known from statistics, *Expectation-Maximization* (EM) algorithm is an efficient procedure to perform maximum likelihood estimation in latent variable model [72]. Generally, two steps need to implement in the procedure alternately: (1) Expectation (E) step where posterior probabilities are calculated for the latent factors based on the current estimates of conditional probability, and (2) Maximization (M) step, where the estimated conditional probabilities are updated and used to maximize the likelihood based on the posterior probabilities computed in the previous E step.

The whole procedure is given as follows:

First, given the randomized initial values of $P(z)$, $P(s_i|z)$, $P(p_j|z)$

then, in E-step, we can simply apply Bayesian formula to generate the following variable based on the usage observation:

$$P(z_k|s_i, p_j) = \frac{P(z_k)P(s_i|z_k)P(p_j|z_k)}{\sum_{z_k \in Z} P(z_k)P(s_i|z_k)P(p_j|z_k)} \tag{6.16}$$

furthermore, in M-step, we compute:

$$P(p_j|z_k) = \frac{\sum_{s_i \in S} m(s_i, p_j)P(z_k|s_i, p_j)}{\sum_{s_i \in S, p_j' \in P} m(s_i, p_j')P(z_k|s_i, p_j')} \tag{6.17}$$

$$P(s_i|z_k) = \frac{\sum\limits_{p_j \in P} m(s_i, p_j)P(z_k|s_i, p_j)}{\sum\limits_{s_i' \in S, p_j \in P} m(s_i', p_j)P(z_k|s_i', p_j)} \quad\quad (6.18)$$

$$P(z_k) = \frac{1}{R} \sum\limits_{s_i \in S, p_j \in P} m(s_i, p_j)P(z_k|s_i, p_j) \quad\quad (6.19)$$

where $R = \sum\limits_{s_i \in S, p_j \in P} m(s_{i,}, p_j)$

Basically, substituting equations (6.17)-(6.19) into (6.14) and (6.15) will result in the monotonically increasing of total likelihood Li of the observation data. The iterative implementation of the E-step and M-step is repeating until Li is converging to a local optimal limit, which means the calculated results can represent the optimal probability estimates of the usage observation data. From the previous formulation, it is easily found that the computational complexity of the *PLSA* model is $O(mnk)$, where m, n and k denote the number of user sessions, Web pages and latent factors, respectively.

By now, we have obtained the conditional probability distribution of $P(z_k)$, $P(s_i|z_k)$ and $P(p_j|z_k)$ by performing the E and M step iteratively. The estimated probability distribution which is corresponding to the local maximum likelihood contains the useful information for inferring semantic usage factors, performing Web user sessions clustering which are described in next sections.

6.2.2 Constructing User Access Pattern and Identifying Latent Factor with PLSA

As discussed in the previous section, note that each latent factor z_k does really represent a specific aspect associated with the usage co-occurrence activities in nature. In other words, for each factor, there might exist a task-oriented user access pattern corresponding to it. We, thus, can utilize the class-conditional probability estimates generated by the *PLSA* model to produce the aggregated user profiles for characterizing user navigational behaviors. Conceptually, each aggregated user profile will be expressed as a collection of pages, which are accompanied by their corresponding weights indicating the contributions to such user group made by those pages. Furthermore, analyzing the generated user profile can lead to reveal common user access interests, such as dominant or secondary "theme" by sorting the page weights.

Partitioning User Sessions

Firstly, we begin with the probabilistic variable , which represents the occurrence probability in the condition of a latent class factor z_k exhibited by a given user session s_i. On the other hand, the probabilistic distribution over the factor space of a specific user session s_i can reflect the specific user access preference over the whole latent factor space, therefore, it may be utilized to uncover the dominant factors by distinguishing the top probability values. Therefore, for each user session s_i, we can further compute a set of probabilities over the latent factor space via Bayesian formula as follows:

$$P(z_k|s_i) = \frac{P(s_i|z_k)P(z_k)}{\sum\limits_{z_k \in Z} P(s_i|z_k)P(z_k)} \quad\quad (6.20)$$

Actually, the set of probabilities $P(z_k|s_i)$ is tending to be "sparse", that is, for a given s_i, typically only few entries are significant different from predefined threshold. Hence we can classify the user into corresponding cluster based on these probabilities greater than a given threshold. Since each user session can be expressed as a pages vector in the original n-dimensional space, we can create a mixture representation of the collection of user sessions within same cluster that associated with the factor z_k in terms of a collection of weighted pages. The algorithm for partitioning user session is described as follows.

Algorithm 6.4: Partitioning user sessions

Input: A set of calculated probability values of $P(z_k|s_i)$, a user session-page matrix SP, and a predefined threshold μ.
Output: A set of session clusters $SCL = (SCL_1, SCL_2, \cdots SCL_k)$
Step 1: Set $SCL_1 = SCL_2 = \cdots = SCL_k = \varphi$,
Step 2: For each $s_i \in S$, select $P(z_k|s_i)$, if $P(z_k|s_i) \geq \mu$, then $SCL_k = SCL_k \cup s_i$,
Step 3: If there are still users sessions to be clustered, go back to step 2,
Step 4: Output session clusters $SCL = \{SCL_k\}$.

Characterizing Latent Semantic Factor

As mentioned in previous section, the core of the PLSA model is the latent factor space. From this point of view, how to characterize the factor space or explain the semantic meaning of factors is a crucial issue in PLSA model. Similarly, we can also utilize another obtained conditional probability distribution by the PLSA model to identify the semantic meaning of the latent factor by partitioning Web pages into corresponding categories associated with the latent factors.

For each hidden factor z_k, we may consider that the pages, whose conditional probabilities $P(p_j|z_k)$ are greater than a predefined threshold, can be viewed to provide similar functional components corresponding to the latent factor. In this way, we can select all pages with probabilities exceeding a certain threshold to form an topic-specific page group. By analyzing the URLs of the pages and their weights derived from the conditional probabilities, which are associated with the specific factor, we may characterize and explain the semantic meaning of each factor. In next section, two examples with respect to the discovered latent factors are presented. The algorithm to generating the topic-oriented Web page group is briefly described as follows:

Algorithm 6.5: Characterizing latent semantic factors

Input: A set of conditional probabilities, $P(p_j|z_k)$, a predefined threshold μ.
Output: A set of latent semantic factors represented by several dominant pages.
Step 1: Set $PCL_1 = PCL_2 = \cdots = PCL_k = \varphi$,
Step 2: For each z_k, choose all Web pages such that $P(p_j|z_k) \geq \mu$ and $P(z_k|p_j) \geq \mu$, then construct $PCL_k = p_j \cup PCL_k$,
Step 3: If there are still pages to be classified, go back to step 2,
Step 4: Output $PCL = \{PCL_k\}$.

Examples of Latent Semantic Factors

In this section, we present some results regarding Web usage pattern and latent semantic factor obtained by conducting experiments on two selected Web log datasets. The first dataset is named KDDCUP [1]. In this data set, the entries in session-page matrix are determined by the number of Web page hits since the number of a user coming back to a specific page is a good measure to reflect the user interest on the page. The second data set is downloaded from msnbc.com [2], which describes the page visits by users who visited msnbc.com on September 28, 1999. This data set is named as "msnbc" dataset.

The experimental results on these two datasets are tabulated in Table 6.1 and 6.2. Table 6.1 first lists 13 extracted latent factors and their corresponding characteristic descriptions from KDDCUP dataset. And Table 6.2 depicts 3 factor examples selected from whole factor space in terms of associated page information including page number, probability and description. From this table, it is seen that factor #3 indicates the concerns about vendor service message such as customer service, contact number, payment methods as well as delivery support. The factor #7 describes the specific progress which may include customer login, product order, express checkout and financial information input such steps occurred in Internet shopping scenario, whereas factors #13 actually captures another focus exhibited by Web content, which reveals the fact that some Web users may pay more attentions to the information regarding department itself..

Table 6.1. Latent factors and their characteristic descriptions from KDDCUP

Factor #	Characteristic title
1	Department_search_results
2	ProductDetailLegwear
3	Vendor_ service
4	Freegift
5	ProductDetailLegcare
6	Shopping_cart
7	Online_shopping
8	Lifestyle_assortment
9	Assortment2
10	Boutique
11	Departmet_replenishment
12	Department_article
13	Home page

As for "msnbc" dataset, it is hard to extract the exact latent factor space as the page information provided is described at a coarser granularity level, i.e. URL category level. Hence we only list two examples of discovered latent factors to illustrate the general usage knowledge

---

[1] www.ecn.purdue.edu/kddcup

[2] http://kdd.ics.uci.edu/databases/

Table 6.2. Factor examples and their associated page information from KDDCUP

Factor #	Page #	$P(p_j|z_k)$	Page description
	10	0.865	main/vendor\.jhtml
	36	0.035	main/cust_serv.jhtml
	37	0.021	articles/dpt_contact\.jhtml
3	39	0.020	articles/dpt_shipping\.jhtml
	38	0.016	articles/dpt_payment\.jhtml
	41	0.016	articles/dpt_faqs\.jhtml
	40	0.013	articles/dpt_returns\.jhtml
	27	0.249	main/login2\.jhtml
	44	0.18	checkout/expresCheckout.jhmt
	32	0.141	main/registration\.jhtml
7	65	0.135	main/welcome\.jhtml
	45	0.135	checkout/confirm_order\.jhtml
	42	0.045	account/your_account\.jhtml
	60	0.040	checkout/thankyou\.jhtml
	12	0.232	articles/dpt_about\.jhtml
	22	0.127	articles/new_shipping\.jhtml
	13	0.087	articles/dpt_about_mgmtteam
13	14	0.058	articles\dpt_about_boardofdirectors
	20	0.058	articles/dpt_affiliate\.jhtml
	16	0.053	articles/dpt_about_careers
	19	0.052	articles/dpt_refer\.jhtml
	23	0.051	articles/new_returns\.jhtml

hidden in the usage data (shown in Table 6.3). The two extracted factors indicate that factor #1 is associated with all kinds of local information that come from miscellaneous information channel such as bbs, while factor #2 reflects the interests or opinions which are often linked with health, sport as well as technical development in physical exercise.

Table 6.3. Factor examples from msnbc data set

Factor #	Category #	$P(p_j|z_k)$	URL category
	4	0.316	local
	7	0.313	misc
1	6	0.295	on-air
	15	0.047	summary
	16	0.029	bbs
	10	0.299	health
2	5	0.262	opinion
	13	0.237	msn-sport
	3	0.203	tech

6.3 Finding User Access Pattern via Latent Dirichlet Allocation Model

In previous sections, we presented the conventional LSI and a variant of LSI model for Web usage mining, which results in discovering usage based user session segments and Web page groups. However, the former one is lack of the capability of capturing latent factor space and suffers from the problems of sparsity of input data, especially in case of a huge number of Web objects appeared in the constructed usage data, while the latter one often incurs in overfitting problem, which is very commonly encountered in the context of data mining and machine learning. To address these difficulties, a new variant LSI-based paradigm, named *Latent Dirichlet Allocation* (LDA) model has been proposed in text mining [35, 205]. In this section, we would like to introduce LDA in Web usage mining.

6.3.1 Latent Dirichlet Allocation Model

To better describe the application of LDA in Web usage mining, we first briefly review the family of generative models and then present the algorithmic description.

Generative Models

Based on the constructed Web usage data model in the forms of weight vectors over the page space, we intend to develop a mechanism to learn the underlying properties of the usage data and extract informative knowledge of Web access behavior to model user access pattern. Before we present LDA model for Web usage mining, it is essential to first review various analytical models used for co-occurrence observation analysis in the context of machine learning [64]. Although these data analysis models are initially proposed for revealing the intrinsic association between documents and words, it is appropriate and reasonable to introduce the basic idea to the identified research problems, which helps us to easily understand the theoretical bases as well as the strengths of the proposed techniques, for accomplishing the required tasks in the context of Web usage mining.

Currently there are generally two kinds of machine learning techniques that can accomplish such mining tasks, namely generative and discriminative approaches. In generative model, we can discover the model of data source through a generating procedure, whereas we learn directly the desired outcome from the training data in descriptive model. In this section, we will be focusing our discussion on using generative model to extract Web usage knowledge.

In particular, here we aim to introduce a recently developed generative model called Latent Dirichlet allocation (LDA), and explore how to employ it to model the underlying correlation amongst usage data. LDA is one kind of generative probabilistic models that is able to effectively generate infinitive sequences of samples according to the probability distribution. The probability inference algorithm is then used to capture the aggregated property of user sessions or Web pages associated with the user access topic, and to reveal the semantics of the topic space via referring to the derived distribution of user session or page object over the latent task space implicitly. In order to easily understand the evolution of generative models, we briefly review the basic generative models used in text mining and summarize the individual strengths and drawbacks.

The generative model, sometimes called Gaussian mixture model, can be generally used to represent user session via a vector expression. In this model, each user session/visit is generated by a mixture of topics, where each topic is represented by a Gaussian distribution with a mean and variation value. The parameters of mean and variation are estimated by an EM algorithm.

Like language model of information retrieval where words are modeled as the co-occurrences in a document, we intend to formulate user hits or duration spent on different pages as a session-page occurrence. Here each user session that consists of a number of weighted Web pages, is considered to be equivalent to a document whereas the whole Web page set is treated as similarly as a "bag-of-word" concept in text domain.

The simplest probability model in text mining is unigram model, where the probability of each word is independent of other words which have already appeared in the document. This model is considered as a single probability distribution U over an entire vocabulary V, i.e. a vector of probabilities, $U(v)$ for each word v in the vocabulary. Under the unigram model, words appeared in every document are randomly taken out from a bag-of-word, then are estimated their values. Therefore, the probability of a observing a sequence of words, $w = w_1, w_2, \cdots, w_n$ is:

$$P_{uni}(w) = \prod_{i=1}^{n} U(w_i) \qquad (6.21)$$

The main limitation of the unigram model is that it assumes all documents are only of homogeneous word collections, that is, all documents are exhibiting a single topic, which is theoretically modeled as the probability distribution U. However, this assumption is often not true in real scenario, since typically, most of documents are in relation to more than one topic, which would be represented by a markedly distinctive set of distributions. Especially, in the context of mining user access pattern, almost every visitor would have different preference rather than only one intention.

In order to handle the heterogeneous property of documents, the mixture model is introduced to overcome the previous problem. In this generative model, we first choose a topic, z, according to a probability distribution, T, and then, based on this topic, we select words according to the probability distribution of zth topic. Similarly, the probability of a observing sequence of words, $w = w_1, w_2, \cdots, w_n$, is formulated as:

$$P_{mix}(w) = \sum_{z=1}^{k} T(z) \prod_{i=1}^{n} U_z(w_i) \qquad (6.22)$$

The main drawback with the mixture model is that it still considers each document to be homogeneous although it could better tackle the heterogeneity in document collection. Similar problem will be occurred in the context of Web usage mining. It is thus needed to develop a better model to tackle the heterogeneity nature of document collection, i.e. multi-topic distribution of probability.

The Probabilistic Latent Semantic Analysis (PLSA) approach is an appropriate model that is capable of handling the multiply topic property in process of Web text or usage mining [118]. In this model, for each word that we observe we pick up a topic according to a distribution, T, which is dependent on the document. The distribution models the mixture of topics for one specific document. And each topic is associated with a probability distribution over the space of word vocabulary and document corpus, derived from a generative process. The probability distribution of an observing sequence $w = w_1, w_2, \cdots, w_n$ is parameterized as:

$$P_{plsa}(w) = \prod_{i=1}^{n} \left(\sum_{z=1}^{k} T_{w_i}(z) U_z(w_i) \right) \qquad (6.23)$$

There are two main problems with *PLSA* model: 1) it is hard to estimate probability of a previously unseen document; 2) due to the linear growth in parameters that depend on the document itself, *PLSA* suffers from over-fitting and inappropriate generative semantics.

To address these problems, *Latent Dirichlet Allocation* (LDA) is introduced by combining the basic generative model with a prior probability on topics to provide a complete generative model for documents. The basic idea of the LDA is that documents are modeled as random mixtures over latent topics with a probability distribution, where each topic is represented by a distribution over word vocabulary. In this sense, any random mixing distribution, $T(z)$ is determined by an underlying distribution thereby representing uncertainty over a particular $\theta(\cdot)$ as $p_k(\theta(\cdot))$, where p_k is defined over all $\theta \in P_k$, the set of all possible $(k-l)$-simplex. That is, the Dirichlet parameters determine the uncertainty, which models the random mixture distribution over semantic topics.

Latent Dirichlet Allocation (LDA)

LDA is a generative probabilistic model of co-occurrence observations. As for a typical application in text analysis, here we utilize the document corpus as the co-occurrence observations to conduct the following formulation. As discussed above, the basic idea of the LDA model is that the documents within the corpus are represented as a random mixture over the latent topics and each topic is characterized by a distribution over the words in the documents. The graphical illustration of the generative procedure of LDA is shown in Fig.6.4. LDA is performed via a sequence of the document generation processes (shown in Fig.6.4 and algorithm 1). The notations used and the generative procedure of LDA model are outlined as follows. Notations:

- M: the number of documents
- K: the number of topics
- V: the size of vocabulary
- α, β: Dirichlet parameters
- θ_m: the topic assignment of the document m
- $\Theta = \theta_m, m = 1, ..., M$: the topic estimations of the corpus, a $M \times K$ matrix
- ϕ_k: the word distribution of the topic k
- $\Phi = \phi_k, k = 1, ..., K$: the word assignments of the topics, a $K \times V$ matrix
- *Dir* and *Poiss* are Dirichlet and Poisson distribution functions respectively

---

Algorithm 6.6: Generation Process of LDA

---

for each of topics
      sample the mixture of words $\phi_k \sim Dir(\beta)$
end
for each of documents $m = 1 : M$
      sample the mixture of topics $\theta_m \sim Dir(\alpha)$
      sample the lengths of documents $N_m \sim Poiss(\xi)$
      for each word $n = 1 : N_m$ in the document m
            sample the topic index of $z_{m,n} \sim Mult(\theta_m)$
            sample the weight of word $w_{m,n} \sim Mult(\phi_{z_{m,n}})$
      end
end

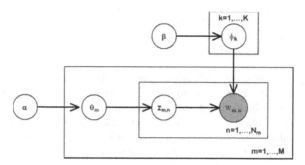

Fig. 6.4. The generative representation of LDA

In LDA, a document $d_m = \{w_{m,n}, n = 1, \cdots, N_m\}$ is generated by picking a distribution over the topics from a Dirichlet distribution ($Dir\,(\alpha)$). And given the topic distribution, we pick the topic assignment of each specific word. Then the topic assignment for each word placeholder $[m,n]$ is calculated by sampling a particular topic from the multinomial distribution of $z_{m,n}$. And finally, a particular word of $w_{m,n}$ is generated for the placeholder $[m,n]$ by sampling its weight from the multinomial distribution of $Mult(\phi_{z_{m,n}})$.

Known from the above description, given Dirichlet parameters α and β, we can formulate a joint distribution of a document d_m, a topic mixture of d_m, i.e. θ_m, and a set of N_m topics, i.e. z_m as follows.

$$P_r(\theta_m, z_m, d_m, \Phi | \alpha, \beta) = P_r(\theta_m | \alpha) P_r(\Phi | \beta) \prod_{n=1}^{N_m} P_r(w_{m,n} | \varphi_{z_{m,n}}) P_r(z_{m,n} | \theta_m) \tag{6.24}$$

Then by integrating over θ_m, $\phi_{z_{m,n}}$ and summing over z_m, we obtain the likelihood of the document d_m:

$$P_r(d_m | \alpha, \beta) = \int \int P_r(\theta_m | \alpha) P_r(\Phi | \beta) \prod_{n=1}^{N_m} P_r(w_{m,n} | \varphi_{z_{m,n}}) P_r(z_{m,n} | \theta_m) d\theta_m d\Phi \tag{6.25}$$

Finally the likelihood of the document corpus $D = \{d_m, m = 1, ..., M\}$ is a product of the likelihood of all documents in the corpus.

$$P_r(D | \alpha, \beta) = \prod_{m=1}^{M} P_r(d_m | \alpha, \beta) \tag{6.26}$$

Dirichlet Parameter Estimation and Topic Inference

In general, estimating the parameters of LDA is performed by maximizing the likelihood of the whole documents. In particular, given a corpus of documents $D = \{d_m, m = 1, ..., M\}$, we aim to estimate the parameters of α and β that maximize the log likelihood of the data:

$$(\alpha_{est}, \beta_{est}) = \max \ell(\alpha, \beta) = \max \sum_{m=1}^{M} \log P_r(d_m | \alpha, \beta) \tag{6.27}$$

However the direct computing for the parameters α and β is intractable due to the nature of the computation. The solution to this is to use various alternative approximate estimation methods. Here we employ the variational EM algorithm [35] to estimate the variational parameters that maximize the total likelihood of the corpus with respect to the model parameters of α and β. The variational EM algorithm is briefly described as follows:

Algorithm 6.7: Variational EM Algorithm

Step 1: (*E*-step) For each document, find the optimizing values of variational parameters θ_m^* and ϕ_m^*.

Step 2: (*M*-step) Maximize the resulting low bound on the likelihood with respect to model parameters α and β. This corresponds to finding the maximum likelihood estimate with the approximate posterior which is computed in the *E*-step.

The *E*-step and *M*-step are executed iteratively until a maximum likelihood value reaches. Meanwhile, the calculated estimation parameters can be used to infer topic distribution of a new document by performing the variational inference. More details with respect to the variational EM algorithm are referred to [35].

Web Usage Data Model

In section 6.1.2, we give a Web data model of session-pageview matrix. Here we use the same data expression, which summarized as:

- $S = \{s_i, i = 1, ..., m\}$: a set of m user sessions.
- $P = \{p_j, j = 1, ..., n\}$: a set of n Web pageviews.
- For each user, a user session is represented as a vector of visited pageviews with corresponding weights: $s_i = \{a_{ij}, j = 1, ..., n\}$, where a_{ij} denotes the weight for page p_j visited in s_i user session. The corresponding weight is usually determined by the number of hit or the amount time spent on the specific page. Here, we use the latter to construct the usage data for the dataset used in experimental study.
- $SP_{m \times n} = \{a_{ij}, i = 1, ..., m, j = 1, ..., n\}$: the ultimate usage data in the form of a weight matrix with a dimensionality of $m \times n$.

6.3.2 Modeling User Navigational Task via LDA

Similar to capturing the underlying topics over the word vocabulary and each document's probability distribution over the mixing topic space, LDA is also able to be used to discover the hidden access tasks and the user preference mixtures over the uncovered task space from user navigational observations. That is, from the usage data, LDA identifies the hidden tasks and represent each task as a simplex of Web pages. Furthermore, LDA characterizes each Web user session as a simplex of these discovered tasks. In other words, LDA reveals two aspects of underlying usage information to us: the hidden task space and the task mixture distribution of each Web user session, which reflect the underlying correlations between Web pages as well as Web user sessions. With the discovered task-simplex expressions, it is viable to model the user access patterns in the forms of weighted page vectors, in turn, to predict the target user's potentially interested pages by employing a collaborative recommendation algorithm. In the following part, we first discuss how to discover the user access patterns in terms of task-simplex expression based on LDA model and how to infer a target user's navigational preference by using the estimated task-simplex space, and then present a collaborative recommendation algorithm by incorporating the inferred navigational task distribution of the target user with the discovered user access patterns to make Web recommendations.

Similar to the implementation of document-topic expression in text mining discussed above, viewing Web user sessions as mixtures of tasks makes it possible to formulate the problem of identifying the set of underlying tasks hidden in a collection of user clicks. Given m Web user sessions containing t hidden tasks expressed over n distinctive pageviews, we can represent $P_r(p|z)$ with a set of t multinomial distributions ϕ over the n Web pages, such that for a hidden task z_k, the associative likelihood on the page p_j is $P_r(p_j|z_k) = \phi_{k,j}, j = 1,...,n, k = 1,...,t$, and $P_r(z|s)$ with a set of m multinomial distributions θ over the t tasks, such that for a Web session s_i, the associative likelihood on the task z_k is $P_r(z_k|s_i) = \theta_{i,k}$.

Here we use the LDA model described above to generate ϕ and θ resulting in the maximum likelihood estimates of LDA model in the Web usage data. The complete probability model is as follows:

$$
\begin{aligned}
\theta_i &\sim Dirichlet(\alpha) \\
z_k|\theta_i &\sim Discrete(\theta_i) \\
\phi_k &\sim Dirichlet(\beta) \\
p_j|\phi_k &\sim Discrete(\phi_k)
\end{aligned}
\tag{6.28}
$$

Here, z_k stands for a specific task, θ_i denotes the Web session s_i's navigational preference distribution over the tasks and ϕ_k represents the specific task z_k's association distribution over the pages. Parameters α and β are the hyper-parameters of the prior variables of θ and ϕ.

We use the variational inference algorithm described above to estimate each Web session's correlation with the multiple tasks (θ), and the associations between the tasks and Web pages (ϕ), with which we can capture the user visit preference distribution exhibited by each user session and identify the semantics of the task space. Interpreting the contents of the prominent pages related to each task based on ϕ will eventually result in defining the nature of each task. Meanwhile, the task-based user access patterns are constructed by examining the calculated user session's associations with the multiple tasks and aggregating all sessions whose associative degrees with a specific task are greater than a threshold. We describe our approach to discovering the task-based user access patterns below.

Given this representation, for each latent task, (1) we can consider user sessions with θ_i exceeding a threshold as the "prototypical" user sessions associated with that task. In other words, these top user sessions contribute significantly to the navigational pattern of this task, in turn, are used to construct this task-specific user access pattern; (2) we select all Web pages as contributive pages of each task dependent on the values of ϕ_k, and capture the semantics of the task by interpreting the contents of those pages.

Thus, for each latent task corresponding to one access pattern, we choose all user sessions with θ_i exceeding a certain threshold as the candidates of this specific access pattern. As each user session is represented by a weighted page vector in the original usage data space, we can create an aggregate of user sessions to represent this task-specific access pattern in the form of weighted page vector. The algorithm of generating the task-specific access pattern is described as follows:

Algorithm 6.8: Building Task-Specific User Access Patterns

Input: the discovered session-task preference distribution matrix θ, m user sessions $S = \{s_i, i = 1,...,m\}$, and the predefined threshold μ.

Output: task-specific user access patterns, $TAP = \{ap_k, k = 1,\cdots,t\}$

Step 1: For each latent task z_k, choose all user sessions with $\theta_{i,k} > \mu$ to construct a user session aggregation R_k corresponding to z_k;

$$
R_k = \{s_i|\theta_{i,k} > \mu, k = 1,\cdots,t\}
\tag{6.29}
$$

Step 2: Within the R_k, compute the aggregated task-specific user access pattern in terms of a weighted page vector by taking the sessions' associations with z_k, i.e. $\theta_{i,k}$, into account:

$$ap_k = \frac{\sum\limits_{s_i \in R_k} \theta_{i,k} \cdot s_i}{|R_k|} \qquad (6.30)$$

where $|R_k|$ is the number of the chosen user sessions in R_k.

Step 3: Output a set of task-specific user access patterns TAP corresponding to t tasks, $TAP = \{ap_k, k = 1, \cdots, t\}$. In this expression, each user access pattern is represented by a weighted page vector, where the weights indicate the relative visit preferences of pages exhibited by all associated user sessions for this task-specific access pattern.

6.4 Co-Clustering Analysis of weblogs using Bipartite Spectral Projection Approach

In previous sections, we broadly discussed Web clustering in Web usage mining. Basically Web clustering could be performed on either Web pages or user sessions in the context of Web usage mining. Web page clustering is one of popular topics in Web clustering, which aims to discover Web page groups sharing similar functionality or semantics. For example, [114] proposed a technique LSH (Local Sensitive Hash) for clustering the entire Web, concentrating on the scalability of clustering. Snippet-based clustering is well studied in [92]. [147] reported using a hierarchical monothetic document clustering for summarizing the search results. [121] proposed a Web page clustering algorithm based on measuring page similarity in terms of correlation. In contrast to Web page clustering, Web usage clustering is proposed to discover Web user behavior patterns and associations between Web pages and users from the perspective of Web user. In practice, Mobasher et al. [184] combined user transaction and pageview clustering techniques, which was to employ the traditional k-means clustering algorithm to characterize user access patterns for Web personalization based on mining Web usage data. In [258] Xu et al. attempted to discover user access patterns and Web page segments from Web log files by utilizing a so-called Probabilistic Semantic Latent Analysis (PLSA) model.

The clustering algorithms described above are mainly manipulated on one dimension (or attribute) of the Web usage data only, i.e. user or page solely, rather than taking into account the correlation between Web users and pages. However, in most cases, the Web object clusters do often exist in the forms of co-occurrence of pages and users - the users from the same group are particularly interested in one subset of Web pages. For example, in the context of customer behavior analysis in e-commerce, this observation could correspond to the phenomenon that one specific group of customers show strong interest to one particular category of goods. In this scenario, Web co-clustering is probably an effective means to address the mentioned challenge. The study of co-clustering is firstly proposed to deal with co-clustering of documents and words in digital library [73]. And it has been widely utilized in many studies which involved in multiple attribute analysis, such as social tagging system [98] and genetic representation [108] etc. In this section, we will propose a co-clustering algorithm for Web usage mining based on bipartite spectral clustering.

6.4.1 Problem Formulation

Bipartite Graph Model

As the nature of Web usage data is a reflection of a set of Web users visiting a number of Web pages, it is intuitive to introduce a graph model to represent the visiting relationship between them. In particular, here we use the Bipartite Graph Model to illustrate it.

Definition 6.1. *Given a graph $G = (V,E)$, where V is a set of vertices $V = \{v_1, \cdots v_n\}$ and E is a set of edges $\{i, j\}$ with edge weight E_{ij}, the adjacency matrix M of the graph G is defined by*

$$M_{ij} = \begin{cases} E_{ij} & \text{if there is an edge } (i,j) \\ 0 & \text{otherwise} \end{cases}$$

Definition 6.2. *(Cut of Graph): Given a partition of the vertex set V into multiple subsets $V_1, \cdots, V_k$, the cut of the graph is the sum of edge weights whose vertices are assigned to two different subsets of vertices:*

$$cut(V_1, V_2, \cdots, V_k) = \sum_{i \in V_i, j \in V_j} M_{ij}$$

As discussed above, the usage data is indeed demonstrated by the visits of Web users on various Web pages. In this case, there are NO edges between user sessions or between Web pages, instead there are only edges between user sessions and Web pages. Thus it is essential that the bipartite graph model is an appropriate graphic representation to characterize their mutual relationships.

Definition 6.3. *(Bipartite Graph Representation): Consider a graph $G = (S,P;E)$ consisting of a set of vertices $V\{s_i, p_j : s_i \in S, p_j \in P; i = 1, \cdots, m, j = 1, \cdots, n\}$, where S and P are the user session collection and Web page collection, respectively, and a set of edges $\{s_i, p_j\}$ each with its weight a_{ij}, where $s_i \in S$ and $p_j \in P$, the links between user sessions and Web pages represent the visits of users on specific Web pages, whose weights indicate the visit preference or significance on respective pages.*

Furthermore, given the $m \times n$ session-by-pageview matrix A such that a_{ij} equals to the edge weight E_{ij}, it is easy to formulate the adjacency matrix M of the bipartite graph G as

$$M = \begin{bmatrix} 0 & A \\ A^t & 0 \end{bmatrix}$$

In this manner, the first m rows in the reconstructed matrix M denote the co-occurrence of user sessions while the last n rows index the Web pages. The element value of M is determined by click times or duration period. Because the ultimate goal is to extract subsets of user sessions and Web pageviews to construct a variety of co-clusters of them such that they possess the closer cohesion within the same cluster but the stronger disjointness from other clusters, it is necessary to model the user session and Web page vectors in a same single unified space. In the coming section, we will discuss how to perform co-clustering on them.

6.4.2 An Example of Usage Bipartite Graph

To better illustrate the bipartite graphic representation of Web usage data, here we present a very simple example. Consider a bipartite graph $G = (S, P; E)$ depicted in Fig.6.5, where the set of user sessions $S = \{s_1, s_2, s_3\}$, the set of Web pages $P = \{p_1, p_2, p_3, p_4\}$ and the set of edges connecting user sessions and Web pages $E = \{a_{ij} : s_i \in S, p_j \in P\}$. Each of edges indicates the relation between the connected user session s_i and Web page p_j, and its weight is set to be the hit number of the page in the user session. According to the definition 2, the cut of the bipartite graph into two subsets is illustrated in Fig.6.6, in which the dash line of s_3 and p_1 indicates the cut degree between them.

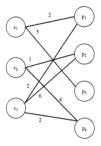

Fig. 6.5. Bipartite graph representation of usage data

Fig. 6.6. Cut of Bipartite graph

6.4.3 Clustering User Sessions and Web Pages

Dual Subset Clustering

Upon the introduction of bipartite graph expression of usage data, we aim to perform the co-clustering of user sessions and Web pageviews. Essentially, the co-clustering could be considered as a problem of Dual Subset Clustering (*DSC*) of user sessions and Web pageviews, that is, the session clustering results in the pageview clustering while the pageview clustering reinforces the session clustering.

Consider a set of disjoint session clusters $S_1, \cdots S_k$ and their associated set of pageview clusters $P_1, \cdots P_k$. Since the usage data is modeled as a bipartite graph of sessions and pageviews, there are no connections between sessions or between pageviews themselves. Thus for a co-clustering operation it is intuitive to assign respective sessions and pageviews into various clusters $C_j = (S_j, P_j), S_j \subset S, P_j \subset P$ such that the sessions have visited the pageviews that are in the same cluster (or the pageviews are visited by the sessions that are in same cluster) but the sessions have less visited the pageviews that from the different clusters (or the pageviews are almost seldom visited by the sessions that from the other clusters). In other words, according to definition 2 of cut of graph, we can further formulate the dual subset clustering of sessions and pageviews as a solution of minimization of graph cut:

$$DSC(C_1, \cdots C_k) = \min_{V_1, \cdots, V_k} cut(V_1, \cdots, V_k)$$

where $V_1, \cdots V_k$ is a k-partitioning of the bipartite graph.

Spectral Co-Clustering Algorithm

Modeling the usage data with a bipartite graph representation motivates us to employ the spectral graph theory to induce the co-clusters, which has been successfully in graph partitioning problem [73]. Spectral graph clustering indeed utilizes the eigenvalues of the adjacency matrix of usage data to map the original inherent relationships of co-occurrence onto a new spectral space, on which the new session or pageview vector is projected. After the projection, the sessions and pageviews are simultaneously partitioned into disjoint clusters with minimum cut optimization.

According to the spectral graph theory proposed in [73], the k left and right singular vectors of the reformed matrix $RA = D_s^{-1/2} A D_p^{-1/2}$ present a best approximation to the projection of row and column vectors on the new spectral space. The D_s and D_p are the diagonal matrices of sessions and pageviews respectively, and are defined as:

$$D_s(i,i) = \sum_{j=1}^{n} a_{ij}, i = 1, \cdots, m, D_p(j,j) = \sum_{i=1}^{m} a_{ij}, j = 1, \cdots, n$$

Let L_s denote the $m \times k$ matrix of the left k singular vectors and R_p the $n \times k$ matrix of the right k singular vectors of RA. As our aim is to conduct a dual subset clustering on both session and pageview attributes, we create a new $(m+n) \times k$ matrix PV to reflect the projection of the row and column vectors on the new spectral space in lower dimension as:

$$PV = \begin{bmatrix} D_s^{-1/2} L_s \\ D_p^{-1/2} R_p \end{bmatrix}$$

The full steps of co-clustering algorithm is summarized in the below Algorithm.

Algorithm 6.10: Spectral Co-Clustering Algorithm

Input: The user session collection S and pageview set P, and the Web log file
Output: A set $C = \{C_1, \cdots C_k\}$ of k subsets of sessions and pageviews such that the cut of k-partitioning of the bipartite graph is minimized.
1. Construct the usage matrix A from the Web usage log, whose element is determined by the visit number or duration of one user on a specific page;
2. Calculate the two diagonal matrices D_s and D_p of A;
3. Form a new matrix $NA = D_s^{-1/2} A D_p^{-1/2}$;
4. Perform SVD operation on NA, and obtain the left and right k singular vectors L_s and R_p, and combine the transformed row and column vectors to create a new projection matrix PV;
5. Execute a clustering algorithm on PV and return the co-clusters of subsets of S and P, $C_j = (S_j, P_j)$.

6.5 Web Usage Mining Applications

Web Usage Mining was intensively studied in last decades for various purposes and was successful in a variety of real applications. One typical applied case in early stage is to help improve website organization and design by utilizing the user access behaviors [233, 203, 204].

With the propagation and popularity of search engine, Web Usage Mining has attracted a lot of interests on how to facilitate the search performance via learning usage knowledge. Moreover, the research of Web community was greatly benefited from the advance of Web Usage Mining. In this section, we will review some studies carried out in this area.

6.5.1 Mining Web Logs to Improve Website Organization

A good design and organization of a website is essential in improving the website's attractiveness and popularity in Web applications. A well designed and organized site is often a basic requirement for securing the success of a site. However, it is not a easy task for every Web designer to satisfy the aims initially designated. There are many reasons, which are associated with the above disappointments. First, different users have their own navigational tasks so following different access traces. Second, even the same user may have different information needs at different times. Third, the website is not logically organized and the individual Web pages are aggregated and placed in inappropriate positions, resulting in the users uneasily locating the needed information; and furthermore, a site may be designed for a particular kind of use, but be used in many different ways in practice; the designer's original intent is not fully realized. All above mentioned reasons will affect the satisfactory degree of a website use. By deeply looking into the causes of such reasons, we can intuitively see that it is mainly because the early website design and organization only reflects the intents of website designers or developers, instead, the user opinions or tastes are not sufficiently taken into account. Inspired by this observation, using Web Usage Mining techniques is intuitively proposed to address the improvement of website design and organization. Essentially the knowledge learned from Web Usage Mining is able to reveal the user navigational behavior and to benefit the site organization improvement by leveraging the knowledge.

Adaptive Web Sites

In [204, 203] the authors proposed an approach to address the above challenges by creating adaptive websites. The approach is to allow Web sites automatically improve their organization and presentation by learning from visitor access patterns. Different from other methods such as customized Web sites, which are to personalize the Web page presentation to individual users, the proposed approach is focused on the site optimization through the automatic synthesis of index pages. The basic idea of the proposed is originated from learning the user access patterns and implemented by synthesizing a number of new index pages to represent the user access interests. The approach was called *PageGather* algorithm. Since the algorithm needs only to explicitly learn usage information rather than to affectively make destructive changes to the original Web sites, the author claimed that the strength of the approach is *nondestructive transformation*.

The PageGather algorithm is based on a basic assumption of visit-coherence: the pages a user visits during one interaction with the site tend to be conceptually related. It uses clustering mining to find the aggregations of related Web pages at a site from the access log. The whole process of the proposed algorithm consists of four sub-steps:

Algorithm 6.11 PageGather algorithm

Step 1. Process the access log into visits.
Step 2. Compute the co-occurrence frequencies between pages and create a similarity matrix.

Step 3. Create the graph corresponding to the matrix, and employ clique(or connected components) finding algorithm in the graph.
Step 4. For each cluster found, create new index Web pages by synthesizing the links to the
documents of pages contained in the cluster.

In the first step, an access log, containing a sequence of hits, or requests to the Web
server, is taken for processing. Each request typically consists of time-stamp made, the URL
requested and the IP address from which the request originated. The IP address in this case
is treated as a single user. Thus a series of hits made in a day period, ordered by the timestamps, is collected as a single session for that user. The obtained user sessions in the form
of requested URLs form the session vector, will be used in the second step. To compute the
co-occurrence frequencies between pages, the conditional probability of each pair of pages P_1
and P_2 is calculated. $P_r(P_1|P_2)$ denotes the probability of a user visiting P_1 if it has already
visited P_2, while $P_r(P_2|P_1)$ is the probability of a user visiting P_2 after having visiting P_1. The
co-occurrence frequency between P_1 and P_2 is the minimum of these values. The reason why
using the minimum of two conditional probabilities is to avoid the problem of asymmetrical
relationships of two pages playing distinct roles in the Web site. Last, a matrix corresponding
to the calculated co-occurrence frequencies is created, and in turn, a graph which is equivalent
to the matrix is built up to reflect the connections of pages derived from the log as well. In
the third step, a clique finding algorithm is employed on the graph to reveal the connected
components of the graph. In this manner, a clique (or called cluster) is the collection of nodes
(i.e. pages) whose members are directly connected with edges. In other words, the subgraph
of the clique, in which each pair of nodes has a connected path between them, satisfies the fact
that every node in the clique or cluster is related to at least one other node in the subgraph.
Eventually, for each found cluster of pages, a new indexing page containing all the links to
the documents in the cluster is generated. From the above descriptions, we can see that the
added indexing pages represent the coherent relationships between pages from the user navigational perspective, therefore, providing an additional way for users to visually know the
access intents of other users and easily browse directly to the needed pages from the provided instrumental pages. Figure 6.7 depicts an example of index page derived by PageGather
algorithm [204].

Mining Web Logs to Improve Website Organization

In [233], the authors proposed a novel algorithm to automatically find the Web pages in a
website whose location is different from where the users expect to find. The motivation behind
the approach is that users will backtrack if they do not find the page where they expect it, and
the backtrack point is where the expected location of page should be. Apparently mining Web
log will provide a possible solution to identifying the backtrack points, and in turn, improving
website organization.

The model of user search pattern usually follows the below procedures [233]:

Algorithm 6.12: backtrack path finding

For a single target page T, the user is expected to execute the following search strategy
1. Start from the root.
2. While (current location C is not the target page T) do
    (a) If any of the links from C is likely to reach T, follow the link that appears most likely

Fig. 6.7. An example of index page derived by PageGather algorithm[204]

to T.

(b) Else, either go back (backtrack) to the parent of C with some possibility, or cease with some possibility.

For a set of target pages $(T_1, T_2, \cdots, T_n)$, the search pattern follows the similar procedure, but after the user identifying T_i, it continues searching T_{i+1}. In this scenario, the hardest task is to differentiate the target page from other pages by simply looking at the Web log. In this study, the authors claimed that the target pages could be separated out based on either whether the targets are content pages or index (or navigational) pages, or setting a time threshold. For the former case, the content pages are most likely to be the target pages for a user. Given a website of portal site, where there is not a clear separation between the content and index pages, resulting in the difficulty in judging the content pages, counting the time spent on a specific page will provide an useful hint to judge this. Here it is known that the user spent more time than the time threshold are considered the target page.

To identify the backtrack points, the Web log is analyzed. However, the browser caching technology brings in unexpected difficulty in differentiating the backtrack points, otherwise, the phenomenon of a page where previous and next pages are the same gives the justification to it. In this work, rather than disabling the browser caching, a new algorithm of detecting backtrack points was devised. The algorithm is motivated by the fact that if there is no link between P_1 and P_2, the user must click the "back" button in the browser to return from P_1 to P_2. Therefore the detection of the backtrack points is becoming the process of detecting whether there is a link between two successive pages in the Web log. To do this, the authors built a hash table of the edges in the website to check the existence of such a link from one page to another. The detailed algorithm description is found in [233].

To demonstrate the results, five examples of expected locations from the Wharton Website [233] are depicted in Fig.6.8. From the Example W1 (in Fig.6.8), it is seen that this page should be relocated in a different place or an additional page should be requested.

Example W1	Target page:	http://www.wharton.upenn.edu/mba/s2s/why_wharton.html
	Actual Location:	http://www.wharton.upenn.edu/mba/s2s/s2s.html
	Expected Location:	http://www.wharton.upenn.edu/mba/s2s/s_qa.html
	Support:	6
	Total Hits:	81
	Explanation:	Visitors expect to find the answer to "Why choose Wharton?" in the "Student-to-Student Program's Question & Answer Session" directory instead of the "Student-to-Student Program's General Description" directory.
Example W2	Target page:	http://www.wharton.upenn.edu/mba/admissions/profile.html
	Actual Location:	http://www.wharton.upenn.edu/mba/admissions/index.html
	Expected Location:	http://www.wharton.upenn.edu/students.html
	Support:	6
	Total Hits:	882
	Explanation:	Visitors expect to find "MBA Student Profiles" under "Student" instead of "MBA Admission".
Example W3	Target page:	http://www.wharton.upenn.edu/whartonnow/calendars.html
	Actual Location:	http://www.wharton.upenn.edu/whartonnow.html
	Expected Location:	http://www.wharton.upenn.edu/programs.html
	Support:	7
	Total Hits:	292
	Explanation:	Visitors expect to find "Calendar" under "Programs" instead of the "WhartonNow" directory.
Example W4	Target page:	http://www.wharton.upenn.edu/undergrad/curriculum/concentrations.html
	Actual Location:	http://www.wharton.upenn.edu/undergrad/curriculum/index.html
	Expected Location:	http://www.wharton.upenn.edu/students.html
	Support:	6
	Total Hits:	293
	Explanation:	Visitors expect to find "Curriculum" under "Students" instead of "Programs".
Example W5	Target page:	http://www.wharton.upenn.edu/mba/curriculum/curriculum.html
	Actual Location:	http://www.wharton.upenn.edu/mba/curriculum/index.html
	Expected Location:	http://www.wharton.upenn.edu/students.html
	Support:	6
	Total Hits:	555
	Explanation:	Visitors expect to find "Curriculum" under "Students" instead of "Programs".

Fig. 6.8. Examples from the Wharton Website for Better Organization[233]

6.5.2 Clustering User Queries from Web logs for Related Query

Clustering Query Refinement by User Intent

Another interesting application of Web Usage Mining is clustering user queries of a search engine [254, 214]. Related search queries is a complementary functionality provided by most of the search engines, such as *Google, Yahoo!* and *Bing*. The motivation of such kind of techniques is to assist users in query issuing by leveraging the navigational behaviors exhibited by other like-minded users. When various users utilize the search engine to find the needed information, the Web log will record the query tracks made by the users as well as the URLs the users following to click after the search results are returned. Thus mining the query logs can implicitly reveal the similar query groups which often serve for the similar search aims with a high co-occurring probability. The related queries are therefore recommended based on finding other queries that co-occur in sessions with the original query. For many popular queries, there may be a large number of related queries found in the query logs. However, given a limited search result window, it is unlikely to present all related queries simultaneously in such a small space. To handle this, an intuitive solution is to cluster the queries contained in the query logs and to present the related queries to the users in the forms of distinctive categories. The user query clustering is normally performed from the perspective of user intent via mining the Web logs.

In [214], the authors proposed a clustering algorithm of query refinements to improve the selection and placement of the query suggestions returned by a search engine. Here the term *"query refinement"* means a particular kind of related queries, which are those queries following the original query in the session. In order to conduct the clustering of query refinements, first an appropriate user query model is essentially needed to construct to capture the relationships among the entries. In this study, a graph representation is used to model the user behavior.

Given a Web log, the whole circle of a user issuing a query and query refinement, and following to click various documents could be modeled a graph, $G(q) = (V, E)$ based on the query and click sequences. In the graph, V is the node set, including query refinements and any clicked documents for the original query q, while E denotes the edge collection, reflecting the sequence order of query refinements and documents for the given original query. The connections within the E are determined by three different scenario, i.e.

- edges from the original query to each of its refinements;
- edges from its refinements to each of its clicked documents;
- edges linking the co-occurring refinements

The idea of the proposed approach is initiated from the assumption that two refinements, r_i and r_j, represents the same underlying intent if the same documents are reached by users in different sessions where q is followed by r_i or r_j. Based on this intuition, it is able to capture the user underlying intent as the representative set of documents reachable from a query refinement r_i, after starting from the original query q. In this manner, each query refinement is conceptually modeled as a document vector determined by the intent. Now the clustering of query refinements is formulated as the problem of clustering by intent. Accordingly, query refinements could be partitioned following the below criterion: queries could be clustered into different groups so that (1) the number of edges between query nodes in different clusters is minimized, and (2) the number of document nodes that have edges from multiple clusters is minimized. Figure 6.9 depicts an example of query refinement graph and its corresponding clustering [214]. As shown, the query refinements are grouped into three clusters. The authors proposed a clustering algorithm of query refinements consisting of four steps[214] as follows:

Algorithm 6.13 query refinement clustering by using user intents

---

(1) initialize transition matrix of $G(q)$;
(2) calculate the limiting distributions;
(3) extract absorption distribution;
(4) cluster vectors.

The inputs of the algorithm are the graph $G(q)$ constructed by the above model and the number of clusters, k. In addition to the inputs, other two parameters used are ε: the document

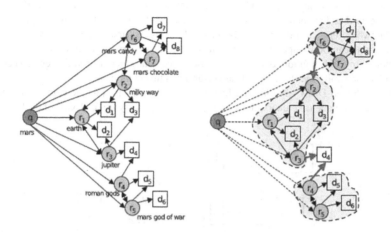

Fig. 6.9. Graph G model of user search behavior and its partition of refinements into three clusters [214]

escape probability, and n, a parameter to the random walk used in the algorithm. More details regarding the algorithm description is referred to [214].

Clustering User Queries of a Search Engine

Clustering user search queries is useful for related query suggestion and Frequently Asked Questions/Queries (FAQs). The classic approaches to information retrieval (IR) would suggest a similarity calculation according to their keywords. However, this approach has some known drawbacks due to the limitations of keywords. Web queries are usually short in length (a couple of words) and ambiguous in meaning expression. The very small word overlap between short Web queries makes it hard to accurately estimate their similarity. One reason is probably that a term may be meant for different meanings by different users (i.e. polysemy), e.g., apple is related to fruit or computer. The other reason is that different terms may have a similar meaning (i.e. synonymy), e.g., car and automobile. New approaches are needed to cluster user search queries effectively. Ji-Rong Wen et al. [254] proposed two clustering principles to solve the above problems.

The first criterion is similar to those used in traditional approaches to document clustering methods based on keywords.

Principle 1 (using query contents): If two queries contain the same or similar terms, they denote the same or similar information needs.

Obviously, the longer the queries, the more reliable the principle 1 is. However, users often submit short queries to search engines. A typical query on the Web usually contains one or two words. In many cases, there is not enough information to deduce users' information needs correctly. Therefore, the second criterion is used as a complement.

The second criterion is similar to the intuition underlying document clustering in IR. Classically, it is believed that closely associated documents tend to correspond to the same query. In their case, they use the intuition in the reverse way as follows:

Principle 2 (using document clicks): If two queries lead to the selection of the same document (which is called a document click), then they are similar.

Document clicks are comparable to user relevance feedback in a traditional IR environment, except that document clicks denote implicit and not always valid relevance judgments.

The two criteria have their own advantages. In using the first criterion, queries of similar compositions can be grouped together. In using the second criterion, we benefit from user's judgments. In [254], authors combine both user clicks and document and query contents to determine the similarity. Better results are result from this combination.

They adopted DBSCAN [88] and Incremental DBSCAN [87] as the core algorithms to construct a comprehensive query clustering tool as shown in Figure 6.10. One of the key prob-

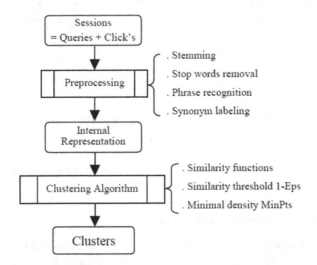

Fig. 6.10. Flow chart of the clustering process.

lems is the choice of similarity function. They utilized two ways to compute similarity. One is based on query contents, such as keywords and strings. The other is based on user feedback, such as clicked documents and their document hierarchy information. Similarities based on query contents and user clicks represent two different points of view. In general, content-based measures tend to cluster queries with the same or similar terms. Feedback-based measures tend to cluster queries related to the same or similar topics. Since user information needs may be partially captured by both query texts and relevant documents, they finally defined a combined measure that takes advantage of both strategies. More details about similarity functions and clustering methods are in [254].

The identification of FAQs is not an easy task; it requires a proper estimation of query similarity. Given the different forms of queries and user intentions, the similarity of queries cannot be accurately estimated through an analysis of their contents alone (i.e. via keywords). Ji-Rong Wen et al. [254] have suggested exploiting user log information (or user document clicks) as a supplement. A new clustering principle is proposed: if two queries give rise to the same document clicks, they are similar. Their initial analysis of the clustering results suggests that this clustering strategy can effectively group similar queries together. It does provide effective assistance for human editors in discovering new FAQs.

6.5.3 Using Ontology-Based User Preferences to Improve Web Search

As we know, different users have different intentions for a same query. In order to satisfy the diverse needs of users, search engines should be adaptive to the individual contexts in which users submit their queries. User preferences consist of a number of attributes, such as what kind of topics that users are interested in, and how much users are interested in each topic, which can be used to personalize search results for better search performance. Each attribute describes a user's favorite in different aspects. In most cases, any individual attribute is deficient in accurately representing user preferences. Combining user knowledge depicted by each attribute can help us understand user preferences well, which finally results in an effective rank mechanism in the Web search.

Now, we will discuss how to get the respective rank lists from the learned use preferences. User preferences are structured as a semantic hierarchy shown in Figure 6.11. For an effective

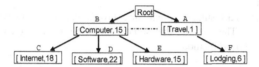

Fig. 6.11. Hierarchical Model of User Preferences.

rank mechanism, the more similar a search result is to user preferences, the higher position it will be put in the final rank list. To produce such a new rank list, hierarchical similarity measures are needed to assess the relatedness between user preferences and search results. Five content-ignorant measures are chosen from [162] because we want to see how much we can benefit from the hierarchical structure. The measures are defined as

$$S_1(i,j) = 2 \cdot M - l, \tag{6.31}$$

$$S_2(i,j) = \alpha S_1(i,j) + \beta h \qquad (\alpha = 0.05, \beta = 1), \tag{6.32}$$

$$S_3(i,j) = e^{-\alpha \cdot l} \qquad (\alpha = 0.25), \tag{6.33}$$

$$S_4(i,j) = \frac{e^{\beta \cdot h} - e^{-\beta \cdot h}}{e^{\beta \cdot h} + e^{-\beta \cdot h}} \qquad (\beta = 0.15), \tag{6.34}$$

$$S_5(i,j) = e^{-\alpha \cdot l} \cdot \frac{e^{\beta \cdot h} - e^{-\beta \cdot h}}{e^{\beta \cdot h} + e^{-\beta \cdot h}} \quad (\alpha = 0.2, \beta = 0.6), \tag{6.35}$$

where h means the depth of the subsumer (the deepest node common to two nodes), l is the naïve distance (the number of edges or the shortest path length between two nodes), i and j are nodes (topics) in Figure 6.11, and M is the maximum depth of topic directory possessed by user preferences. The values in parentheses are the optimal values of parameters [162].

Then two user-centered rank lists are calculated plus the result list returned by Google for rank-based fusion.

(1)**Hierarchical Semantic Similarity** User preferences include a number of topics (nodes) in Figure 6.11. The semantic similarity between one search result and one user are further defined as the maximum value among all the values computed by any one of Equations 6.31-6.35. The search results then are re-ranked and form a rank list in order of one attribute of user preferences (i.e., the topics a user is interested in).

(2) **Degree of User Interests** The more times a user clicks one topic, the more interested the user is in it. The user's clicked times can produce a complementary rank list of search results.

(3) **Google List** Google applies its patented PageRank technology on the Google Directory to rank the sites. To keep our rank aggregation from missing the high quality Web pages in Google, the original rank list of Google Directory Search is considered as well.

In [159] authors study the problem of combining sets of rank lists from different attributes of user preferences into a single rank list. Voting provides us with a traditional class of algorithms to determine the aggregated rank list. The most common voting theory, named after its creator, is known as Borda's rule [38] which argues that the majority opinion is the truth, or at least the closest that we can come to determining it [266]. However, the problem with Borda's rule is that it does not optimize any criterion. Footrule distances [74] is used to weigh edges in a bipartite graph and then find a minimum cost matching. This method was proved in [82] to approximate the optimal ranking that approximately minimizes the number of disagreements with the given inputs.

In [159] experimental results on a real click-through data set demonstrated the effectiveness of their methods. They argued that some rank-based aggregation methods performed better than the *Socre-Based* method.

Summary

In this chapter, we have reviewed and summarized a number of Web usage mining algorithms. The reported algorithms are mainly related to two kinds of well studied data mining paradigms, namely clustering and latent semantic analysis. In first section, we have described the procedures of modeling user interest and capturing user clusters. In the following two sections, we have elaborated the combination of latent semantic analysis into Web usage mining. In section 6.4, we have reported the study of co-clustering of weblogs. Section 6.5 listed a couple of Web usage mining applications in real world. In this chapter, besides the technical coverage on algorithmic issues, some interesting and insightful experimental investigations have also been presented.

Social Networking and Web Recommendation:
Techniques and Applications

Part III

Extracting and Analyzing Web Social Networks

In previous two parts, we intensively discussed the theoretical backgrounds of Web data mining and the engaged techniques of three kinds of Web data mining. These contents provide the comprehensive descriptions from the perspective of principles and approaches. In this part, we change to discuss the possible applications of such techniques in a broader extent. The application potentials cover a variety of application areas. In particular, in this part we will discuss several interesting topics of social networking, Web community and Web recommender systems.

Though social network analysis seems to be a traditional topic in the areas of psychology, sociology and behavior science, it is becoming an active and popular topic in computer science domain due to its interdisciplinary research essence recently, especially with the propagation of Web 2.0 technology. In this chapter, we concentrate on the research issues of social networks on the Web. We will discuss the issues of extracting and analyzing Web social networks, analyzing the temporal changes of Web communities, and capturing the dynamic evolution patterns of Web networked structures, and an empirical study of identifying social sense from a large scale Web log archive.

7.1 Extracting Evolution of Web Community from a Series of Web Archive

Recent advances in storage technology make it possible to store and keep a series of large Web archives. It is now an exciting challenge for us to observe evolution of the Web, since it has experienced dramatic growth and dynamic changes in its structure. We could see a lot of phenomena in the Web, which correspond to social activities in the real world. For example, if some topic becomes popular in the real world, many pages about the topic are created, then good quality pages are pointed to by public bookmarks or link lists for that topic, and these pages become densely connected.

M.Toyoda and M. Kitsuregawa [244] proposed a method for observing the evolution of Web communities. A Web community is a collection of Web pages created by individuals or associations with a common interest on a topic, such as fan pages of a baseball team, and official pages of computer vendors. Recent research on link analysis [52, 55, 70, 93, 99, 137, 153] shows that we can identify a Web community on a topic by extracting densely connected structure in the Web graph, in which nodes are Web pages and edges are hyperlinks. The

G. Xu et al., *Web Mining and Social Networking*,
DOI 10.1007/978-1-4419-7735-9_7, © Springer Science+Business Media, LLC 2011

Web community slightly differs from a community of people, for example, a Web community may include competing companies. Since a Web community represents a certain topic, we can understand when and how the topic emerged and evolved in the Web.

As introduced in Section 5.4, there are several algorithms for finding Web communities. Here, the extraction of Web community utilizes Web community chart that is a graph of communities, in which related communities are connected by weighted edges. The main advantage of the Web community chart is existence of relevance between communities. We can navigate through related communities, and locate evolution around a particular community.

M.Toyoda and M. Kitsuregawa explain how Web communities evolve, and what kinds of metrics can measure degree of the evolution, such as growth rate and novelty. They first explain the details of changes of Web communities, and then introduce evolution metrics that can be used for finding patterns of evolution. Here the notations used are summarized in this section.

$t_1, t_2, ..., t_n$: Time when each archive crawled. Currently, a month is used as the unit time.
$W(t_k)$: The Web archive at time t_k.
$C(t_k)$: The Web community chart at time t_k.
$c(t_k), d(t_k), e(t_k), ...$: Communities in $C(t_k)$.

7.1.1 Types of Changes

Emerge: A community $c(t_k)$ emerges in $C(t_k)$, when $c(t_k)$ shares no URLs with any community in $C(t_{k-1})$. Note that not all URLs in $c(t_k)$ newly appear in $W(t_k)$. Some URLs in $c(t_k)$ may be included in $W(t_{k-1})$, and do not have enough connectivity to form a community.
Dissolve: A community $c(t_{k-1})$ in $C(t_{k_1})$ has dissolved, when $c(t_{k-1})$ shares no URLs with any community in $C(t_k)$. Note that not all URLs in $c(t_{k-1})$ disappeared from $W(t_{k-1})$. Some URLs in $c(t_{k-1})$ may still be included in $W(t_k)$ losing connectivity to any community.
Grow and shrink: When $c(t_{k-1})$ in $C(t_{k-1})$ shares URLs with only $c(t_k)$ in $C(t_k)$, and vice versa, only two changes can occur to $c(t_{k-1})$. The community grows when new URLs are appeared in $c(t_k)$, and shrinks when URLs disappeared from $c(t_{k-1})$. When the number of appeared URLs is greater than the number of disappeared URLs, it grows. In the reverse case, it shrinks.
Split: A community $c(t_{k-1})$ may split into some smaller communities. In this case, $c(t_{k-1})$ shares URLs with multiple communities in $C(t_k)$. Split is caused by disconnections of URLs in SDG. Split communities may grow and shrink. They may also merge (see the next item) with other communities.
Merge: When multiple communities ($c(t_{k-1})$), $d(t_{k-1})$, ...) share URLs with a single community $e(t_k)$, these communities are merged into $e(t_k)$ by connections of their URLs in SDG. Merged community may grow and shrink. They may also split before merging.

7.1.2 Evolution Metrics

Evolution metrics measure how a particular community $c(t_k)$ has evolved. For example, we can know how much $c(t_k)$ has grown, and how many URLs newly appeared in $c(t_k)$. The proposed metrics can be used for finding various patterns of evolution described above. To measure changes of $c(t_k)$, the community is identified at time t_{k-1} corresponding to $c(t_k)$. This corresponding community, $c(t_{k-1})$, is defined as the community that shares the most URLs with $c(t_k)$. If there were multiple communities that share the same number of URLs, a community that has the largest number of URLs is selected.

The community at time t_k corresponding to $c(t_{k-1})$ can be reversely identified. When this corresponding community is just $c(t_k)$, they call the pair $(c(t_{k-1}))$, $c(t_k)$) as main line. Otherwise, the pair is called as branch line. A main line can be extended to a sequence by tracking such symmetrically corresponding communities over time. A community in a main line is considered to keep its identity, and can be used for a good starting point for finding changes around its topic.

The metrics are defined by differences between $c(t_k)$ and its corresponding community $c(t_{k-1})$. To define metrics, the following attributes are used to represent how many URLs the focused community obtains or loses.

$N(c(t_k))$: the number of URLs in the $c(t_k)$.

$Nsh(c(t_{k-1}), c(t_k))$: the number of URLs shared by $c(t_{k-1})$ and $c(t_k)$.

$Ndis(c(t_{k-1}))$: the number of disappeared URLs from $c(t_{k-1})$ that exist in $c(t_{k-1})$ but do not exist in any community in $C(t_k)$).

$Nsp(c(tk_1), c(t_k))$: the number of URLs split from $c(t_{k-1})$ to communities at t_k other than $c(t_k)$.

$Nap(c(t_k))$: the number of newly appeared URLs in $c(t_k)$) that exist in $c(t_k)$ but do not exist in any community $C(t_{k-1})$.

$Nmg(c(t_{k-1}), c(t_k))$: the number of URLs merged into $c(t_k)$) from communities at t_{k-1} other than $c(t_{k-1})$.

Then evolution metrics are defined as follows. The *growth rate*, $R_{grow}(c(t_{k-1}), c(t_k))$, represents the increase of URLs per unit time. It allows us to find most growing or shrinking communities. The growth rate is defined as follows. Note that when $c(t_{k-1})$ does not exist, zero is used as $N(c(t_{k-1}))$.

$$R_{grow}(c(t_{k-1}), c(t_k)) = \frac{N(c(t_k)) - N(c(t_{k-1}))}{t_k - t_{k-1}}. \tag{7.1}$$

The *stability*, $R_{stability}(c(t_{k-1}), c(t_k))$, represents the amount of disappeared, appeared, merged and split URLs per unit time. When there is no change of URLs, the stability becomes zero. Note that $c(t_k)$ may not be stable even if the growth rate of $c(t_k)$ is zero, because $c(t_k)$ may lose and obtain the same number of URLs. A stable community on a topic is the best starting point for finding interesting changes around the topic. The stability is defined as:

$$R_{stability}(c(t_{k-1}), c(t_k)) = \frac{N(c(t_k)) + N(c(t_{k-1})) - 2N_{sh}(c(t_{k-1}), c(t_k))}{t_k - t_{k-1}}. \tag{7.2}$$

The *disappearance rate*, $R_{disappear}(c(t_{k-1}), c(t_k))$, is the number of disappeared URLs from $c(t_{k-1})$ per unit time. Higher disappear rate means that the community has lost URLs mainly by disappearance. The disappear rate is defined as

$$R_{disappear}(c(t_{k-1}), c(t_k)) = \frac{N_{dis}(c(t_{k-1}))}{t_k - t_{k-1}}. \tag{7.3}$$

The *merge rate*, $R_{merge}(c(t_{k-1}), c(t_k))$, is the number of absorbed URLs from other communities by merging per unit time. Higher merge rate means that the community has obtained URLs mainly by merging. The merge rate is defined as follows.

$$R_{merge}(c(t_{k-1}), c(t_k)) = \frac{N_{mg}(c(t_{k-1}))}{t_k - t_{k-1}}. \qquad (7.4)$$

The *split rate*, $R_{split}(c(t_{k-1}), c(t_k))$, is the number of split URLs from $c(t_{k-1})$ per unit time. When the split rate is low, $c(t_k)$ is larger than other split communities. Otherwise, $c(t_k)$ is smaller than other split communities. The split rate is defined as follows.

$$R_{split}(c(t_{k-1}), c(t_k)) = \frac{N_{sp}(c(t_{k-1}))}{t_k - t_{k-1}}. \qquad (7.5)$$

By combining these metrics, some complex evolution patterns can be represented. For example, a community has stably grown when its growth rate is positive, and its disappearance and split rates are low. Similar evolution patterns can be defined for shrinkage.

Longer range metrics (more than one unit time) can be calculated for main lines. For example, the novelty metrics of a main line $(c(t_i), c(t_{i+1}), ..., c(t_j))$ is calculated as follows. Other metrics can be calculated similarly.

$$R_{novelty}(c(t_i), c(t_j)) = \frac{\sum_{k=i}^{j} N_{ap}(c(t_k))}{t_j - t_i}. \qquad (7.6)$$

7.1.3 Web Archives and Graphs

For experiments, M.Toyoda and M. Kitsuregawa used four Web archives of Japanese Web pages (in jp domain) crawled in 1999, 2000, 2001, and 2002 (See Table 1). The same Web crawler was used in 1999 and 2000, and collected about 17 million pages in each year. In 2001, the number of pages became more than twice of the 2000 archive through improving the crawling rate. The used crawlers collected pages in the breadth-first order.

From each archive, a Web graph is built with URLs and links by extracting anchors from all pages in the archive. The graph included not only URLs inside the archive, but also URLs outside pointed to by inside URLs. As a result, the graph included URLs outside jp domain, such as com and edu. Table 1 also shows the number of links and the total URLs. For efficient link analysis, each Web graph was stored in a main-memory database that provided out-links and in-links of a given URL. Its implementation was similar to the connectivity server [30]. The whole system was implemented on Sun Enterprise Server 6500 with 8 CPU and 4GB memory. Building the connectivity database of 2002 took about one day.

By comparing these graphs, the Web was extremely dynamic. More than half URLs disappeared or changed its location in one year. They first examined how many URLs in our Web graphs were changed over time, by counting the number of URLs shared between these graphs. About 60% of URLs disappeared from both 1999 and 2000 graphs. From 2001 to 2002, about 30% of URLs disappeared in four months. The number of URLs surviving through four archives was only about 5 million. In [63], Cho reported that more than 70% of pages survived more than one month in their four month observation. This result is close to their results from 2001 to 2002 (30% disappearance in four months). Although it is not easy to estimate the rate for one year from [63], they say that their results does not deviate so much.

7.1.4 Evolution of Web Community Charts

The global behavior of community evolution is described now. From the above four Web graphs, four community charts are built using the technique described in Chapter 5(Section 5.4).

Table 7.1. The number of seeds and communities

Year	Period	Seeds	Communities
1999	Jul. to Aug.	657K	79K
2000	Jun. to Aug.	737K	88K
2001	Early Oct.	1404K	156K
2002	Early Feb.	1511K	170K

To compare Web community charts in the same condition, they fixed values of parameters, IN and N, for the chart building algorithm. IN is 3, that is, they selected seeds that have in-links from three or more different servers. Using a larger value than 3 drastically decreased seeds, because of its power-law distribution. N is 10, that is, top 10 results by Companion- were used for calculating relevance between seeds. It took about a half day to build the chart for 2002. Most of the time was spent on calculating related pages of seeds by Companion-. Table 7.1 shows the number of seeds and communities in the chart created for each year. In the following, evolution statistics of Web community charts are shown.

Size distribution

The size distribution of communities also follows the power law and its exponent did not change so much over time. Figure 7.1 shows log-log plots of the communities size distributions for all charts.

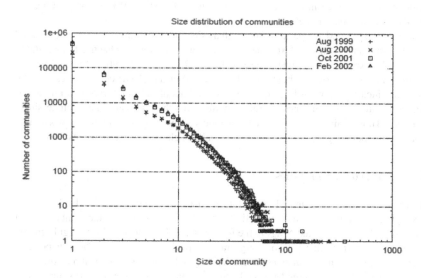

Fig. 7.1. Size distribution of communities.

All four curves roughly fit to a power law distribution with exponent 2.9 to 3.0. This result is similar to distributions of connected components in the Web graph reported in [44].

Table 7.2. umber of main lines in split or merged communities

	tk_1: Aug. 99	Aug. 00	Oct. 01
	tk: Aug. 00	Oct. 01	Feb. 02
# Branch lines at tk_1	28,467	32,490	41,501
# Main lines	26,723	34,396	83,771
# Branch lines at tk	29,722	41,752	44,305

Types of Changes

Although the size distribution of communities is stable, the structure of communities changes dynamically. Figure 6 shows how many communities are involved in each type of changes from tk_1 to tk. Each bar represents the number of communities in charts at the time. Bars at 2000 and 2001 are split vertically, since they have the previous and the next charts to be compared. Each block represents the number of communities involved in a particular change. Dotted blocks represent dissolved communities from tk_1, and white blocks represent emerged communities. Gray blocks represent communities that are involved in split or merge. Finally, black blocks represent single communities that are not involved in these changes, but may grow or shrink.

The structure of the chart changes mainly by split and merge, in which more than half of communities are involved. The number of single communities is small (10% in 1999, 14% in 2000, and 25% in 2001). Since the seed sets of the charts are stable parts in our archives, the number of communities dissolved from each chart is rather small. About 24% to 30% of communities are dissolved in one year from 1999 to 2001, while 20% of communities are dissolved in four months from 2001.

Changes by split and merge are complicated, since split communities may be merged with other communities in the next time. However, it is not totally chaotic. Rather stable communities by extracting main lines are seen. Table 7.2 shows the number of main lines and branch lines in each intervals. About half of survived (not dissolved) communities in 1999 and 2000 are included in main lines for one year, and about 66% of survived communities in 2001 are included in main lines for four months. Note that the main lines include single communities. Those main lines can be used as a good starting point for finding changes around the topic. In the following section, we show the detailed behavior of each changes.

Split and Merged Communities

The distributions of the split rate and merge rate are fist shown in Figure 7.2 and 7.3.

They plot the number of split or merged communities as a function of the number of split and merged URLs (i.e., Nsp and Nmg) in the log-log scale. Both distributions roughly follow the power law, and show that split or merge rate is small in most cases. Their shapes and scales are also similar. That is, when communities at tk_1 split with a split rate, almost the same number of communities are merged at tk with the same rate as the split rate. This symmetry is part of the reason why the size distribution of communities does not change so much.

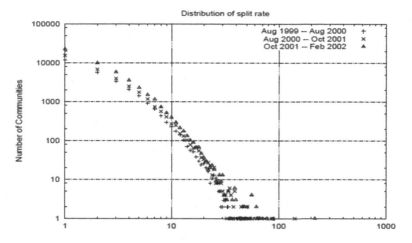

Fig. 7.2. Distribution of split rate.

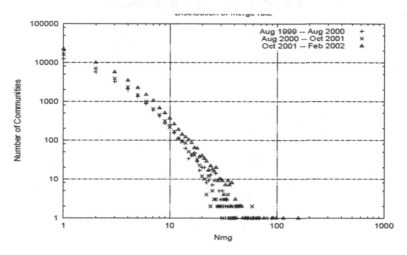

Fig. 7.3. Distribution of split rate.

Emerged and Dissolved Communities

The size distributions of emerged and dissolved communities also follow the power law, and contribute to preserve the size distribution of communities. Figure 7.4 and 7.5 show these distributions for all periods in the log-log scale.

In most cases, the exponent of the power law is greater than 3.2, while the exponent of the whole chart is around 3.0. This means that small communities are easy to emerge and dissolve.

Growth Rate

Finally, the distribution of the growth rate is examined. Figure 7.6 shows the number of communities as a function of the growth rate.

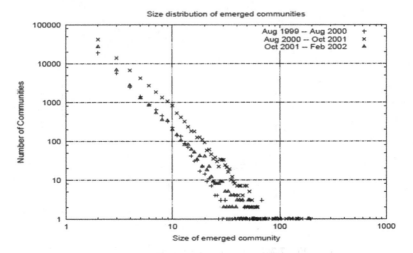

Fig. 7.4. Size distribution of emerged communities.

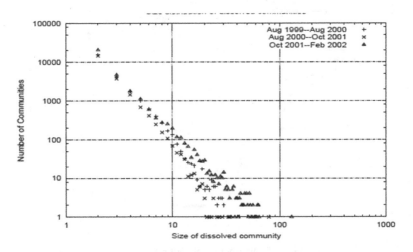

Fig. 7.5. Size distribution of dissolved communities.

A log scale is used on the y-axis. For simplicity, the growth rates of main lines are plotted in this graph. The growth rate is small for most of communities, and the graph has clear y-axis symmetry. This is also part of the reason why the size distribution of communities is preserved over time.

Combining evolution metrics and relevance, evolution around a particular community can be located. The experiments have been performed against four Japanese Web archives (in jp domain) crawled from 1999 to 2002 with 119M pages in total, and statistics of Web graphs and community evolution are examined. They have found that the size distribution of communities followed the power-law, and its exponent did not change so much over time. This is because

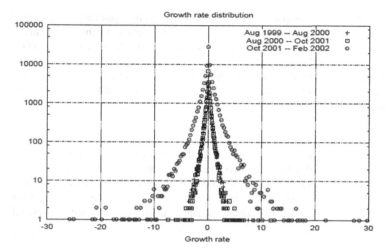

Fig. 7.6. Distribution of growth rate.

most of changes in communities follow the power-law, and the changes are symmetric between split and merge, and between growth and shrinkage.

7.2 Temporal Analysis on Semantic Graph using Three-Way Tensor Decomposition

A social network is a graphical representation of the relationships existing within a community [23]. The relationships amongst the members are measured by a number of metrics, such as size, density, centrality and so on. Social networks provide us a tool to study collaboration, in particular through theory developed in social network analysis [251, 221, 217]. Recently social network analysis is becoming increasingly popular and hot in many fields besides sociology, including intelligence analysis [220], marketing [48] and recommender systems [197].

Within social network analysis, using the social relationships or friendships to identify the network structures embedded in the communities is emerging as an important topic. More interestingly, the dynamic analysis of social networks over an evolution is able to capture the changes of networks over time. Sarkar and Moore [217] proposed an approach of dynamic social network analysis using latent semantic space. They embedded an evolving friendship graph in p-dimensional space using multidimensional scaling, and analyze the network structure shift in this space over time. In [15] Bader et al. aimed to address the temporal analysis of semantic graphs using three-way tensor. With the additional temporal dimension, compared to traditional graph-based approaches, their algorithm looks quite interesting and promising. In this section, we will briefly present their proposed algorithm and a few selected experimental results reported in [15].

7.2.1 Background

This study introduced a new algorithm, called ASALSAN, for computing DEDICOM (DEcomposition into DIrectional Components) [109]. The goal of the algorithm is to provide information on latent semantic components in data and the pattern of asymmetric relationships among these components. The novelty of this study is the introduction of a third-dimensional mode (i.e. temporal) into the social network analysis, which extends the two-way analytic model to a three-way DEDICOM model for large-scale data.

The model is described as follows. Given a directed graph with n vertices whose adjacency matrix X contains a nonzero entry x_{ij} for each edge $[i, j]$, the two-way DEDICOM model applied to X could be generally approximated as

$$X \approx ARA^T$$

where $A \in^{n \times p}$ is a loading matrix (or "weights") for the n vertices on $p < n$ dimension and $R \in^{n \times p}$ is a matrix that reflects the asymmetric mutual relationships on the p latent dimensions. More mathematically, the two-way DEDICOM model is equivalent to a SVD (Singular Value Decomposition) approximate transformation of an symmetric adjacency matrix. Thus the model is visualized in Fig.7.7. In considering the temporal analysis, it is intuitive to extend

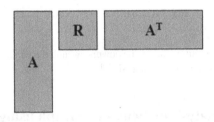

Fig. 7.7. Two-way DEDECOM model [15]

the two-way model to three-way DEDICOM by using time as the third mode. Suppose there are m discrete time edge labels in the graph, then we can construct an adjacency matrix X_k for each edge label, $k = 1, \cdots, m$, and stack the k adjacency matrices as an array $X \in^{n \times n \times m}$. The three-way model of X is approximated as

$$X_k \approx AD_k RD_k A^T, k = 1, \cdots, m \qquad (7.7)$$

where X_k is the kth adjacency matrix in X, $A \in^{n \times p}$ is the loading matrix, D_k is a diagonal matrix that indicates the weights of the columns of A for each discrete stamp in the third time mode, and $R \in^{n \times p}$ is the asymmetric matrix that captures the overall trends of networks over the time. The approximation illustration of the three-way DEDICOM model is shown in Fig.7.8. From the figure, it is seen that after the three-way approximation, the latent components are projected into a small-size three-way array, i.e. D, and R represents the aggregate property of latent semantic components mined from the large-scale data. The interpretation of the three-way decomposition has multiple ways. One of interesting and simplified meanings is that the model takes a large data array and condenses the mutual relationships into an aggregated structure of R. Each row of matrix A corresponds to the contribution made by a node (e.g. an individual person in a social network), and the contributed weights represent the closeness of the node to the all latent components. In real applications, such kind of weights is able to capture the user communities in the social network.

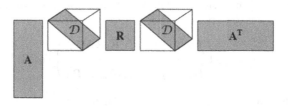

Fig. 7.8. Three-way DEDECOM model [15]

7.2.2 Algorithms

Notations

To exactly formulate the mathematical problems in the three-way model, the following similar notations that are discussed Chapter 2 are introduced. Scalars are denoted by lowercase letters, e.g. a. Vectors are denoted by boldface lowercase letter, e.g. $\mathbf{a}$, the ith element of $\mathbf{a}$ is denoted by a_i. Matrices are denoted by boldface capital letters, e.g. $\mathbf{A}$. The jth column of $\mathbf{A}$ is denoted by $\mathbf{a}_j$ and the entry (i,j) by a_{ij}. The three-way array is denoted by a tensor symbol, e.g. X, the element (i,j,k) of a three-way array X is denoted by x_{ijk}, and the kth frontal slice of X is denoted by $\mathbf{X}_k$ [15].

The symbol $\otimes$ denotes the matrix Kroneck product, and the symbol $*$ denotes the Hadamard matrix product. The Frobenius norm of a matrix, $\|Y\|_F$, is the square root of the sum of squares of its all elements [15].

Algorithm

As discussed before, the proposed algorithm is in fact to find the best approximation of the original data, $\mathbf{X}_k$. In this manner, the solution to the three-way DEDICOM model is equivalent to an optimization problem, i.e. finding a best approximation to X. To fit the three-way DEDICOM model, we need to tackle the following minimization problem,

$$\min_{\mathbf{A},\mathbf{R},\mathbf{D}} \sum_{k=1}^{m} \left\| \mathbf{X}_k - \mathbf{A}\mathbf{D}_k\mathbf{R}\mathbf{D}_k\mathbf{A}^T \right\|_F^2 \tag{7.8}$$

To solve Eq.7.8, there are a few algorithms. Here Bader et al. [15] proposed an alternating optimization algorithm, which is called ASALSAN (for Alternating Simultaneous Approximation, Least Square, and Newton). The improvement of the algorithm claimed by the authors is the capability of dealing with large and sparse arrays.

The algorithm is composed of one initialization step and three updating steps. The initialization step starts with randomly selecting $\mathbf{A}$, $\mathbf{R}$ and $\mathbf{D}_k = \mathbf{I}$. Then the algorithm updates $\mathbf{A}$, $\mathbf{R}$ and $\mathbf{D}$ in an alternating manner as follows.

- Updating $\mathbf{A}$: First obtain all front slices of X by stacking the data side by side, i.e. $\mathbf{X}_k$, $k = 1, \cdots, m$; then update $\mathbf{A}$ with the following formula:

$$A \leftarrow \left[\sum_{k=1}^{m} \left(X_k A D_k R^T D_k + X_k^T A D_k R D_k \right) \right]_{normalized} \tag{7.9}$$

- Updating **A**: vectorizing X and **R**, and stacking them in an array such that the optimization criterion of Eq.7.8 is changed to

$$f(R) = \left\| \begin{pmatrix} Vec(X_1) \\ \cdots \\ Vec(X_m) \end{pmatrix} - \begin{pmatrix} \mathbf{R}_1 \otimes \mathbf{AD}_1 \\ \cdots \\ \mathbf{AD}_m \otimes \mathbf{AD}_m \end{pmatrix} Vec(\mathbf{R}) \right\| \quad (7.10)$$

where $Vec(\mathbf{R})$ is the normalized $\sum_{k=1}^{m} Vec\left(D_k A^T X_k A D_k\right)$.

- Updating **D**: by alternating over various slices $\mathbf{D}_k$, and holding **A** and **R**, the following minimization condition is reached

$$\min_{D_k} \sum_{k=1}^{m} \left\| X_k - AD_k RD_k A^T \right\|_F^2 \quad (7.11)$$

The algorithm runs iteratively until a convergence is reached, i.e. $f(\mathbf{A},\mathbf{R},\mathbf{D}) / \|X\|_F^2$ does not change any more according to a threshold value or the maximum number of iteration is executed. in the other words, the iterative execution of the algorithm makes the optimization criterion satisfactory and converged to a stable value.

7.2.3 Examples of Formed Community

In [15], two applications are investigated to demonstrate the temporal analysis of the social network structure. The first is a small case of international trade data and the second one is a relatively large email communications within the Enron corporation that are publicly available during the federal investigation.

The world trade data consists of import/export data among 18 nations in European, North American, and the Pacific Rim countries from 1981 to 1990. A semantic graph of this data is corresponding to a densely connected adjacency array X of size $18 \times 18 \times 10$. The Enron email communication data contains 34,427 emails communicated between 184 email addresses during 44 months from 13-Nov-1998 to 21-Jun-2002. The final processed data is a graph corresponding to a sparse adjacency array X of size $184 \times 184 \times 44$. On these two semantic graphs, the authors employed the proposed algorithm to analyze the semantic network structures and the temporal shifts of the networks.

First, let's see the aggregated networks derived from the international trade dataset. Figure 7.9 depicts the aggregated trade patterns (or trade networks) in terms of **R** matrix. It is seen from Fig.7.9 that three major latent components corresponding to mostly three geographical regions, namely North America, Europe and Japan, are revealed from the analysis of **R** and **A** matrices. There are dense self cycle connections within North American or European countries, indicating the higher international trade amongst the countries within these two regions. And the trade patterns amongst different regions are asymmetric. For example, the export trade amount of North America to Europe is bigger than that in reverse direction. In addition, Fig.7.10 gives the scales in **D** for different trade regions, which indicate the temporal changes of commerce over time. Interestingly, the increase of scale of Japan during the middle 80's provides evidence of Japanese economic booming during that period. For Enron dataset, Fig.7.11 indicates the four latent user roles are captured from the communications' frequencies and directional modes (i.e. sender/recipients). During the period, the email conversations within legal parties or Executive and Government Affairs. And again, the communication is dramatically asymmetric in that the r_{23} is significantly larger than r_{32}. Figure 7.12 talks about the comparisons of communication patterns among the four roles between October 2000 to

	#1	#2	#3
#1 North America	4589	187	178
#2 Europe	126	896	89
#3 Japan	60	168	37

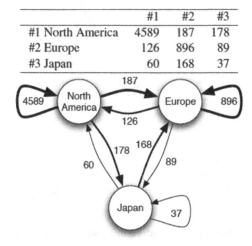

Fig. 7.9. The results of world trade patterns [15]

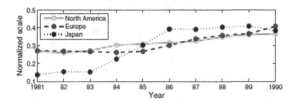

Fig. 7.10. The temporal changes of trade over time [15]

October 2001. The interesting finding from this figure is that the intra-role communications in the government affairs and legal parties substantially decrease over this time period, while it increases in the executive and pipeline roles due to the fact of being investigated. More insights discovered could be further found in [15]. In summary, the proposed three-way decomposition algorithm provides a useful means for capturing the latent aggregated components and the temporal analysis.

7.3 Analysis of Communities and Their Evolutions in Dynamic Networks

For many social network datasets, the commonly used representation is graph model, where the nodes denote the individual members and the edges represent the relationships and interaction between the nodes. For example, a co-authorship network could be modeled as an undirected graph, each node representing one specific author while the edge between two nodes giving the co-authorship fact. In such applications, thus, one important typical task of social network analysis is finding the communities embedded in the social network datasets, and moreover, analyzing the evolutions of the communities in dynamic networks. The evolution pattern as one kind of temporal analysis aspect sometimes could provide us an interesting

	#1	#2	#3	#4
#1 (Legal)	440.2	13.4	-7.9	-5.6
#2 (Exec/Gov't Affairs)	13.8	286.7	157.8	0.4
#3 (Executive)	-23.6	93.5	211.6	-4.8
#4 (Pipeline)	-4.8	-5.9	-6.5	172.4

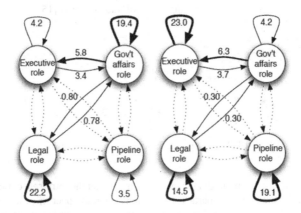

Fig. 7.11. The results of Enron email communication patterns [15]

Fig. 7.12. The communication pattern change in October (pre-crisis, left) and October 2001 (during crisis, right) of Enron [15]

insight from the perspective of social behavior. Recently, a considerable amount researches have been done on this topic. In this section, we will present an innovative solution on this proposed by Lin et al.[164].

7.3.1 Motivation

In tradition analysis of social network analysis, the network analyzed is usually associated with a *static* graph, where the graph is either derived from aggregating the data subjects or taken as a frozen snapshot of data at a specific time stamp. Such kinds of approaches have been broadly adopted in many studies, ranging from well known social network analysis [250] to state-of-the-art applications [137]. The treatment of network as a static model will of course simplify the analysis difficulty. However, it undoubtedly deteriorates the analysis quality of outcomes. The reason is that one of the essential and crucial aspect of social networks, i.e. their dynamic feature, is not fully taken into account. This leads to the major analytical limitations of traditional social network analysis techniques.

Recently there has been an increasing number of studies on the analysis of communities and their evolutions in *dynamic* networks [13, 144, 155, 244]. However, a common weakness of these approaches is the split of analysis process on communities and their evolutions. The commonly observed process is that after a set of community structures are independently determined from the consecutive timestamps, then the evolutions of these community structures are analyzed to reveal the evolutionary characteristics. In such a manner, the coherent connections between the communities have not been fully and simultaneously considered in the community finding, resulting in the incapability of temporal analysis in dynamic networks. Lin et al. [164] proposed a unified framework of social network detecting and evolution analysis to address this.

7.3.2 Problem Formulation

To model the networked data with discrete timestamps, we first use a snapshot graph to represent the interactions between nodes at a specific timestamp t, i.e. $G_t(V_t, E_t)$, where each node $v_i \in V_t$ denotes an individual and each edge $e_{ij} \in E_t$ denotes the presence of interaction between v_i and v_j. Suppose G_t has n nodes, we generate a matrix $W \in R^{n \times n}$ to represent the similarity between nodes in G_t. $w_{ij} > 0$ if $e_{ij} \in E_t$, otherwise $w_{ij} = 0$, and $\sum_{i,j} w_{ij} = 1$. Thus for a set of discrete timestamps, we obtain a sequence of snapshot graphs $\{G_1, \cdots, G_t, \cdots\}$.

Formulation

The main idea of the proposed approach is to analyze communities and their evolutions in a unified fashion. To fulfill this, the community structure found by the approach is via such a process that the evolution from time stamp $t - 1$ to t is not unreasonably dramatic but following a certain criterion. That is, we propose to use the community structure at timestamp $t - 1$ (already extracted) to regularize the community structure at time stamp t (to be extracted). To measure the community quality at time stamp t, here a cost function is introduced as follows, which consists of two components - a snapshot cost and a temporal cost [49].

$$\cos t = \alpha \cdot CS + (1 - \alpha) CT \tag{7.12}$$

In this cost function, the snapshot cost CS measures how well the snapshot graph characterizes the interaction between the individuals, i.e. the matrix W. The temporal cost CT reveals how consistently the community structure evolves from the historic state (i.e. $t - 1$) to the current state t.

Snapshot Cost

The aim of snapshot cost is to allow the community structure found at time stamp t as close as possible to matrix W. Below we describe how to compute the difference between the W and the found community structure.

Assume there exist m communities at time stamp t. The derived interaction magnitude w_{ij} from the given community structure is a combined effect of all the m communities, which is approximated as $w_{ij} \approx \sum_{k=1}^{m} p_k \cdot p_{k \to i} \cdot p_{k \to j}$, where p_k is the prior probability that the interaction due to the k-th community, $p_{k \to i}$ and $p_{k \to j}$ are the probabilities that an interaction in community k involves nodes v_i and v_j, respectively. Written in a form of matrix, it changes to $W \approx X\Lambda X^T$, where $X \in R^{n \times m}$ is a non-negative matrix with $x_{ik} = p_{k \to i}$ and $\sum_i x_{ik} = 1$. Λ is a $m \times m$ nonnegative matrix with $\lambda_k = p_k$ [267]. As such, the interaction (i.e. similarity) matrix W is approximated via the community structures.

Based on above formulations, the snapshot cost CS is defined as the error introduced by such an approximation, i.e.,

$$CS = D\left(W \,\middle\|\, X\Lambda X^T\right) \tag{7.13}$$

where $D(A \| B)$ is the KL-divergence between distribution A and B.

Temporal Cost

As discussed above, the community structure is formulated by $X\Lambda$. The temporal cost means the community structure change from time stamp $t-1$ to t, thus it is measured by the difference between the community structures at two states, i.e.,

$$CT = D(X_{t-1}\Lambda_{t-1} \| X\Lambda) \tag{7.14}$$

A Combined Cost

By combining the snapshot cost and temporal cost into a unified scheme, we eventually formulate the analysis of communities and their evolutions as an optimization problem of best community structure at time stamp t, which is expressed by X and Λ. Apparently, the minimization of the following equation leads to the final solution.

$$cost = \alpha \cdot D\left(W \,\middle\|\, X\Lambda X^T\right) + (1-\alpha) \cdot D(X_{t-1}\Lambda_{t-1} \| X\Lambda) \tag{7.15}$$

7.3.3 Algorithm

To solve the above optimization, the authors used an iterative algorithm by updating the values of X and λ alternatively until the Eq.7.15 converges. The algorithm works as follows:

- Updating X given W, X and λ

$$x_{ik} \leftarrow x_{ik} \cdot 2\alpha \cdot \sum_j \frac{w_{ij} \cdot \lambda_k \cdot x_{jk}}{(X\Lambda X^T)_{ij}} + (1-\alpha) \cdot y_k \tag{7.16}$$

then normalize such that $\sum_i x_{ik} = 1, \forall k$

- Updating λ given updated X

$$\lambda_k \leftarrow \lambda_k \cdot \alpha \cdot \sum_j \frac{w_{ij} \cdot \lambda_k \cdot x_{jk}}{(X\Lambda X^T)_{ij}} + (1-\alpha) \cdot \sum_i y_{ik} \tag{7.17}$$

then normalize such that $\sum_k \lambda_k = 1$

It is proved that the iterative running of the algorithm that updating X and Λ alternatively results in the monotonic decrease of the cost function. More detailed regarding the proof is referred to [164].

7.3.4 Community Discovery Examples

In [164], an interesting result given is based on a NEC blog dataset. The blog data was collected by an NEC in-house crawler. The crawled blog dataset contains 148,681 entry-to-entry links between 407 blogs over 12 consecutive month (one month corresponds to one time stamp in the networked dataset) between August 2005 and September 2006. To determine the number of communities, *Soft Modularity* metric [191] is introduced to measure the goodness of the communities derived. The larger the soft modularity value the better result of community partition is obtained. Thus first the blog dataset is transformed into a single networked graph and its soft modularity values Q_s are calculated and plotted in Fig.7.13(a). As seen from the figure, a clear peak of Q_s is located at the community number being 4. Then, based on this optimized community number, four aggregated community structures were extracted by using the graph partition algorithm [164], which are shown in Fig.7.13. In addition to the aggregated commu-

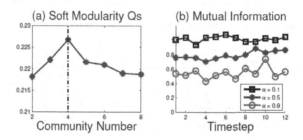

Fig. 7.13. (a) Soft modularity and (b) mutual information under different α for the NEC dataset [164]

nity structures, in Fig.7.14 the top keywords measured by the *tf/idf* scores that contained in four corresponding communities are listed as well. Furthermore, by interpreting the top keywords (i.e. the representatives of communities), we can see the essential properties of various communities. For example, $C1$ is about technology, $C2$ about politics, $C3$ about entertainment, and $C4$ about digital libraries [164]. With the derived community structures as ground truth of communities, the proposed algorithm is employed to determine the community memberships by taking the evolutions of community into consideration. By comparing the difference of the ground truth and dynamically extracted results, the mutual information between them is plotted in Fig.7.13(b) under different α values. The plots indicate that when α increases, emphasizing less on the temporal smoothness, the extracted community structures are much deviated from the ground truth at each time stamp and have high variation over time. As a result, the concluded results reveal the dynamic evolutions of communities in-depth, which again justifies the strong capability of social network analysis in dynamic environments. More analysis insights are seen in [164].

7.4 Socio-Sense: A System for Analyzing the Societal Behavior from Web Archive

M. Kitsuregawa et al. [136] introduce a Socio-Sense Web analysis system. The system applies structural and temporal analysis methods to long term Web archive to obtain insight into the

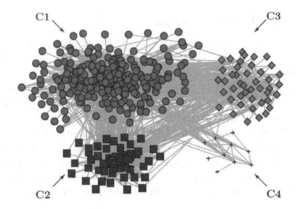

Fig. 7.14. Four aggregated communities derived from the NEC dataset [164]

C1	adsense, beta, skype, firefox, msn, rss, aol, yahoo, google, ebay, desktop, wordpress, voip, feeds, myspace, podcasting, technorati, search, engine, browser, ads, gmail, windows, os, developer, venture, marketing, apple, podcasts, developers, engines, mac, publishers, ceo, linux
C2	gop, uranium, hezbollah, democrats, rove, cia, republicans, saddam, qaeda, tax, republican, iraqi, roberts, bush, clinton, iraq, senate, troops, terrorists, administration, terrorist, wilson, conservative, taxes, liberal, intelligence, israel, terror, iran, weapons, war, soldiers
C3	shanghai, robots, installation, japan, japanese, architecture, art, chinese, china, saudi, phones, filed, mobile, games, korea, rfid, sex, green, camera, sound, cell, body, africa, phone, entertainment, film, gay, india, fuel, archive, design, elections, flash, device, water, wireless, south
C4	library, learning, digital, resources, collection, conference, staff, communities, students, session, books, database, access, survey, university, science, canada, myspace, articles, education, technologies, knowledge, filed, virtual, tools, research, david, learn, services, flickr, computers

Fig. 7.15. Top keywords contained in the four aggregated communities derived from the NEC dataset [164]

real society. They present an overview of the system and core methods followed by excerpts from case studies on consumer behavior analyses.

Socio-Sense is a system for analyzing the societal behavior based on exhaustive Web information, regarding the Web as a projection of the real world. The Web is inundated with information issued from companies, governments, groups, and individuals, and various events in the real world tend to be reflected on the Web very quickly. Understanding the structure of the cyber space and keeping track of its changes will bring us deep insight into the background and the omen of real phenomena. Such insight cannot be achieved with current search engines, which mainly focus on providing plain facts.

The system has been developed from the ground up in the following directions:

1. Web archive consisting of 9 years' worth of Japanese-centric Web contents, which enable long term historical analyses.
2. Web structure analysis methods based on graph mining algorithms and natural language processing techniques. By grouping topically related Web pages, one can browse and navigate the cyber space at a macroscopic level. On the other hand, microscopic information such as product reputations can also be identified.

3. Web temporal analysis methods to capture events in the cyber space such as emergence, growth, decay, and disappearance of some topic, or split and merger among topics.

The above elements have been integrated into the system to conduct case studies assuming corporate users' needs, such as tracking of reputations of brands or companies, grasping of consumer preferences, and analysis of consumers' lifestyles.

7.4.1 System Overview

At the base of the system is the Web archive, which consists of Japanese-centric Web contents [237] and their derivatives accumulated in a bunch of storage devices. The archived contents span 9 years now.

The Web archive started as a mere collection of yearly snapshots obtained from each run of a batch-mode crawler, and has evolved towards a general temporal database, where new versions of each Web page are independently appended. The associated crawler, which keeps running on a bunch of servers, now operates in the continuous mode, estimating update intervals of Web pages to visit them adaptively. As a result, the minimum time resolution between versions has been reduced to a day.

The URL-time index of the Web archive supports tracking of history of a URL, and cross-cutting of whole URLs at arbitrary times. Contents of different periods can be uniformly searched with full text queries. Thus, history of occurrence frequency of specific words can be easily obtained.

Though the Web archive supports exporting of its subset in one of general archive formats such as tar, the system tightly couples the Web archive with an analysis cluster to avoid overhead of moving around huge amount of data. With this parallel scanning mechanism, contents are extracted from the Web archive and dispatched on the fly to one of the cluster nodes, where an instance of application-specific content processing loop is running. The system also takes care of load balancing among the cluster nodes.

The results of the analyses are significantly reduced in size compared with their input, but they tend to be still too complicated to present on space-limited desktop screens. Thus, they built a display wall with 5k x 3k pixels to visualize complex results nicely. Figure 7.16 shows the display wall showing the results from structural and temporal analyses which are described next.

7.4.2 Web Structural Analysis

Topically related Web pages tend to be connected with relatively large number of hyper-links and reside topologically near in the Web graph. Leveraging this property, they obtained sets of related pages by extracting dense subgraphs from the whole Web space. Each set of related pages is called a Web community. Subgraphs dense enough to comprise Web communities are commonly observed in various areas, from home pages of companies in the same category of industry, to personal pages mentioning the same hobbies.

After having extracted the Web communities exhaustively, communities were linked to each other according to the sparse part of the Web graph. This resulted in an associative graph with communities as nodes and degrees of relationship among communities as edges. This high level graph is called a community chart and serves as a map of the cyber space in terms of communities. Figure 7.17 is a subset of the community chart which relates to a term "computer".

Fig. 7.16. Display wall at the front end of the system

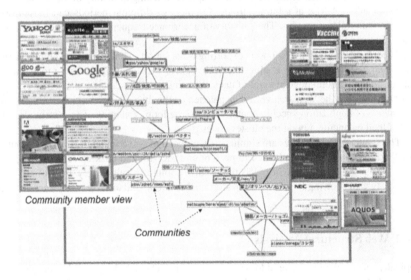

Fig. 7.17. Community chart on "computers"

Each rectangle represents a community and related communities are connected with links. Member pages are also shown for four communities, namely computer hardware vendor community, software vendor community, security information/vendor community, and portal/search engine community (from right-bottom to lefttop). This can be regarded as inter-industry relationship exposed on the Web. A graphical frontend is provided to explore the community chart, modifying the visible communities and their layout interactively.

In addition to the relationships among Web pages, it is also important to analyze textual data in the Web pages themselves. One challenge is reputation extraction. The Web text

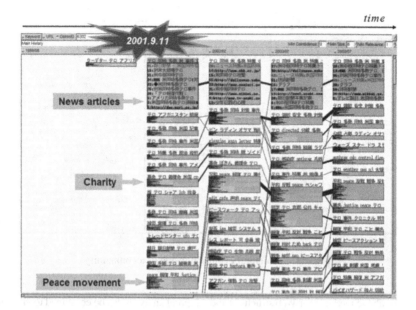

Fig. 7.18. Evolution of communities on "terror"

contains consumer-originated reputations of products and companies, which are useful for marketing purpose. However, extracting reputations is not trivial. It requires huge lexicon that exhaustively lists up affective words and phrases, and it is costly or even impractical to build such lexicon by hand. To tackle this problem, M. Kitsuregawa et al. [136] employed linguistic patterns and a statistical measure in order to automatically build the lexicon from the Web archive [131]. Using this lexicon they developed a reputation extraction tool. In this tool, reputations of a query are extracted from the archive and displayed to users. Besides original texts, the number of positive/negative reputations and facets on topic are also presented. These functions provide users brief overview of the result.

7.4.3 Web Temporal Analysis

By arranging community charts derived for different times side-by-side, the evolution process of the same communities can be tracked. Linking communities of different times can be accomplished by regarding the member URL set as the identity of a community. Some URLs join and leave a community over time, and sometimes communities split and merge. The lack of counterpart of a community implies emergence or disappearance of the community.

Figure 7.18 shows a screenshot of a tool for visualizing the evolution process of communities. Each column corresponds to different times and each rectangle represents a community with its member URLs shown inside. Inter-community links between adjacent time slots are depicted instead of links within each time slice. This example reveals that right after the September 11 attacks, terror-related communities emerged abruptly. The method can be applied to investigate emeregence of new information, transitions of topics, and sociological phenomena.

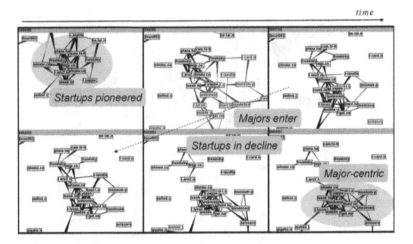

Fig. 7.19. Structural evolution inside of a community

The above methods for Web structural and temporal analyses can be combined to visualize the evolution of graph structures themselves [245]. This is most useful for Web graphs at page granularity in that subgraphs not dense enough to form a community can be captured. The characteristics of graph structures can be observed at embryonic stage of community formation and at stage of community growth.

Figure 7.19 shows evolution of the graph structure inside Japanese mobile search engine communities. Each of 6 panes displays the graph structure at the corresponding time. Each pane is layed out in a "synchronized" manner, where corresponding pages (nodes) are located at similar positions in each pane. What has happened at each stage can be easily identified by interactively manipulating the graphs. At the early stage, search services for mobile phones in Japan were mainly provided by startups or individuals. It can be observed that, however, after major companies entered the industry, the center of the community has gradually moved to such companies.

A lot of new words are born and die every day on the Web. It is interesting to observe and analyze dynamics of new words from linguistic perspective. To analyze the dynamics of words, the frequency of new words in each year is estimated. Because Japanese does not have word separator and it is often difficult for conventional technique to accurately estimate the frequency of new words, Support Vector Machine (SVM) is employed to extract new verbs and adjectives from the Web. Since verbs and adjectives usually inflect regularly, character n-gram was used as features of SVM.

Figure 7.20 shows evolution of new verb gugu-ru (Google in Japanese). The y-axis represents the normalized frequency in the Web archive.It can be seen that gugu-ru has become popular in recent years although it was not frequently used in 1999.

7.4.4 Consumer Behavior Analysis

Prevalence of blogs drastically reduced the burden for individuals to express their opinions or impressions, and blogs have been recognized as an influential source for decision making of individuals because blogs have agility and reality in contrast to information originated in

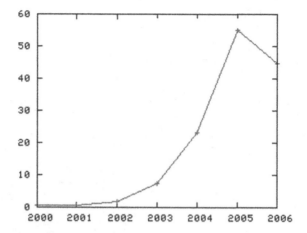

Fig. 7.20. Evolution of new verb gugu-ru (Google in Japanese)

companies and mass media. Companies also start recognizing significance of blogs as a tool for grasping consumers' behavior and for communicating with consumers more intimately.

Because of this situation, the methods for Web structural and temporal analyses are applied to analysis of consumer behavior based on blog information. As a consequence, a visualization tool is obtained for inter-blog links. This tool can visualize link structure at arbitrary time, which can be intuitively adjusted with a slide bar. The temporal evolution of link relationships can be easily replayed [246].

Considering inter-blog links as an indication of topic diffusion, it can be observed how word-of-mouth information has spread out via blogs. For example, we succeeded in identifying a source blog for a book which got drastic popularity gain through WOM. Figure 7.21 shows temporal changes in links to the source blog (circled). It can be observed that, over time, the site gets more and more links.

For companies, it's more important to figure out how they and their products are perceived. Figure 7.22 shows a link structure among blog entries and Web sites of commodity brands in the same industry. Blogs mentioning (linking to) a brand gather around the brand's site. Thus, attractive brands can be easily identified (in this case, brands A and C).

In conclusion, Socio-Sense system combines the long term Web archive, graph mining algorithms, and natural language processing techniques enabled the system to figure out structure and evolution process of the cyber space. Through various case studies, it is demonstrated that the proposed system is effective for understanding behavior of the society and people.

Summary

In this chapter, we have reported the main recent progresses of social network analysis from the perspective of data mining and machine learning. The research issues of extracting, detecting and analyzing Web social networks have been intensively addressed. A considerable attention has been given to the temporal and evolution analysis of Web networked structures. The real world case study described in this chapter highlights the emphasis of application potential in future time.

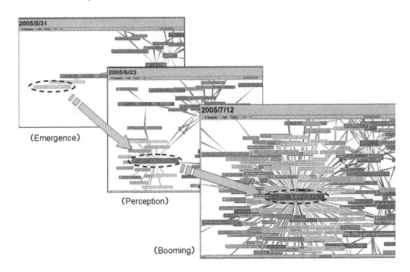

Fig. 7.21. Popularity evolution of a WOM source

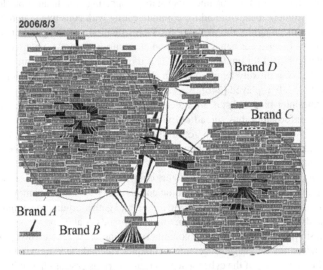

Fig. 7.22. Comparison of commodity brands

8

Web Mining and Recommendation Systems

In last chapter, we have selectively addressed several interesting topics on Web community and social network detecting, forming and analysis, especially temporal and evolutionary analysis. We have discussed the motivations of such kinds of techniques, the algorithmic issues, and the experimental studies as well as the insightful findings and results. In this chapter, we will shift to another important application of Web data mining: Web recommendation.

8.1 User-based and Item-based Collaborative Filtering Recommender Systems

Nowadays the Internet has been well known as a big data repository consisting of a variety of data types as well as a large amount of unseen informative knowledge, which can be discovered via a wide range of data mining or machine learning paradigms. Although the progress of the Web-based data management research results in developments of many useful Web applications or services, like Web search engines, users are still facing the problems of information overload and drowning due to the significant and rapid growth in amount of information and the number of users. In particular, Web users usually suffer from the difficulties of finding desirable and accurate information on the Web due to two problems of low precision and low recall caused by above reasons.

Web (data) mining could be partly used to solve the problems mentioned above directly or indirectly. In principle, Web mining is the means of utilizing data mining methods to induce and extract useful information from Web data information. By utilizing the informative knowledge learned from Web mining, we can substantially improve the Web search performance and user satisfaction. Additionally, another most promising technique for this is Web recommendation.

Web recommendation or personalization could be viewed as a process that recommends customized Web presentation or predicts tailored Web content to Web users according to their specific tastes or preferences. To-date, there are two kinds of approaches commonly used in recommender systems, namely content-based filtering and collaborative filtering systems [81, 117]. Content-based filtering systems such as WebWatcher [129] and client-side agent Letizia [163] usually generate recommendation based on the pre-constructed user profiles by measuring the similarity of Web content to these profiles, while collaborative filtering systems make recommendation by referring other users' preference that is closely similar to current

G. Xu et al., *Web Mining and Social Networking*,
DOI 10.1007/978-1-4419-7735-9_8, © Springer Science+Business Media, LLC 2011

one. Recently collaborative filtering has been widely adopted in Web recommendation applications and have achieved great successes as well [116, 139, 224]. In the following sections, we first present introductions on collaborative filtering based recommender systems.

8.1.1 User-based Collaborative Filtering

The basic idea of collaborative filtering (CF) based recommendation algorithm is to provide item recommendation or prediction based on the common opinion of other like-minded users. The opinion of users is usually expressed explicitly by user rating or implicitly by other implicit measures. As such user rating data is the most common data format used in CF-based algorithm. Below let's first look at the data organization of user rating data.

User Rating Data Format and Collaborative Filtering Process

Since a collaborative filtering algorithm makes recommendation based on the user's previous likings and the choosing of other like-minded users, the data format used in CF-based algorithm provides a fundamental start to understand the collaborative filtering process. Given a typical CF scenario, there are a collection of m users $U = \{u_1, u_2, \cdots, u_m\}$ and a collection of n items $I = \{i_1, i_2, \cdots, i_n\}$. The favorite degree of each item i_j by user u_i is explicitly given by a *rating score*, generally represented by a certain numerical scale, e.g. a scale range of 1-5. In this fashion, the relationships between users and items are modeled as two-way matrix, where each row corresponds to a user u_i and each column an item i_j. The entry of user u_i on item i_k denotes the favorite degree (i.e. rating scale). Figure 8.1 gives the schematic diagram of the rating data format as well as the collaborative filtering process [218]. Note that in the rating matrix, if the user did not rate the item yet, the corresponding scale score is set to 0. As shown in the figure, the aim of collaborative filtering process could be prediction: assigning a numerical score, expressing the predicted likeliness of each item the target user did not rate yet; or recommendation: presenting a list of top-N items that the target user will like the most but did not rate before. In the context of collaborative filtering, there are usually two main categories

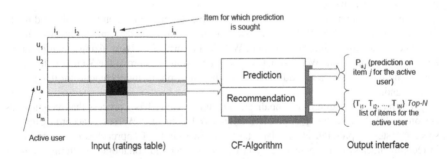

Fig. 8.1. The user rating data and CF process [218]

of algorithms - *Memory-based (User-based)* and *Model-based (Item-based)* algorithm. In this part, we first briefly discuss the principle of the former one.

Memory-based algorithm starts from the whole user-item database to make predictions. These systems employ statistical learning techniques to determine a set of users, known as neighbors, who have the similar intent or preference to the target user (i.e. like-minded users). After the neighborhood of the target user is determined, the historic preference of the like-minded users are utilized to make a prediction or recommend a list of top-N items to the target user. Since the main idea of such techniques are based on the preference of nearest neighbors (or like-minded users), it is also called as *nearest-neighbor* or user-based collaborative filtering. User-based CF algorithms are popular and widely used in a variety of applications [212].

Major Challenges of Memory-based CF Algorithms

Although user-based collaborative filtering algorithms have been successful in practice, they suffer from some potential challenges exhibited in real applications, such as

- Sparsity: In practice, the rating datasets used in recommender systems are extremely big, probably containing several hundred thousands users and millions of item. In these systems, however, even active users may have chosen to rate or purchase a very small ratio of total items or products, saying well below 1%. This makes the collected rating datasets very sparse, resulting in the big challenges to such recommender systems. Thus a recommender system based on user-based CF may be unable to make any item recommendation for any user, and the performance of recommendations may be quite limited.
- Scalability: User-based CF algorithms need to compute the nearest neighbors in a huge space of millions users and millions items. And the consistent growth of user and item number due to the commercial expansion adds the extra computational difficulties to the recommendations. The scalability problems suffer the user-based CF recommender systems significantly.

8.1.2 Item-based Collaborative Filtering Algorithm

The item-based (or model-based) algorithms were first proposed by Sarwar et al. [218]. The main idea of the approach is to calculate the similarity between different items based on the user-item rating data and then to compute the prediction score for a given item based on the calculated similarity scores. The intuition behind the proposed approach is that a user would be interested in items that are similar to the items, which the user has exhibited interests or purchased before. Thus in order to make recommendations, an item similarity (or an equivalent model) matrix needs to learn first or the recommendation is based on item computation. From the perspective of data analysis target, such approach is named item-based or model-based collaborative filtering.

Since the item similarity matrix is computed in advance and no nearest neighbor computation needs, item-based CF approach has the less significant scalability problems and is fast in running the recommendations. Thus item-based CF approach has shown strength in practice [41, 185, 212]. In the following part, we will discuss the item-based collaborative filtering algorithm reported in [218].

Item Similarity Computation

There are a number of different measures to compute the similarity between two items, such as cosine-based, correlation-based and adjusted cosine-based similarity. Below the definitions of them are given respectively [17, 218].

Cosine-based Similarity

In this case, two items are treated as two vectors in the form of m-dimensional user space. The similarity between two items i and j is formulated as the cosine of the angle between two vectors:

$$sim(i,j) = \cos\left(\vec{i}, \vec{j}\right) = \frac{\vec{i} \cdot \vec{j}}{\left\|\vec{i}\right\|_2 \times \left\|\vec{j}\right\|_2} \tag{8.1}$$

where "·" denotes the dot product of two vectors.

Correlation-based Similarity

In this case, similarity between two items i and j is computed by the *Pearson* correlation $corr_{ij}$ coefficient. To calculate it, the user set who co-rated both item i and j are chosen. Let the user set be U the the correlation coefficient is defined by

$$sim(i,j) = corr_{ij} = \frac{\sum_{u \in U}\left(R_{u,i} - \overline{R_i}\right)\left(R_{u,j} - \overline{R_j}\right)}{\sqrt{\sum_{u \in U}\left(R_{u,i} - \overline{R_i}\right)^2 \sum_{u \in U}\left(R_{u,j} - \overline{R_j}\right)^2}} \tag{8.2}$$

where $R_{u,i}$ denotes the rating score on item i by user u, $\overline{R_i}$ is the average rating of the ith item.

Adjusted Cosine Similarity

In the case of cosine-based similarity computation, one possible problem existed in the calculation is that the difference in rating score between different users are not fully taken into consideration, which brings in the biased weights to the users who always made higher rating scores. To overcome such rating score bias, an adjust cosine-based similarity is introduced to offset the impact of relative rating score difference by subtracting the corresponding user average from each co-rated item pair. Thus the similarity between two item i and j is given by

$$sim(i,j) = \frac{\sum_{u \in U}\left(R_{u,i} - \overline{R_u}\right)\left(R_{u,j} - \overline{R_u}\right)}{\sqrt{\sum_{u \in U}\left(R_{u,i} - \overline{R_u}\right)^2 \sum_{u \in U}\left(R_{u,j} - \overline{R_u}\right)^2}} \tag{8.3}$$

where $\overline{R_u}$ is the average score of the uth user's rating.

Prediction Computation

After defining the similarity measures, they can be used to compute the prediction or recommendation scores. Here, the authors of [218] proposed two methods, namely weighted sum and regression.

Weighted Sum

The weighted sum scheme is to calculate the final rating score of an item i for the target user u by averaging the sum of the total rating scores of items that are similar to item i given by the user. And each rating is weighted by the corresponding similarity s_{ij} between item i and j. The predicted rating score of item i is defined by

$$P_{u,i} = \frac{\sum_{j \in I_i} \left(sim\left(i,j\right) \times R_{u,j} \right)}{\sum_{j \in I_i} \left(\left| sim\left(i,j\right) \right| \right)} \tag{8.4}$$

where I_i is the set items that are similar to item i, $\|$ denotes the size of the set. The illustration of item-based collaborative filtering algorithm is depicted in Fig.8.2. Actually it is further concluded that the weighted sum approach predicts the overall rating preference of the target item for the user by referring to the similar items determined by analyzing the co-rating data.

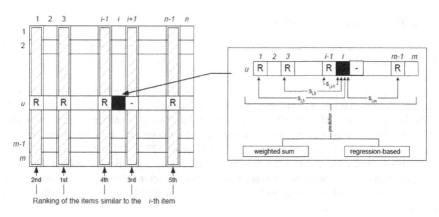

Fig. 8.2. The item-based collaborating filtering recommendation process [218]

Regression

This approach follows the similar prediction principle but with different calculation strategy. Instead of using the "raw" rating scores of similar items in computing the weighted sum, this approach uses an approximation of the ratings based on regression model. The initiated motivation behind is the fact that in practice even the calculated similarity between two items using cosine or correlation is quite high, the rating vectors may be distant (in Euclidean space). In this case using the raw rating scores of the similar items may result in the poor prediction performance. An intuitive solution is to use formulated rating scores rather than the raw ones of similar item for computing the weighted sum. This process is realized by a linear regression model. If the target item and the similar items are denoted by R_i and R_j respectively, the linear regression model can be expressed as

$$\overline{R'_j} = \alpha \overline{R_i} + \beta + \varepsilon \tag{8.5}$$

The regression model parameters α and β are empirically determined. ε is the regression error.

In comparison to user-based collaborative filtering algorithms, one significant advantage of model-based algorithms is the scalability of the recommendations. In user-based CF (or neighborhood-based CF) systems, the neighborhood computation is very time consuming especially in case of larger e-commerce sites, making it almost unsuitable in real time applications. However, model-based CF systems have the potential to be employed recommender systems operating at a large scale. The solid solution to this problem is to separate the whole recommendation process into two stages: one offline stage and one online stage. The model learning is able to train the model (i.e. the item similarity matrix) before the real recommendation making, largely avoiding the computational difficulty and high time cost. Upon the learned model, the further recommendation operation could be performed in a short time period, making the online recommendation feasible and operational. More importantly, such two-stage recommendation scheme has become a well-adopted strategy for many recommender system later. Basically the computational complexity of such model-based CF systems requires an $O(n^2)$ for a setting of n items.

8.1.3 Performance Evaluation

In [218], comprehensive experiments are carried out to evaluate the proposed model-based CF systems. In the following section, we briefly review the experimental setting and some representative results.

The dataset used in the experiments is from the *MovieLens* recommender system. MovieLens is a Web-based research recommender system built up in Fall 1997. Since Sagwar et al. published their work using the MovieLens dataset, later many researchers on recommender system research are continuing the use of this dataset for comparative studies. Even recently some latest recommendation work use it as a benchmark [222]. The dataset chosen for experiments contains 943 users, 1682 movies and 100,000 ratings. For the chosen dataset, a certain percentage of whole dataset is separated for the model training purpose, while the rest of dataset is left out for the test. In the experiments, different separation ratio values x are empirically investigated.

Here we select several experimental results to present. Figure 8.3 depicts the impact of train/test separation ratio values and the neighborhood size on MAE using the two recommendation strategies: item-item weighted sum and regression. Known from the figure, the bigger separation ratio values of train/test dataset always achieve the better recommendation performance, indicating the larger training dataset is essential for an accurate recommendation. While for the selection of neighborhood size, the recommendation accuracy increases when the neighborhood size is becoming bigger, and becomes stable after the neighborhood size reaches a certain value. The observed result implies that an appropriate neighborhood size achieves the best recommendation outcome, suggesting that the choosing a large number of neighbors will only increase the computation cost but not benefit the recommendations. Similarly, in Fig.8.4, the recommendation comparisons of model-based and user-based CF al-

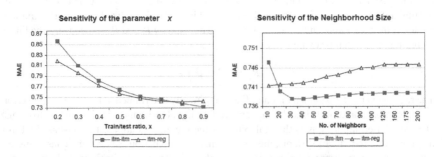

Fig. 8.3. The impact of parameter x and neighborhood size [218]

gorithms are carried out in terms of parameter x and neighborhood size. From the figure, it is seen that the proposed model-based CF algorithms consistently outperform the user-based CF algorithms.

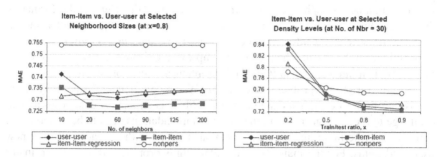

Fig. 8.4. The recommendation comparisons of item-based and user-based collaborative filtering algorithms [218]

8.2 A Hybrid User-based and Item-based Web Recommendation System

In this section, we will introduce a strategy which is the combination of the User-based and Item-based Web recommendation system reported in [212]. Collaborative Filtering (CF)-based recommender systems are indispensable tools to find items of interest from the unmanageable number of available items. Moreover, companies who deploy a CF-based recommender system may be able to increase revenue by drawing customers' attention to items that they are likely to buy. However, many algorithms proposed thus far, where the principal concern is recommendation quality, may be too expensive to operate in a large-scale system. To address this, a hybrid strategy which combine user-based and item-based recommender system is proposed by Rashid et al. [212]. Such strategy is simple and intuitive which is well suited for large data sets. In this section, we discuss CLUSTKNN, a hybrid CF algorithm based on clustering techniques, as a way to overcome this saclability challenge. By applying complexity analysis, we analytically demonstrate the performance advantages that CLUSTKNN has over traditional CF algorithms. In addition, we present some empirical measurements of the performance and recommendation accuracy of CLUSTKNN and several other algorithms.

8.2.1 Problem Domain

As it is introduced in the last section, a collaborative filtering domain consists of a set of n customers of users $\{u_1, u_2, ..., u_n\}$, a set of m products or items $\{a_1, a_2, ..., a_m\}$, and users' preferences on items. Typically, each user only expresses her preferences for a small number of items. In other words, the corresponding *user* × *item* matrix is very sparse.

However, users' preferences can be in terms of *explicit* ratings on some scale including a binary like/dislike, or they can be *implicit*. For instance, a customer's purchase history or her browsing patterns is *implicit*. A recommender system may also maintain demographic and other information about the users, and information about item features such as actors, directors, and genres in the case of a movie. This additional content information can be used to create *user − based(content − based)*filtering[181, 216], which can help improve a CF system, particularly where rating data is limited or absent (Cold start problem-new user or new item).

We now turn to the problem statement. A Web recommender system may easily involve millions of customers and products[165]. This amount of data poses a great challenge to the CF algorithms in that the recommendations need to be generated in real-time. Furthermore, the algorithm also has to cope with a steady influx of new users and items. For the majority of the algorithms proposed to date, the primary emphasis has been given into improving recommendation accuracy. While accuracy is certainly important and can affect the profitability of the company, the operator simply cannot deploy the system if it does not scale to the vast data of the site.

8.2.2 Hybrid User and Item-based Approach

Before we introduce the hybrid approach, we briefly discuss user-based and item-based algorithm and describe how hybrid approach leverages the advantages of both types of algorithms.

There are two workaround in **User-based** recommender system. **One** is to only consider a subset of the preference data in the calculation, but doing this can reduce both recommendation quality and the number of items due to data being omitted from the calculation. **Another** is to perform as much of the computation as possible in an offline setting. However, this may make it difficult to add new users to the system on a real-time basis, which is a basic necessity of most online systems. Furthermore, the storage requirements for the precomputed data could be high.

On the other hand, **Item-based** algorithm is time-consuming and is only done periodically. The disadvantage is that adding new users, items, or preferences can be tantamount to recomputing.

The Hybrid Approach-CLUSTKNN has the advantages from both types. One of the goals is to maintain simplicity and intuitiveness throughout the approach. It is important for the recommendation presentation [227]. This is achieved by utilizing a straightforward *partitional clustering* algorithm [122] for modeling users. A nearest-neighbor algorithm is used to generate recommendations from the learned model. Since the data is greatly compressed after the model is built, recommendations can be computed quickly, which solves the scalability challenge.

The algorithm has a tunable parameter, the number of clusters k which can be adjusted to trade off accuracy for time and space requirements. In addition, the algorithm also has two phases: model building (offline) and generation of predictions or recommendations (online).

Model Building

- Select the number of user-clusters k, considering the effect on the recommendation accuracy and resource requirements.
- Perform BISECTING k−MEANS clustering on the user-preference data.
- Build the model with k *surrogate* users, directly derived from the *kcentroids*: $\{c_1, c_2, ...c_k\}$, where each c_i is a vector of size m, the number of items. That is $c_i = (\tilde{R}_{c_i,a1}, \tilde{R}_{c_i,a2}, ..., \tilde{R}_{c_i,aj})$, where $\tilde{R}_{c_i,aj}$ is the element in the centroid vector c_i corresponding to the item a_j. Further, since $\tilde{R}_{c_i,aj}$ is essentially an average value, it is 0 if nobody in the i-th cluster has rated a_j.

Prediction Generation

In order to compute the rating prediction $\hat{R}_{c_t,at}$ for the target(user, item) pare (u_t, a_t), the following steps are taken.

- Compute similarity of the target user with each of the surrogate model users who have rated a_t using the Pearson correlation coefficient:

$$w_{u_t,c_i} = \frac{\Sigma_{a\in\tau}(R_{u_t,a} - \bar{R}_{u_t})(\tilde{R}_{c_i,a} - \bar{R}_{c_i})}{\sqrt{\Sigma_{a\in\tau}(R_{u_t,a} - \bar{R}_{u_t})^2 \Sigma_{a\in\tau}(\tilde{R}_{c_i,a} - \bar{R}_{c_i})^2}} \tag{8.6}$$

  where τ is the set of items reated by both the target user and i-th surrogate user.
- Find up to l surrogate users most similar to the target user.
- Compute prediction using the adjusted weighted average:

$$\hat{R}_{u_t,a_t} = \bar{R}_{u_t} + \frac{\Sigma_{i=1}^{l}(\tilde{R}_{c_i,a_t} - \bar{R}_{c_i})w_{u_t,c_i}}{\Sigma_{i=1}^{l}w_{u_t,c_i}} \tag{8.7}$$

Note that any *partitionalclustering* [122] techniques can be used for model-building in this hybrid approach. BISECTING k−MEANS is an extension to and an improved version of the basic k-MEANS algorithm. The algorithm starts by considering all data points as a single cluster. Then it repeats the following steps $(k-1)$ times to produce k clusters.

- Pick the largest cluster to split
- Apply the basic k-MEANS (2MEANS , to be exact)clustering to produce 2 sub-clusters.
- Repeat step 2 for j times and take the best split, one way of determining which is looking for the best *intra*-cluster similarity.

At this stage, it is straightforward to derive the time-complexity. Note that the time complexity of CF algorithm can be divided into two parts: one for the offline modeling-building, and the other for the online generation of recommendations.

Time-complexity

The time-complexity of the basic k-MEANS is reported to be $O(n)$ that can be seen in [122]; since the *similarity* or*distance* between the data points and centroids as a constant in the basic one, the time-complexity in Hybrid approach becomes $O(mn)$ because that cost is $O(m)$. So the offline time-complexity of Hybrid approach is $O(mn)$.

During the online stage, $O(k)$ similarity weight calculations are needed for the target user, each of which takes $O(m)$times; so, the online time-complexity is $O(km) \simeq O(m)$

8.2.3 Experimental Observations

In [212], the authors gave the evaluation results of recommendation. The two datasets i.e. ML1N and MLCURRENT used in the experiments are from the same data source described in Sec.8.1. Here we select a few conclusive results presented. Figure 8.5 plots the predictive performance of Hybrid approach - CLUSTKNN both for the metrics *NMAE* and *EU* used in [212], and for both of the datasets. Since such Hybrid approach can be regarded as approximating user-based KNN with the two becoming equivalent when k equals the number of user in the system, we have also included the predictive performance of user-based KNN in the plots a line as the upper bound for such Hybrid approach. It is seen that the hybrid approach of user-based and item-based algorithm consistently outperforms the classic user-based algorithm alone.

8.3 User Profiling for Web Recommendation Based on PLSA and LDA Model

In Chap.6, we have discussed using latent semantic analysis for Web usage mining. The results of Web usage mining are the user profiles that are in the forms of user session clusters. In this section, we will describe how to utilize the user profiles for Web recommendation based on PLSA and LDA model, respectively. In previous sections, we have derived user access patterns and user profiles via a probability inference algorithm. In the following parts, we aim to incorporate the discovered usage knowledge with the collaborative filtering algorithm into the Web recommendation algorithm.

8.3.1 Recommendation Algorithm based on PLSA Model

As discussed in previous sections, Web usage mining will result in a set of user session clusters $SCL = \{SCL_1, SCL_2, \cdots SCL_k\}$, where each SCL_i is a collection of user sessions with similar access preference. And from the discovered user session clusters, we can then generate their corresponding centroids of the user session clusters, which are considered as usage profiles, or user access patterns. The complete formulation of usage profiling algorithm is expressed as follows:

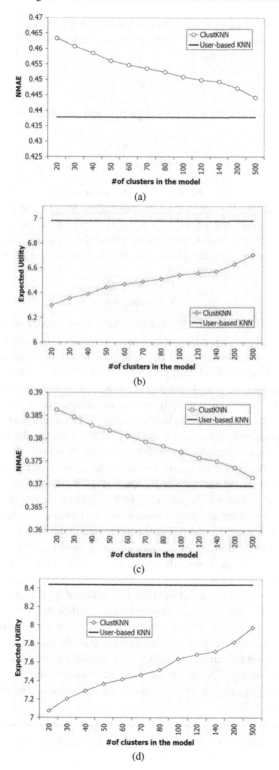

Fig. 8.5. Prediction performance of Hybrid approach:(a)-(b) on ML1M , and (c)-(d) on MLCURRENT dataset. Results of user-based KNN are shown for comparison.

Given a user session cluster SCL_i, the corresponding usage profile of the cluster is represented as a sequence of page weights, which are dependent on the mean weights of all pages engaged in the cluster

$$up_i = \left(w_1^i, w_2^i, \cdots w_n^i\right) \tag{8.8}$$

where the contributed weight, w_j^i, of the page p_j within the user profile up_i is:

$$w_j^i = \frac{1}{|SCL_i|} \sum_{t \in SCL_i} a_{tj} \tag{8.9}$$

And a_{tj} is the element weight of page p_j in user session s_t, $s_t \in SCL_i$. To further select the most significant pages for recommendation, we can use filtering method to choose a set of dominant pages with weights exceeding a certain value as an expression of user profile, that is, we preset a threshold μ and filter out those pages with weights greater than the threshold for constructing the user profile. Given w_j^i, then

$$w_j^i = \begin{cases} w_j^i & w_j^i > \mu \\ 0 & \text{otherwise} \end{cases} \tag{8.10}$$

This process performs repeatedly on each user session cluster and finally generates a number of user profiles, which are expressed by a weighted sequence of pages. These usage patterns are then used into collaborative recommending operation.

Generally, Web recommendation process is to predict and customize Web presentation in a user preferable style according to the interests exhibited by individual or groups of users. This goal is usually carried out in two ways. On the one hand, we can take the current active user's historic behavior or pattern into consideration, and predict the preferable information to this specific user. On the other hand, by finding the most similar access pattern to the current active user from the learned usage models of other users, we can recommend the tailored Web content. The former one is sometime called memory-based approach, whereas the latter one is called model-based recommendation, respectively. In this work, we adopt the model-based technique in our Web recommendation framework. We consider the usage-based user profiles generated in Sect.6.2 and 6.3 as the aggregated representations of common navigational behaviors exhibited by all individuals in same particular user category, and utilize them as a usage knowledge base for recommending potentially visited Web pages to the current user.

Similar to the method proposed in [184] for representing user access interest in the form of n-dimensional weighted page vector, we utilize the commonly used cosine function to measure the similarity between the current active user session and discovered usage pattern. We, then, choose the best suitable profile, which shares the highest similarity with the current session, as the matched pattern of current user. Finally, we generate the top-N recommendation pages based on the historically visited probabilities of the pages by other users in the selected profile. The detailed procedure is described as follows:

Algorithm 8.1: User profiling algorithm for Web recommendation based on PLSA

Input: An active user session s_a and a set of user profiles $up = \{up_j\}$.

Output: The top-N recommendations $REC_{PLSA}(s_a) = \{p_j^{mat} \mid p_j^{mat} \in P, j = 1, \ldots, N\}$.

Step 1: The active session s_a and the discovered user profiles up are viewed as n-dimensional vectors over the page space within a site, i.e. $up_j = [w_1^j, w_2^j, \cdots, w_n^j]$, where w_i^j is the significant weight contributed by page p_i in the up user profile, similarly $s_a = [w_1^a, w_2^a, \cdots w_n^a]$, where $w_i^a = 1$, if page p_i is already accessed, and otherwise $w_i^a = 0$,

Step 2: Measure the similarities between the active session and all derived usage profiles, and choose the maximum one out of the calculated similarities as the most matched pattern:

$$sim(s_a, up_j) = (s_a \cdot up_j)/\|s_a\|_2 \|up_j\|_2 \tag{8.11}$$

where $s_a up_j = \sum_{i=1}^n w_i^j w_i^a$, $\|s_a\|_2 = \sqrt{\sum_{i=1}^n (w_i^a)^2}$, $\|up_j\|_2 = \sqrt{\sum_{i=1}^n (w_i^j)^2}$.

$$sim(s_a, up_{mat}) = \max_j(sim(s_a, up_j)) \tag{8.12}$$

Step 3: Incorporate the selected profile up_{mat} with the active session s_a, then calculate the recommendation score $rs(p_i)$ for each page p_i:

$$rs(p_i) = \sqrt{w_i^{mat} \times sim(s_a, up_{mat})} \tag{8.13}$$

Thus, each page in the profile will be assigned a recommendation score between 0 and 1. Note that the recommendation score will be 0 if the page is already visited in the current session,

Step 4: Sort the calculated recommendation scores in step 3 obtained in a descending order, i.e. $rs = (w_1^{mat}, w_2^{mat}, \cdots, w_n^{mat})$, and select the N pages with the highest recommendation score to construct the top-N recommendation set:

$$REC_{PLSA}(s_a) = \{p_j^{mat} \mid rs(p_j^{mat}) > rs(p_{j+1}^{mat}), j = 1, 2, \cdots N - 1\} \tag{8.14}$$

8.3.2 Recommendation Algorithm Based on LDA Model

In this section, we present a user profiling algorithm for Web recommendation based on LDA generative model. As introduced in Sect.6.2, LDA is one of the generative models, which is to reveal the latent semantic correlation among the co-occurred activities via a generative procedure. Similar to the Web recommendation algorithm proposed in previous section, we, first, discover the usage pattern by examining the posterior probability estimates derived via the LDA model, then, measure the similarity between the active user session and the usage patterns to select the most matched user profile, and eventually make the collaborative recommendation by incorporating usage pattern with collaborative filtering, i.e. referring to other users' visiting preference, who have similar navigational behavior. Likewise, we employ the top-N weighted scoring scheme algorithm in the collaborative recommendation process, to predict user's potentially interested pages via referring to the page weight distribution in the closest access pattern. In the following part, we explain the details of the algorithm.

Given a set of user access models and current active user session, the algorithm of generating the top-N most weighted pages recommendation is outlined as follows:

Algorithm 8.2: User profiling for Web recommendation based on LDA model

---

Input: An active user session s_a, the computed session-topic preference distribution θ and a predefined threshold μ.
Output: The top-N recommendation pages $REC_{lda}(s_a) = \{p_j^{rec}|p_j^{rec} \in P, j = 1, \cdots N - 1\}$.
Step 1: Treat the active session s_a as a n-dimensional vectors: $s_a = [w_1^a, w_2^a, \cdots, w_n^a]$, where $w_i^a = 1$, if page p_i is already clicked, and otherwise $w_i^a = 0$,
Step 2: For each latent topic z_j, choose all user sessions s_i with $\theta_{z_j}^{s_i} \geq \mu$ to construct a user session aggregation R and compute the usage pattern as

$$up_j = \frac{\sum_{s_i \in R} \theta_{z_j}^{s_i} \cdot s_i}{|R|} \tag{8.15}$$

Step 3: Measure the similarities between the active session and all learned user access models, and choose the maximum one out of the calculated similarities as the most closely matched access pattern:

$$sim(s_a, up_j) = (s_a \cdot up_j)/\|s_a\|_2 \|up_j\|_2 \tag{8.16}$$

where $s_a \cdot up_j = \sum_{i=1}^n w_i^a w_i^j$, $\|s_a\|_2 = \sqrt{\sum_{i=1}^n (w_i^a)^2}$, $\|up_j\|_2 = \sqrt{\sum_{i=1}^n (w_i^j)^2}$

$$sim(s_a, up_{rec}) = \max_j(sim(s_a, up_j)) \tag{8.17}$$

Step 4: Refer to the page weight distribution in the most matched access pattern up_{rec}, and calculate the recommendation score $RS(p_i)$ for each page p_i:

$$RS(p_i) = \sqrt{w_i^{rec} \times sim(s_a, up_{rec})} \tag{8.18}$$

Thus, each page in the matched pattern will be assigned a recommendation score between 0 and 1. Note that the recommendation score will be 0 if the page is already visited in the current session,
Step 5: Sort the calculated recommendation scores obtained in step 4 in a descending order, i.e. $RS = (w_1^{rec}, w_2^{rec}, \cdots, w_n^{rec})$, and select the N pages with the top-N highest recommendation scores to construct the top-N recommendation set:

$$REC_{LDA}(s_a) = \{p_j^{rec} | RS(p_j^{rec}) > RS(p_{j+1}^{rec}), j = 1, 2, \cdots N - 1\} \qquad (8.19)$$

8.4 Combing Long-Term Web Achieves and Logs for Web Query Recommendation

The conventional approaches of finding related search engine queries rely on the common terms shared by two queries to measure their relatedness. However, search engine queries are usually short and the term overlap between two queries is very small. Using query terms as a feature space cannot accurately estimate relatedness. Alternative feature spaces are needed to enrich the term based search queries.

Query enrichment is an effective method to find semantically related queries, which enriches the representation of a query by alternative feature spaces, instead of using terms in the query itself. Consequently, how to get suitable feature spaces becomes a key in this method. In this paper, given a search query, first we extract the Web pages accessed by users from Japanese Web access logs which store the users' individual and collective behavior. From these accessed Web pages we usually can get two kinds of feature spaces, i.e, content-sensitive (e.g., nouns) and content-ignorant (e.g., URLs) which can be used to enrich the expressions of search queries. Then, the relatedness between search queries can be estimated on their enriched expressions, e.g., the overlap of their feature spaces. Our experimental results show that the URL feature space produces lower precision scores than the noun feature space which, however, is not applicable, at least in principle, in settings including: non-text pages like multimedia (image) files, Usenet archives, sites with registration requirement, and dynamic pages returned in response to a submitted query and so forth. It is crucial to improve the quality of the URL (content-ignorant) feature space since it is generally available in all types of Web pages. The problem of the URL feature space is that even though two queries share no common URLs in their accessed Web pages, they may be related since Web pages with different URLs may semantically related.

It is important to find a novel content-ignorant feature space for query enrichment. The whole Web can be considered as a graph where nodes are Web pages and edges are hyperlinks. Recent research on link analysis has shown the existence of numerous Web communities [1] The idea given in [157] is that a query can be enriched by the Web communities that the respective accessed Web pages belong to, instead of using the URLs of Web pages directly. Web communities from a Japanese Web page archive are create by only exploiting link analysis, thus they are regarded an alternative content-ignorant feature space. The proposed Web community feature space is novel, different from the traditional URL and noun feature spaces which are

---

[1] In the field of social network, Web community is also used to mean a set of users having similar interests, which slightly differs from the definition in this paper.

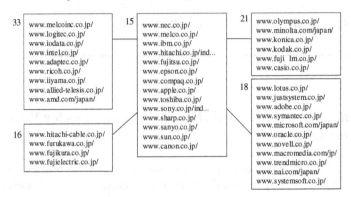

Fig. 8.6. A part of Web community chart

widely used in the literature [16, 25, 61, 68, 253, 259]. Experimental results show that the novel Web community feature space generates much better results than the traditional URL feature space.

It is understandable that even though the URLs of two Web pages are different, their contents may be related. L. Li et al. [157] think if we can cluster related Web pages into a Web community which is a collection of Web pages sharing common interest on a specific topic, each query will be represented by the Web communities which the accessed Web pages belong to. Their experimental results show that the Web community based query enrichment largely improves the precision of finding related queries over the URL based one.

Web communities are created using only linkage information between pages without taking into account the contents of Web pages. This means that a Web page archive is needed to store the hyperlink information among Web pages. These Web pages are not only the accessed Web pages in our access logs, but also other Web pages on the Web during the period of collecting our logs. Thus, Web pages can be clustered using their linkage information. A large-scale snapshot of a Japanese Web page archive they used was built in February 2002. 4.5 million Web pages are crawled. A connectivity database is built to search outgoing and incoming links of a given Web page in the archive. To create Web communities, a manually maintained page list is used as a seed set which includes 4~691 pages of companies, organizations and schools. And the seed set is extended by applying *Companion*– which was described in [243].

A part of the community chart built in [157] is illustrated in Figure 8.6 where the number represents the community ID. In the center of Figure 8.6 there is a major community of computer manufactures (15) surrounded by software (18), peripheral device (33 and 16), and digital camera communities (21). It is understandable that even if there are no common URLs of Web pages shared by two enriched queries, they may be related to some extent provided that some Web pages are clustered into a same Web community, e.g., the different Web pages in the computer manufactures (15) community. Each Web page in our data set is labelled by a community ID. Given the accessed Web pages of a query, their corresponding community IDs compose the Web community feature space of the query.

We give a concrete example to understand their idea clearly. For the two search queries "bank" and "deposit", using the Web community feature space, their enriched representations are got as follow (number denotes Web community ID):

q_{bank}={37652,7968,1105,38251,9650,118781,140963,57665,150439,35392,37750,47811},
$q_{deposit}$={9650,140963,40786,38251,46820,37652,35392,1105}.

Based on our log data, the sum of the weights of all elements in the community space of "bank" is 113 and the sum of "deposit" is 13. Then, the normalized weights of these elements are

$$C_{q_{bank}}=\{\tfrac{7}{113},\tfrac{3}{113},\tfrac{3}{113},\tfrac{2}{113},\tfrac{2}{113},\tfrac{1}{113},\tfrac{1}{113},\tfrac{1}{113},\tfrac{1}{113},\tfrac{1}{113},\tfrac{1}{113},\tfrac{1}{113}\},$$
$$C_{q_{deposit}}=\{\tfrac{2}{13},\tfrac{2}{13},\tfrac{1}{13},\tfrac{1}{13},\tfrac{1}{13},\tfrac{1}{13},\tfrac{1}{13},\tfrac{1}{13}\}.$$

For example, in $\tfrac{7}{113}$, 7 is the value of the occurrences of the Web community 37652 multiplied by the submit times of the query *bank* and 113 is the sum of weights of all the communities in $C_{q_{Bank}}$. The intersection of the two enriched queries includes six communities listed as follows:

$$C_{q_{bank}} \cap C_{q_{deposit}}=\{37652,1105,38251,9650,140963,35392\}.$$

Therefore, the normalized weighted Jaccard score of the two queries, "bank" and "deposit" is: $\frac{0.142+0.615}{2}=0.378$.

The experiments are conducted on a Japanese Web access log data, also called *"panel logs"* which are provided by *Video Research Interactive Inc.*. The collecting method and statistics of this panel logs are described in [194]. The proposed community based feature space shows much better results than the URL based feature space in [157]. Their experimental results show, although the noun feature space can find more related search queries than the URL and Web community spaces, it is not generally available in the case of non-text pages.

8.5 Combinational CF Approach for Personalized Community Recommendation

Social networking products are flourishing. Sites such as MySpace, Facebook, and Orkut attract millions of visitors a day, approaching the traffic of Web search sites [2]. These social networking sites provide tools for individuals to establish communities, to upload and share user generated content, and to interact with other users. In recent articles, users complained that they would soon require a full-time employee to manage their sizable social networks. Indeed, take Orkut as an example. Orkut enjoys 100+ million communities and users, with hundreds of communities created each day. A user cannot possibly view all communities to select relevant ones.

Chen et al. [60] tackle the problem of community recommendation for social networking sites. Such a problem fits in the framework of collaborative filtering (CF), which offers personal recommendations (of e.g., Web sites, books, or music) based on a user's profile and prior information access patterns. What differentiates their

---

[2] Alexa internet. http://www.alexa.com/.

work from prior work is that they propose a fusion method, which combines information from multiple sources. Their method is named as CCF for Combinational Collaborative Filtering. CCF views a community from two simultaneous perspectives: a bag of users and a bag of words. A community is viewed as a bag of participating users; and at the same time, it is viewed as a bag of words describing that community. Traditionally, these two views are independently processed. Fusing these two views provides two benefits. First, by combining bags of users with bags of words, CCF can perform personalized community recommendations, which the bags of words alone model cannot. Second, augmenting bags of users with bags of words, CCF achieves better personalized recommendations than the bags of users alone model, which may suffer from information sparsity.

8.5.1 CCF: Combinational Collaborative Filtering

We start by introducing the baseline models. We then show how our CCF model combines baseline models. Suppose we are given a collection of co-occurrence data consisting of communities $C = \{c_1, c_2, \cdots, c_N\}$, community descriptions from vocabulary $D = \{d_1, d_2, \cdots, d_V\}$, and users $U = \{u_1, u_2, \cdots, u_M\}$. If community c is joined by user u, we set $n(c, u) = 1$; otherwise, $n(c, u) = 0$. Similarly, we set $n(c, d) = R$ if community c contains word d for R times; otherwise, $n(c, d) = 0$. The following models are latent aspect models, which associate a latent class variable $z \in Z = \{z_1, z_2, \cdots, z_K\}$.

Before modeling CCF, we first model community-user co-occurrences (C-U), shown in Figure 8.7(a); and community-description co-occurrences (C-D), shown in Figure 8.7(b). Our CCF model, shown in Figure 8.7(c), builds on C-U and C-D models. The shaded and unshaded variables in Figure 8.7 indicate latent and observed variables, respectively. An arrow indicates a conditional dependency between variables.

8.5.2 C-U and C-D Baseline Models

The C-U model is derived from PLSA and for community-user co-occurrence analysis. The co-occurrence data consists of a set of community-user pairs (c; u), which are assumed to be generated independently. The key idea is to introduce a latent class variable z to every community-user pair, so that community c and user u are rendered conditionally independent. The resulting model is a mixture model that can be written as follows:

$$P(c, u) = \sum_z P(c, u, z) = P(c) \sum_z P(u|z)P(z|c), \tag{8.20}$$

where z represents the topic for a community. For each community, a set of users is observed. To generate each user, a community is c chosen uniformly from the community set, then a topic z is selected from a distribution $P(z|c)$ that is specific to the community, and finally a user u is generated by sampling from a topic-specific distribution $P(u|z)$.

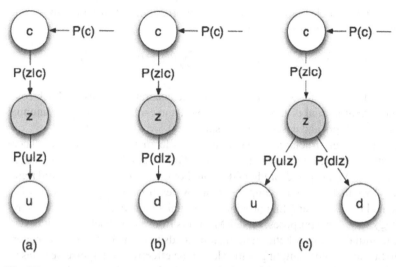

Fig. 8.7. (a) Graphical representation of the Community-User (C-U) model. (b) Graphical representation of the Community-Description (C-D) model. (c) Graphical representation of Combinational Collaborative Filtering (CCF) that combines both bag of users and bag of words information.

The second model is for community-description co-occurrence analysis. It has a similar structure to the C-U model with the joint probability written as:

$$P(c,d) = \sum_z P(c,d,z) = P(c)\sum_z P(d|z)P(z|c), \qquad (8.21)$$

where z represents the topic for a community. Each community's interests are modeled with a mixture of topics. To generate each description word, a community c is chosen uniformly from the community set, then a topic z is selected from a distribution $P(z|c)$ that is specific to the community, and finally a word d is generated by sampling from a topic-specific distribution $P(d|z)$.

Remark: One can model C-U and C-D using LDA. Since the focus of this work is on model fusion, we defer the comparison of PLSA vs. LDA to future work.

8.5.3 CCF Model

In the C-U model, we consider only links, i.e., the observed data can be thought of as a very sparse binary $M \times N$ matrix W, where $W_{i,j} = 1$ indicates that user i joins (or linked to) community j, and the entry is unknown elsewhere. Thus, the C-U model captures the linkage information between communities and users, but not the community content. The C-D model learns the topic distribution for a given community, as well as topic-specific word distributions. This model can be used to estimate how similar two communities are in terms of topic distributions. Next, we introduce our CCF model, which combines both the C-U and C-D.

For the CCF model (Figure 8.7(c)), the joint probability distribution over community, user, and description can be written as:

$$P(c,u,d) = \sum_z P(c,u,d,z) = P(c)\sum_z P(u|z)P(d|z)P(z|c), \qquad (8.22)$$

The CCF model represents a series of probabilistic generative processes. Each community has a multinomial distribution over topics, and each topic has a multinomial distribution over users and descriptions, respectively.

Given the model structure, the next step is to learn model parameters. There are some standard learning algorithms, such as Gibbs sampling [96], Expectation-Maximization (EM) [72], and Gradient descent. For CCF, we propose a hybrid training strategy: We first run Gibbs sampling for a few iterations, then switch to EM. The model trained by Gibbs sampling provides the initialization values for EM. This hybrid strategy serves two purposes. First, EM suffers from a drawback in that it is very sensitive to initialization. A better initialization tends to allow EM to find a "better" optimum. Second, Gibbs sampling is too slow to be effective for large-scale datasets in high-dimensional problems [34]. A hybrid method can enjoy the advantages of Gibbs and EM.

Chen et al. [60] devised two strategies to speed up training of CCF. First, they employed a hybrid training strategy, which combined Gibbs sampling with the Expectation-Maximization (EM) algorithm. Their empirical study showed that Gibbs sampling provided better initialization for EM, and thus could help EM to converge to a better solution at a faster pace. Their second speedup strategy was to parallelize CCF to take advantage of the distributed computing infrastructure of modern data centers. Their scalability study on a real-world dataset of 312k active users and 109k popular communities demonstrated that their parallelization scheme on CCF was effective. CCF could achieve a near linear speedup on up to 200 distributed machines, attaining 116 times speedup over the training time of using one machine. CCF is attractive for supporting large-scale personalized community recommendations, thanks to its effectiveness and scalability. Readers can refer to [60] for the specific algorithms of Gibbs & EM hybrid training and parallelization.

To test CCF's performance, Chen et al. [60] conducted experiments on a large Orkut data set. The experimental results demonstrate that their approaches successfully produce better quality recommendations, and accurately cluster relevant communities/users with similar semantics.

Summary

This chapter covers an interesting extension of Web data mining, i.e. Web recommendation. Several traditional recommender systems have been thoroughly discussed. Following the current progresses in Web recommendation, we have further explored the combination of Web data mining with Web recommendation. We have given considerable discussions on Web recommendation from the algorithmic and developmental perspective.

9

Conclusions

9.1 Summary

Nowadays World Wide Web has become an indispensable part of our daily life. We heavily rely on the Internet for everyday's work, study, entertainment and even almost every aspect of our life. We use the Internet to search the interested information and find the needed service; make prompt and real time communications with friends, families and colleagues via email; use a lot of new information services based on Web 2.0 technology such as Facebook, Twitter and Flicker for social and collaborative activities. As such World Wide Web is becoming a huge information or knowledge "ocean" containing massive data, which has not been sufficiently exploited. On the other hand, due to the lag of technical development of Web research, today people who use the Web significantly suffer from the dramatic expansion of data volume over the Web and the unprecedented growth of Web user population. In particular, Web users usually suffer from the difficulties of finding desirable and accurate information on the Web due to two problems of low precision and low recall caused by above reasons. Facilitating ordinary Web users to locate the needed information accurately and promptly and making the Internet use as friendly and conveniently as possible is always kept as a first priority research question to Web research academia and industrial partners. Furthermore, with propagation and popularity of Web 2.0 technologies, human has become the reigning role during the interaction between users and computers. A large amount of newly emerging Web information services possess the social and collaborative essence and the human behavior patterns are embedded in the human-machine interactions. Analyzing the social media data is able to reveal the underlying social and societal characteristics of human behavior and real world structure. Thus, the emerging of Web has put forward a great deal of challenges to Web researchers for Web-based information management and retrieval.

This book starts with a foundation part consisting of two chapters of some preliminary background knowledge for better understanding of the succeeding chapters. In theoretical backgrounds chapter, various Web data models in the context of Web textual, linkage and usage analysis are discussed and some matrix concepts and theo-

G. Xu et al., *Web Mining and Social Networking*,
DOI 10.1007/978-1-4419-7735-9_9, © Springer Science+Business Media, LLC 2011

ries commonly used in matrix-based analysis are presented accordingly, such as matrix eigenvalue, eigenvector; norm, singular value decomposition (SVD) of matrix as well as three-way tensor expression and decomposition. In addition, a number of well known performance evaluation metrics in the context of information retrieval and recommendation are reviewed, and the basic concepts in social networks are summarized as well. The chapter of algorithms and techniques covers three main aspects of contents - fundamental data mining algorithms, such as association rules, sequential patterns, Markov models and Bayesian networks, clustering and classification; Web recommendation algorithms, e.g. content-based, user-based, model-based and kNN; and the detection and evolution analysis algorithms of social networks. Then, the book presents comprehensive materials on two-level focuses of how to utilize Web data mining to capture the inherent cohesion between various Web pages and between pages and users, and how to exploit or extend Web data mining in social and collaborative applications.

The former is covered in Chapter.4, Chapter.5 and Chapter.6, in which we systematically discuss the research and application issues of Web mining from the different perspectives of Web content, linkage and usage mining. Chapter 4 presents materials about Web content mining. Following the vector space model, Web search is first addressed to cover the methodologies of crawling, archiving and indexing content, and searching strategies. To overcome the challenges of sparse and low overlapping of textual features embedded in pages, feature enrichment and latent semantic analysis methods are given sequentially. Moreover, two extended applications of content analysis in automatic topic extraction and opinion mining from Web documents are demonstrated the application potentials in this domain. Chapter 5 is mainly talking about another important issue in Web mining, i.e. Web linkage mining. Starting with the principles of co-citation and bibliographic coupling, which is from information science, this chapter presents highly summarized materials on two well-known algorithms in Web search, namely PageRank and HITS, which are thoroughly and substantially investigated and cited in a large amount of literatures after the great success of *Google* search engine. In addition to these two algorithms, this chapter also present the topic of Web community discovery as well. The concepts and algorithms like bipartite cores, network flow, cut-based notations of communities and Web community chart are substantially discussed along with the theories of Web graph measurement and modeling. An extended application of Web linkage analysis for Web page classification is proposed to show how the linkage analysis facilitates Web page organization and presentation. Different from Chap.4 and Chap.5, in which the Web mining is mainly performed on Web pages standalone, Chapter 6 reports the research and application progresses from the point of view of interaction between users and machines, i.e. Web usage mining. By introducing the usage data model of user-pageview matrix, this chapter first gives the idea of modeling user navigation interest in terms of page-weight pair vector, and propose clustering-based algorithms to measure the similarity of user interest, and in turn, to find user navigational patterns. In additional to clustering, latent semantic analysis and its variants are explored to be employed in Web usage mining. Two recently well studied latent semantic analysis algorithms, namely PLSA and LDA, are presented and elaborated to show the procedures of capturing the underlying navigation tasks and forming the user access patterns from Web logs via probability inference approaches. The combination of clustering and latent semantic analysis is fully addressed as well. Then a number of Web usage mining applications are reviewed in this chapter to emphasize the application potentials along with some experimental studies.

The latter mission of this book is reflected in Chapter.7 and Chapter.8, where two recently active and popular topics - social networks and Web recommendation, are covered. Following the basic backgrounds discussed in Chap.2 and Chap.3, Chapter 7 concentrates mainly on a few important technical issues of social networking. It presents some algorithms with respect to detecting, extracting and analyzing the Web community structures and social networks and their dynamic evolutions by using Web data mining. We discuss the approach of using Web archive and graph to capture the Web community and its evolution, which is based on graph mining and Web community discovery approaches. In addition, we report the studies of temporal analysis of Web networked structures using three-way tensor analysis. The additional dimension of temporal feature makes it possible to capture the dynamic change of networked structures at a high level of spatial-temporal space. The reported work on combining social network discovery and evolution analysis provides an instructive hint in a unified fashion of social network analysis. We aim to present the materials of social network analysis from the perspectives of longitudinal, evolutionary and unified aspects. Apart from the algorithmic researches, we also give an real world study of social network analysis in the context of societal and social behavior in e-commerce. Chapter 8 talks about the topic of Web recommendation. We aim to present materials following a thread of Web data mining. After introducing algorithms and techniques of the traditional recommender systems, such as user-base, item-based and a hybrid recommender systems, we aim to illustrate how Web mining is able to help improve the recommendation. Especially we report several studies in Web recommendation via Web mining. In usage-based user profiling approaches, we discuss the algorithmic descriptions on using the user access patterns derived with Web usage mining to predict the users' more interested contents. We also review the study of combining Web archives and logs (i.e. the combination of Web content and usage mining) for Web query recommendation. With th potential capability of Web recommendation in improving user satisfaction and enterprise market value, this chapter prepares a progressive landscaping of the start-of-the-art Web recommendation. Next, we will outline some future research directions in the area of Web mining and social networking, focusing on the issues of combination of these two aspects, and social media and social network computing because it attracts a large volume of attentions from various disciplines.

9.2 Future Directions

With the coming era of Web 2.0 and propagation of related technologies and applications, social media mining and social network computing is becoming an active interdisciplinary area, which attracts attention from different research areas, such as computer science, artificial intelligence, natural language processing, information science and social science. As such one of significant directions is along this thread. Nowadays human has played a major role in various kinds of social media, such as Facebook, Twitter and collaborative social tagging systems. The huge involvement of human role makes the data source more complicated and collaborative than any precedented stages. The complex and rich characteristics of social media data require a more automated and unified analysis way to take the different aspects of the social data into account. Different from the tradition Web mining approaches, social media mining gives much attention to the combination of human role in mining procedure. Apparently the better identification of user intent and behavior will reveal insightful and in-depth opinion and motivation behind the user activities, which is hard to achieve by only using content analysis standalone. In a word, combining the social aspects of human with the rich expressions of Web contents in a unified analytical way is the most promising means in future Web mining, especially social media mining and social network computing.

Another interesting issue is semantic Web. The current research is purely based on analysis of explicit data expressions, such as Web content, linkage and usage data, rather than, taking the semantics of Web into consideration, even latent semantic analysis has achieved a considerable amount of successes. It is belied that semantic Web research is probably able to foster new opportunities in Web mining. With the development of semantic Web and ontology research, therefore, ontology knowledge of Web pages can provide deeper understanding or semantic linking of Web page as a result of conveying the conceptual information. Ontology knowledge could be viewed as a high-level knowledge representation over the intuitive content knowledge. Hence, integrating the ontology knowledge with the usage knowledge will substantially improve the effectiveness and efficiency of Web data mining.

Recently *Cloud Computing* becomes a buzz word catching public attention. Cloud computing refers to a Internet-based computing infrastructure that providing shared softwares, data and services to the connected computer or other devices on demand. Academically, we may consider that is merely a new bottle of old wine. However, its impact will be very profound rather than some catching words. It represents a paradigm shift that because of 1) the widely availability of stable and broad bandwidth, and 2) the major cost for end users and enterprises is the maintenance and management (rather than hardware) such like anti-virus, cataloging, backups, data mining and etc, more and more services and data will be centralized. Even some people forecast that the Microsoft era of personal computing is ending. This paradigm shift means the infrastructure would be rather stable and limited to some high end IT professionals. Majority system development and maintenance are at the application level or more precisely service level: to provide various customized services offered on reasonably transparent infrastructure. In the context of cloud computing, service-oriented computing is essentially a basic challenge in delivering better quality services to various types of end users. The usage of Web services provided forms an important data sources, which Web data mining is able to help improve the service optimization. From the end user perspective, cloud computing produces a great amount of research opportunities to Web data mining.

The following research questions need to be thoroughly studied and addressed in the future:

- Q1.What model is suitable for capturing the relationships between Web documents and human behavior information?
- Q2. How do we conduct social media mining and social network computing based on such a model
- Q3. How do we devise new paradigms or extend the existing algorithms in related research context?
- Q4. How do we integrate Web data mining and social network computing together to better analyze the human behavior and social structure?
- Q5. How do we apply the theoretical researches into the real world applications in the context of social computing?

As Web and its usage grow, it will continue to generate evermore content, structure, and usage data, and the value of Web mining will keep increasing. In particular, outlined below are some possible research directions that must be pursued to ensure that we continue to develop Web mining technologies that will enable this value to be realized.

Web services optimization

As services over the Web continue to grow, there will be a need to make them robust, scalable, efficient, etc. Web mining can be applied to better understand the behavior of these services, and the knowledge extracted can be useful for various kinds of optimizations. Research is needed in developing Web mining techniques to improve various other aspects of Web services. In the context of cloud computing, particularly, Web mining could help organize various Web services in an efficient way and facilitate end users to reach the requested Web service promptly and economically.

Fraud and threat analysis

The anonymity provided by the Web has led to a significant increase in attempted fraud, from unauthorized use of individual credit cards to hacking into credit card databases for blackmail purposes. Yet another example is auction fraud, which has been increasing on popular sites like eBay. Since all these frauds are being perpetrated through the Internet, Web mining is the perfect analysis technique for detecting and preventing them. Research issues include developing techniques to recognize known frauds, and characterize and then recognize unknown or novel frauds, etc. The issues in cyber threat analysis and intrusion detection are quite similar in nature.

Web mining and privacy

While there are many benefits to be gained from Web mining, a clear drawback is the potential for severe violations of privacy. Public attitude towards privacy seems to be almost schizophrenic - i.e. people say one thing and do quite the opposite. Some researches have demonstrated that people were willing to provide fairly personal information about themselves, which was completely irrelevant to the task at hand, if provided the right stimulus to do so. Furthermore, explicitly bringing attention information privacy policies had practically no effect. One explanation of this seemingly contradictory attitude towards privacy may be that we have a bi-modal view of privacy, namely that "I would be willing to share information about myself as long as I get some (tangible or intangible) benefits from it, as long as there is an implicit guarantee that the information will not be abused". The research issue generated by this attitude is the need to develop approaches, methodologies and tools that can be used to verify and validate that a Web service is indeed using an end-user's information in a manner consistent with its stated policies.

Temporal evolution of the Web

Society's interaction with the Web is changing the Web as well as the way the society interacts. While storing the history of all of this interaction in one place is clearly too staggering a task, at least the changes to the Web are being recorded by the pioneering Internet Archive project. Research needs to be carried out in extracting temporal models of how Web content, Web structures, Web communities, authorities, hubs, etc. are evolving. Large organizations generally archive (at least portions of) usage data from there Web sites. With these sources of data available, there is a large scope of research to develop techniques for analyzing of how the Web evolves over time. In another aspect, the analysis of Web structure evolution reveal the insight of social networking changes in the social network analysis.

Combining natural language processing and machine learning for really large and dynamic Web data

The inherent heterogeneity and complex characteristics of Web data nature makes it not an easy job for employing simply traditional data mining algorithms in Web mining tasks. Natural language processing techniques provide additional assistance in such kinds of tasks, which leverages the simulated human intelligent capabilities to understand the observed Web data. It is believed the strengths of natural language processing substantially reinforce the Web mining approaches. In real world applications, the analysis scalability and affordability problems of really large and dynamic Web data largely impair the creditability of Web data mining. To overcome such scenarios, practical machine learning approaches is indeed the necessaries. Undoubtedly, the integration of data mining, machine learning and natural language processing techniques would significantly deepen and broaden the Web mining and social network analysis landscapes and potentials.

The exploration of research experience and techniques obtained from various disciplines, such as database, information retrieval, Web community and data mining, social network analysis, social behavior computing, is needed to discover the underlying relationships among Web communities or Web users for social media mining and social networking computing.

References

1. http://dms.irb.hr/.
2. http://en.wikipedia.org/wiki/.
3. http://www.ibm.com/developerworks/linux/library/l-neural/ ?open&l=805, t=grl, p=NeuralNets.
4. M. a. Carreira-perpinan and R. S. Zemel. Proximity graphs for clustering and manifold learning. In *Advances in Neural Information Processing Systems 17*, pages 225–232. MIT Press, 2005.
5. C. C. Aggarwal, F. Al-Garawi, and P. Yu. Intelligent crawling on the world wide web with arbitrary predicates. In *the 10th Intl. World Wide Web Conf. (WWW01)*, pages 96–105, 2001.
6. R. Agrawal, T. Imieliński, and A. Swami. Mining association rules between sets of items in large databases. In *SIGMOD '93: Proceedings of the 1993 ACM SIGMOD international conference on Management of data*, pages 207–216, New York, NY, USA, 1993. ACM.
7. R. Agrawal, H. Mannila, R. Srikant, H. Toivonen, and A. I. Verkamo. Fast discovery of association rules. *Advances in knowledge discovery and data mining*, pages 307–328, 1996.
8. R. Agrawal and R. Srikant. Fast algorithms for mining association rules in large databases. In *Proceedings 20th International Conference on Very Large Data Bases*, pages 487–499, 1994.
9. R. Agrawal and R. Srikant. Fast algorithms for mining association rules in large databases. In *Proceedings of the 20th International Conference on Very Large Data Bases (VLDB)*, pages 487–499, Santiago, Chile, 1994. Morgan Kaufmann.
10. R. Agrawal and R. Srikant. Mining sequential patterns. In P. S. Y. Chen and A. S. P., editors, *Proceedings of the International Conference on Data Engineering (ICDE)*, pages 3–14, Taipei, Taiwan, 1995. IEEE Computer Society Press.
11. R. Agrawal and R. Srikant. Mining sequential patterns. In *Proceedings of International Conference on Data Engineering*, pages 3–14, 1995.
12. R. Albert, H. Jeong, and A. Barabasi. The diameter of the world wide web. *Nature*, 401:130, 1999.
13. S. Asur, S. Parthasarathy, and D. Ucar. An event-based framework for characterizing the evolutionary behavior of interaction graphs. In *KDD '07: Proceedings of the 13th ACM SIGKDD international conference on Knowledge discovery and data mining*, pages 913–921, New York, NY, USA, 2007. ACM.

G. Xu et al., *Web Mining and Social Networking*,
DOI 10.1007/978-1-4419-7735-9, © Springer Science+Business Media, LLC 2011

14. J. Ayres, J. Gehrke, T. Yiu, and J. Flannick. Sequential pattern mining using a bitmap representation. In *Proceedings of ACM SIGKDD International Conference on Knowledge Discovery and Data Mining*, pages 429–435, 2002.

15. B. W. Bader, R. A. Harshman, and T. G. Kolda. Temporal analysis of semantic graphs using asalsan. In *ICDM '07: Proceedings of the 2007 Seventh IEEE International Conference on Data Mining*, pages 33–42, Washington, DC, USA, 2007. IEEE Computer Society.

16. R. A. Baeza-Yates, C. A. Hurtado, and M. Mendoza. Improving search engines by query clustering. *JASIST*, 58(12):1793–1804, 2007.

17. R. A. Baeza-Yates and B. Ribeiro-Neto. *Modern Information Retrieval*. Addison-Wesley Longman Publishing Co., Inc., Boston, MA, USA, 1999.

18. T. L. Bailey and C. Elkan. Fitting a mixture model by expectation maximization to discover motifs in biopolymers. In *Proceedings of International Conference on Intelligent Systems for Molecular Biology*, pages 28–36, 1994.

19. M. F. Balcan, A. Blum, P. P. Choi, J. Lafferty, B. Pantano, M. R. Rwebangira, and X. Zhu. Person identification in webcam images: An application of semi-supervised learning. In *ICML 2005 Workshop on Learning with Partially Classified Training Data*, 2005.

20. P. Baldi, P. Frasconi, , and P. Smyth. *Modeling the internet and the web: probabilistic methods and algorithms*. John Wiley & Sons, 2003.

21. E. Balfe and B. Smyth. An analysis of query similarity in collaborative web search. In *Advances in Information Retrieval, 27th European Conference on IR Research, (ECIR'05)*, pages 330–344, Santiago de Compostela, Spain, 2005.

22. A. Barabsi and R. Albert. Emergence of scaling in random networks. *Science*, 286(5439):509512, 1999.

23. J. Barnes. *Social Networks Reading*. MA: Addison-Wesley, 1972.

24. R. J. Bayardo. Efficiently mining long patterns from databases. In *Proceedings of the ACM SIGMOD International Conference on Management of Data*, pages 85–93, 1998.

25. D. Beeferman and A. L. Berger. Agglomerative clustering of a search engine query log. In *Proceedings of the 6th ACM SIGKDD International Conference on Knowledge discovery and data mining (KDD'00)*, pages 407–416, Boston, MA, USA, 2000.

26. M. Belkin and P. Niyogi. Semi-supervised learning on riemannian manifolds. *Machine Learning*, 1-3(56):209–239, 2004.

27. M. Belkin, P. Niyogi, and V. Sindhwani. Manifold regularization: A geometric framework for learning from labeled and unlabeled examples. *Journal of Machine Learning Research*, 7:2399–2434, 2006.

28. D. Bergmark, C. Lagoze, and A. Sbityakov. Focused crawls, tunneling, and digital libraries. In *ECDL '02: Proceedings of the 6th European Conference on Research and Advanced Technology for Digital Libraries*, pages 91–106, London, UK, 2002. Springer-Verlag.

29. P. Berkhin. Survey of clustering data mining techniques. Technical report, Accrue Software, Inc., 2002.

30. K. Bharat, A. Broder, M. Henzinger, P. Kumar, and S. Venkatasubramanian. The connectivity server: fast access to linkage information on the web. *Comput. Netw. ISDN Syst.*, 30(1-7):469–477, 1998.

31. K. Bharat and M. R. Henzinger. Improved algorithms for topic distillation in a hyperlinked environment. In *SIGIR '98: Proceedings of the 21st annual international ACM SIGIR conference on Research and development in information retrieval*, pages 104–111, New York, NY, USA, 1998. ACM.

32. D. Billsus and M. J. Pazzani. A hybrid user model for news story classification. In *Proceedings of the 7th International Conference on User modeling (UM'99)*, pages 99–108, Secaucus, NJ, USA, 1999.

33. C. M. Bishop. *Pattern Recognition and Machine Learning (Information Science and Statistics)*. Springer-Verlag New York, Inc., 2006.

34. D. M. Blei and M. I. Jordan. Variational methods for the dirichlet process. In *ICML '04: Proceedings of the twenty-first international conference on Machine learning*, page 12, New York, NY, USA, 2004. ACM.

35. D. M. Blei, A. Y. Ng, and M. I. Jordan. Latent dirichlet allocation. *Journal of Machine Learning Research*, 3(1):993–1022, 2003.

36. A. Blum, J. Lafferty, M. R. Rwebangira, and R. Reddy. Semi-supervised learning using randomized mincuts. In *Proceedings of the twenty-first international conference on Machine learning*, page 13, 2004.

37. A. Blum and T. Mitchell. Combining labeled and unlabeled data with co-training. In *the eleventh annual conference on Computational learning theory, the Workshop on Computational Learning Theory*, pages 92–100, 1998.

38. J. Borda. Mémoire sur les élections au scrutin. *Comptes rendus de l'Académie des sciences*, 44:42–51, 1781.

39. J. Borges and M. Levene. Data mining of user navigation patterns. In *WEBKDD '99: Revised Papers from the International Workshop on Web Usage Analysis and User Profiling*, pages 92–111, London, UK, 2000. Springer-Verlag.

40. A. Borodin, G. O. Roberts, J. S. Rosenthal, and P. Tsaparas. Finding authorities and hubs from link structures on the world wide web. In *WWW '01: Proceedings of the 10th international conference on World Wide Web*, pages 415–429, New York, NY, USA, 2001. ACM.

41. J. S. Breese, D. Heckerman, and C. Kadie. Empirical analysis of predictive algorithms for collaborative filtering. In *In Proceedings of the 14th Annual Conference on Uncertainty in Artificial Intelligence (UAI98)*, pages 43–52. Morgan Kaufmann, 1998.

42. S. Brin, R. Motwani, and C. Silverstein. Beyond market baskets: generalizing association rules to correlations. In *Proceedings of the ACM SIGMOD International Conference on Management of Data*, pages 265–276, 1997.

43. S. Brin and L. Page. The anatomy of a large-scale hypertextual web search engine. *Computer Networks*, 30(1-7):107–117, 1998.

44. A. Broder, R. Kumar, F. Maghoul, P. Raghavan, S. Rajagopalan, R. Stata, A. Tomkins, and J. Wiener. Graph structure in the web. In *Proceedings of the 9th international World Wide Web conference on Computer networks : the international journal of computer and telecommunications netowrking*, pages 309–320, Amsterdam, The Netherlands, The Netherlands, 2000. North-Holland Publishing Co.

45. A. Z. Broder, S. C. Glassman, M. S. Manasse, and G. Zweig. Syntactic clustering of the web. In *Selected papers from the sixth international conference on World Wide Web*, pages 1157–1166, Essex, UK, 1997. Elsevier Science Publishers Ltd.

46. A. G. Büchner and M. D. Mulvenna. Discovering internet marketing intelligence through online analytical web usage mining. *SIGMOD Rec.*, 27(4):54–61, 1998.

47. D. Cai, S. Yu, J.-R. Wen, and W.-Y. Ma. Block-based web search. In *SIGIR '04: Proceedings of the 27th annual international ACM SIGIR conference on Research and development in information retrieval*, pages 456–463, New York, NY, USA, 2004. ACM.

48. J. J. Carrasco, J. Joseph, C. Daniel, C. Fain, K. J. Lang, and L. Zhukov. Clustering of bipartite advertiser-keyword graph, 2003.

49. D. Chakrabarti, R. Kumar, and A. Tomkins. Evolutionary clustering. In *KDD '06: Proceedings of the 12th ACM SIGKDD international conference on Knowledge discovery and data mining*, pages 554–560, New York, NY, USA, 2006. ACM.

50. S. Chakrabarti. Data mining for hypertext: a tutorial survey. *SIGKDD Explor. Newsl.*, 1(2):1–11, 2000.

51. S. Chakrabarti. Integrating the document object model with hyperlinks for enhanced topic distillation and information extraction. In *WWW '01: Proceedings of the 10th international conference on World Wide Web*, pages 211–220, New York, NY, USA, 2001. ACM.

52. S. Chakrabarti. Integrating the document object model with hyperlinks for enhanced topic distillation and information extraction. In *Proceedings of the 10th international conference on World Wide Web(WWW'01)*, pages 211–220, 2001.

53. S. Chakrabarti. *Mining the Web: Discovering Knowledge from Hypertext Data*. Morgan-Kauffman, 2002.

54. S. Chakrabarti, B. Dom, and P. Indyk. Enhanced hypertext categorization using hyperlinks. In *Proceedings of ACM SIGMOD International Conference on Management of Data (SIGMOD'98)*, pages 307–318, Seattle, Washington, USA, 1998.

55. S. Chakrabarti, B. Dom, P. Raghavan, S. Rajagopalan, D. Gibson, and J. Kleinberg. Automatic resource compilation by analyzing hyperlink structure and associated text. In *WWW7: Proceedings of the seventh international conference on World Wide Web 7*, pages 65–74, Amsterdam, The Netherlands, The Netherlands, 1998. Elsevier Science Publishers B. V.

56. S. Chakrabarti, M. M. Joshi, K. Punera, and D. M. Pennock. The structure of broad topics on the web. In *WWW '02: Proceedings of the 11th international conference on World Wide Web*, pages 251–262, New York, NY, USA, 2002. ACM.

57. S. Chakrabarti, K. Punera, and M. Subramanyam. Accelerated focused crawling through online relevance feedback. In *the 11th Intl. World Wide Web Conf. (WWW02)*, pages 148–159, 2002.

58. G. Chang, M. Healey, J. McHugh, and T. Wang. *Mining the World Wide Web: An Information Search Approach*. Springer, 2001.

59. O. Chapelle, B. Schölkopf, and A. Zien, editors. *Semi-Supervised Learning*. MIT Press, Cambridge, MA, 2006.

60. W.-Y. Chen, D. Zhang, and E. Y. Chang. Combinational collaborative filtering for personalized community recommendation. In *KDD '08: Proceeding of the 14th ACM SIGKDD international conference on Knowledge discovery and data mining*, pages 115–123, New York, NY, USA, 2008. ACM.

61. P.-A. Chirita, C. S. Firan, and W. Nejdl. Personalized query expansion for the web. In *Proceedings of the 30th Annual International ACM SIGIR Conference on Research and Development in Information Retrieval (SIGIR'07)*, pages 7–14, Amsterdam, The Netherlands, 2007.

62. P. A. Chirita, W. Nejdl, R. Paiu, and C. Kohlschütter. Using ODP metadata to personalize search. In *Proceedings of the 28th Annual International ACM SIGIR Conference on Research and Development in Information Retrieval (SIGIR'05)*, pages 178–185, Salvador, Brazil, 2005.

63. J. Cho and H. Garcia-Molina. The evolution of the web and implications for an incremental crawler. In *Proceedings of the 26th International Conference on Very Large Data Bases(VLDB'00)*, pages 200–209, 2000.

64. D. A. Cohn and T. Hofmann. The missing link - a probabilistic model of document content and hypertext connectivity. In *NIPS*, pages 430–436, 2000.

65. R. Cooley, B. Mobasher, and J. Srivastava. Data preparation for mining world wide web browsing patterns. *KNOWLEDGE AND INFORMATION SYSTEMS*, 1:5–32, 1999.

66. T. H. Cormen, C. E. Leiserson, R. L. Rivest, and C. Stein. *Introduction to algorithms.* McGraw-Hill, 2002.

67. M. Craven, D. DiPasquo, D. Freitag, A. McCallum, T. Mitchell, K. Nigam, and S. Slattery. Learning to extract symbolic knowledge from the world wide web. In *AAAI '98/IAAI '98: Proceedings of the fifteenth national/tenth conference on Artificial intelligence/Innovative applications of artificial intelligence*, pages 509–516, Menlo Park, CA, USA, 1998. American Association for Artificial Intelligence.

68. H. Cui, J.-R. Wen, J.-Y. Nie, and W.-Y. Ma. Query expansion by mining user logs. *IEEE Trans. Knowl. Data Eng.*, 15(4):829–839, 2003.

69. B. Datta. *Numerical Linear Algebra and Application.* Brooks/Cole Publishing Company, 1995.

70. J. Dean and M. R. Henzinger. Finding related pages in the world wide web. *Computer Networks*, 31(11-16):1467–1479, 1999.

71. S. Deerwester, S. T. Dumais, G. W. Furnas, T. K. Landauer, and R. Harshman. Indexing by latent semantic analysis. *Journal American Society for information retrieval*, 41(6):391–407, 1990.

72. A. P. Dempster, N. M. Laird, and D. B. Rubin. Maximum likelihood from incomplete data via the em algorithm. *JOURNAL OF THE ROYAL STATISTICAL SOCIETY, SERIES B*, 39(1):1–38, 1977.

73. I. S. Dhillon. Co-clustering documents and words using bipartite spectral graph partitioning. In *KDD '01: Proceedings of the seventh ACM SIGKDD international conference on Knowledge discovery and data mining*, pages 269–274, New York, NY, USA, 2001. ACM.

74. P. Diaconis and R. L. Graham. Spearman's footrule as a measure of disarray. *Journal of the Royal Statistical Society. Series B (Methodological)*, 39(2):262–268, 1977.

75. L. Dietz, S. Bickel, and T. Scheffer. Unsupervised prediction of citation influences. In *ICML '07: Proceedings of the 24th international conference on Machine learning*, pages 233–240, 2007.

76. M. Diligenti, F. Coetzee, S. Lawrence, C. L. Giles, and M. Gori. Focused crawling using context graphs. In *26th Intl. Conf. on Very Large Databases (VLDB00)*, page 527?534, 2000.

77. C. Ding, X. He, P. Husbands, H. Zha, and H. D. Simon. Pagerank, hits and a unified framework for link analysis. In *Ding, Chris: Proceedings of the 25th annual international ACM SIGIR conference on Research and development in information retrieval*, pages 353–354, New York, NY, USA, 2002. ACM.

78. G. Dong and J. Li. Efficient mining of emerging patterns: discovering trends and differences. In *Proceedings of ACM SIGKDD International Conference on Knowledge Discovery and Data Mining*, pages 43–52, 1999.

79. Z. Dou, R. Song, and J.-R. Wen. A large-scale evaluation and analysis of personalized search strategies. In *Proceedings of the 16th International Conference on World Wide Web (WWW'07)*, pages 581–590, Banff, Alberta, Canada, 2007.

80. Dou.Shen, Jian-Tao.Sun, Qiang.Yang, and Zheng.Chen. A comparison of implicit and explicit links for web page classification. In *the 15th international conference on World Wide Web(WWW'06)*, pages 643–650, 2006.

81. M. Dunja. Personal web watcher: Design and implementation (report). Technical Report IJS-DP-7472, Department of Intelligent Systems, J. Stefan Institute, Slovenia, 1996.

82. C. Dwork, R. Kumar, M. Naor, and D. Sivakumar. Rank aggregation methods for the web. In *Proceedings of the 10th International Conference on World Wide Web (WWW'01)*, pages 613–622, Hong Kong, China, 2001.

83. J. M. E. B. Hunt and P. Stone. *Experiments in induction*. Academic Press, 1966.

84. R. J. Elliott, J. B. Moore, and L. Aggoun. *Hidden Markov Models. Estimation and Control*. New York: Springer-Verlag, 1995.

85. E. Erosheva, S. Fienberg, and J. Lafferty. Mixed membership models of scientific publications. In *Proceedings of the National Academy of Sciences*, volume 101, pages 5220–5227, 2004.

86. E. Eskin and P. Pevzner. Finding composite regulatory patterns in dna sequences. In *Proceedings of International Conference on Intelligent Systems for Molecular Biology*, pages 354–363, 2002.

87. M. Ester, H.-P. Kriegel, J. Sander, M. Wimmer, and X. Xu. Incremental clustering for mining in a data warehousing environment. In *Proceedings of the 24rd International Conference on Very Large Data Bases(VLDB'98)*, pages 323–333, 1998.

88. M. Ester, H.-P. Kriegel, J. Sander, and X. Xu. A density-based algorithm for discovering clusters in large spatial databases with noise. In *Proc. of 2nd International Conference on Knowledge Discovery and*, pages 226–231, 1996.

89. M. Ester, H. peter Kriegel, J. S, and X. Xu. A density-based algorithm for discovering clusters in large spatial databases with noise. In *SIGKDD*, pages 226–231, 1996.

90. A. Farahat, T. LoFaro, J. C. Miller, G. Rae, and L. A. Ward. Authority rankings from hits, pagerank, and salsa: Existence, uniqueness, and effect of initialization. *SIAM J. Sci. Comput.*, 27(4):1181–1201, 2006.

91. U. M. Fayyad, G. Piatetsky-Shapiro, P. Smyth, and R. Uthurusamy. *Advances in Knowledge Discovery and Data Mining*. AAAI/MIT Press, 1996.

92. P. Ferragina and A. Gulli. A personalized search engine based on web-snippet hierarchical clustering. In *WWW '05: Special interest tracks and posters of the 14th international conference on World Wide Web*, pages 801–810, New York, NY, USA, 2005. ACM.

93. G. W. Flake, S. Lawrence, and C. L. Giles. Efficient identification of web communities. In *KDD '00: Proceedings of the sixth ACM SIGKDD international conference on Knowledge discovery and data mining*, pages 150–160, New York, NY, USA, 2000. ACM.

94. J. Fürnkranz. Exploiting structural information for text classification on the www. In *the Third International Symposium on Advances in Intelligent Data Analysis(IDA'99)*, pages 487–498, 1999.

95. M. N. Garofalakis, R. Rastogi, and K. Shim. Spirit: Sequential pattern mining with regular expression constraints. In *Proceedings of International Conference on Very Large Data Bases*, pages 223–234, 1999.

96. S. Geman and D. Geman. *Stochastic relaxation, Gibbs distributions, and the Bayesian restoration of images*. Morgan Kaufmann Publishers Inc., San Francisco, CA, USA, 1990.

97. R. Ghani and A. Fano. Building recommender systems using a knowledge base of product semantics. In *in Proceedings of the Workshop on Recommendation and Personalization in E-Commerce, at the 2nd International Conference on Adaptive Hypermedia and Adaptive Web Based Systems*, 2002.

98. E. Giannakidou, V. A. Koutsonikola, A. Vakali, and Y. Kompatsiaris. Co-clustering tags and social data sources. In *WAIM*, pages 317–324, 2008.

99. D. Gibson, J. Kleinberg, and P. Raghavan. Inferring web communities from link topology. In *HYPERTEXT '98: Proceedings of the ninth ACM conference on Hypertext and*

hypermedia : links, objects, time and space—structure in hypermedia systems, pages 225–234, New York, NY, USA, 1998. ACM.

100. N. S. Glance. Community search assistant. In *Proceedings of the 2001 International Conference on Intelligent User Interfaces (IUI'01)*, pages 91–96, Santa Fe, NM, USA, 2001.

101. E. J. Glover, K. Tsioutsiouliklis, S. L. andDavid M. Pennock, and G. W. Flake. Using web structure for classifying and describing web pages. In *the Eleventh International World Wide Web Conference (WWW'02)*, pages 562–569, 2002.

102. B. Goethals. Survey on frequent pattern mining. Technical report, 2002.

103. G. H. Golub and C. F. V. Loan. *Matrix computations*. The Johns Hopkins University Press, 1983.

104. A. Gruber, M. Rosen-Zvi, and Y. Weiss. Latent topic models for hypertext. In *Uncertainty in Artificial Intelligence (UAI)*, pages 230–240, 2008.

105. J. Han, G. Dong, and Y. Yin. Efficient mining of partial periodic patterns in time series database. In *Proceedings of International Conference on Data Engineering*, pages 106–115, 1999.

106. J. Han and M. Kambe. *Data Mining: Concepts and Techniques*. Morgan Kaufmann Publishers, 2000.

107. J. Han, J. Pei, and Y. Yin. Mining frequent patterns without candidate generation. In *Proceedings of the 2000 ACM SIGMOD international conference on Management of data*, pages 1–12, 2000.

108. D. Hanisch, A. Zien, R. Zimmer, and T. Lengauer. Co-clustering of biological networks and gene expression data. In *ISMB*, pages 145–154, 2002.

109. R. A. Harshman. Models for analysis of asymmetrical relationships among n objects or stimuli. In *In First Joint Meeting of the Psychometric Society and the Society for Mathematical Psychology, McMaster University, Hamilton, Ontario*, 1978.

110. J. A. Hartigan and M. A. Wong. Algorithm as 136: A k-means clustering algorithm. *Royal Statistical Society, Series C (Applied Statistics)*, 1(28):100–108, 1979.

111. T. Hastie, R. Tibshirani, and J. Friedman. *The elements of statistical learning: data mining, inference and prediction*. Springer, 2 edition, 2008.

112. T. H. Haveliwala. Topic-sensitive pagerank. In *WWW '02: Proceedings of the 11th international conference on World Wide Web*, pages 517–526, New York, NY, USA, 2002. ACM.

113. T. H. Haveliwala. Topic-sensitive pagerank: A context-sensitive ranking algorithm for web search. *IEEE Trans. Knowl. Data Eng.*, 15(4):784–796, 2003.

114. T. H. Haveliwala, A. Gionis, and P. Indyk. Scalable techniques for clustering the web (extended abstract). In *WebDB2000, Third International Workshop on the Web and Databases, In conjunction with ACM SIGMOD2000*, 2000.

115. M. Hein and M. Maier. Manifold denoising. In *Advances in Neural Information Processing Systems 19*, 2006.

116. J. L. Herlocker, J. A. Konstan, A. Borchers, and J. Riedl. An algorithmic framework for performing collaborative filtering. In *SIGIR '99: Proceedings of the 22nd annual international ACM SIGIR conference on Research and development in information retrieval*, pages 230–237, New York, NY, USA, 1999. ACM.

117. J. L. Herlocker, J. A. Konstan, L. G. Terveen, and J. T. Riedl. Evaluating collaborative filtering recommender systems. *ACM Transaction on Information Systems (TOIS)*, 22(1):5 – 53, 2004.

118. T. Hofmann. Probabilistic latent semantic analysis. In *In Proc. of Uncertainty in Artificial Intelligence, UAI99*, pages 289–296, 1999.

119. J. Hou and Y. Zhang. Constructing good quality web page communities. In *ADC '02: Proceedings of the 13th Australasian database conference*, pages 65–74, Darlinghurst, Australia, Australia, 2002. Australian Computer Society, Inc.

120. J. Hou and Y. Zhang. Effectively finding relevant web pages from linkage information. *IEEE Trans. on Knowl. and Data Eng.*, 15(4):940–951, 2003.

121. J. Hou and Y. Zhang. Utilizing hyperlink transitivity to improve web page clustering. In *Proceedings of the 14th Australasian Database Conferences (ADC2003)*, volume 37, pages 49–57, Adelaide, Australia, 2003. ACS Inc.

122. A. K. Jain, M. N. Murty, and P. J. Flynn. Data clustering: a review. *ACM Comput. Surv.*, 31(3):264–323, 1999.

123. K. Järvelin and J. Kekäläinen. Cumulated gain-based evaluation of ir techniques. *ACM Trans. Inf. Syst.*, 20(4):422–446, 2002.

124. G. Jeh and J. Widom. Scaling personalized web search. In *Proceedings of the 12th International World Wide Web Conference (WWW'03)*, pages 271–279, Budapest, Hungary, 2003.

125. F. Jelinek. *Statistical methods for speech recognition*. MIT Press, 1997.

126. X. Jin and B. Mobasher. Using semantic similarity to enhance item-based collaborative filtering. In *in Proceedings of The 2nd International Conference on Information and Knowledge Sharing*, 2003.

127. X. Jin, Y. Zhou, and B. Mobasher. A unified approach to personalization based on probabilistic latent semantic models of web usage and content. In *Proceedings of the AAAI 2004 Workshop on Semantic Web Personalization (SWP'04)*, San Jose, 2004.

128. X. Jin, Y. Zhou, and B. Mobasher. A maximum entropy web recommendation system: Combining collaborative and content features. In *Proceedings of the ACM SIGKDD Conference on Knowledge Discovery and Data Mining (KDD'05)*, pages 612–617, Chicago, 2005.

129. T. Joachims, D. Freitag, and T. Mitchell. Webwatcher: A tour guide for the world wide web. In *The 15th International Joint Conference on Artificial Intelligence (IJCAI'97)*, pages 770–777, Nagoya, Japan, 1997.

130. M. I. Jordan, editor. *Learning in graphical models*. MIT Press, Cambridge, MA, USA, 1999.

131. N. Kaji and M. Kitsuregawa. Building lexicon for sentiment analysis from massive collection of html documents. In *Proceedings of the 2007 Joint Conference on Empirical Methods in Natural Language Processing and Computational Natural Language Learning (EMNLP-CoNLL'07)*, pages 1075–1083, 2007.

132. M. Kamber, J. Han, and J. Chiang. Metarule-guided mining of multi-dimensional association rules using data cubes. In *Proceedings of ACM SIGKDD International Conference on Knowledge Discovery and Data Mining*, pages 207–210, 1997.

133. S. D. Kamvar, T. H. Haveliwala, C. D. Manning, and G. H. Golub. Extrapolation methods for accelerating pagerank computations. In *WWW '03: Proceedings of the 12th international conference on World Wide Web*, pages 261–270, New York, NY, USA, 2003. ACM.

134. H. R. Kim and P. K. Chan. Learning implicit user interest hierarchy for context in personalization. In *Proceedings of the 2003 International Conference on Intelligent User Interfaces (IUI'03)*, pages 101–108, Miami, FL, USA, 2003.

135. H.-r. Kim and P. K. Chan. Personalized ranking of search results with learned user interest hierarchies from bookmarks. In *Proceedings of the 7th WEBKDD workshop on Knowledge Discovery from the Web (WEBKDD'05)*, pages 32–43, Chicago, Illinois, USA, 2005.

136. M. Kitsuregawa, T. Tamura, M. Toyoda, and N. Kaji. Socio-sense: a system for analysing the societal behavior from long term web archive. In *Proceedings of the 10th Asia-Pacific web conference on Progress in WWW research and development(APWeb'08)*, pages 1–8, 2008.

137. J. M. Kleinberg. Authoritative sources in a hyperlinked environment. In *Proc. of the Ninth Annual ACM-SIAM Symposium on Discrete Algorithms (SODA'98)*, pages 668–677, 1998.

138. M. Klemettinen, H. Mannila, P. Ronkainen, H. Toivonen, and A. I. Verkamo. Finding interesting rules from large sets of discovered association rules. In *Proceedings of ACM Conference on Information and Knowledge Management*, pages 401–407, 1994.

139. J. Konstan, B. Miller, D. Maltz, J. Herlocker, L. Gordon, and J. Riedl. Grouplens: Applying collaborative filtering to usenet news. *Communications of the ACM*, 40:77–87, 1997.

140. R. Kosala and H. Blockeel. Web mining research: a survey. *SIGKDD Explor. Newsl.*, 2(1):1–15, 2000.

141. A. Krogh, M. Brown, I. Mian, K. Sjolander, and D. Haussler. Hidden markov models in computational biology. applications to protein modeling. *Journal of Computational Biology*, 235:1501–1531, 1994.

142. D. Kulp, D. Haussler, M. G. Reese, and F. H. Eeckman. A generalized hidden markov model for the recognition of human genes in dna. In *Proceedings of the Fourth International Conference on Intelligent Systems for Molecular Biology*, pages 134–142. AAAI Press, 1996.

143. H. C. Kum, J. Pei, W. Wang, and D. Duncan. Approxmap: Approximate mining of consensus sequential patterns. In *Proceedings of SIAM International Conference on Data Mining*, pages 311–315, 2003.

144. R. Kumar, J. Novak, and A. Tomkins. Structure and evolution of online social networks. In *KDD '06: Proceedings of the 12th ACM SIGKDD international conference on Knowledge discovery and data mining*, pages 611–617, New York, NY, USA, 2006. ACM.

145. R. Kumar, P. Raghavan, S. Rajagopalan, and A. Tomkins. Extracting large-scale knowledge bases from the web. In *VLDB '99: Proceedings of the 25th International Conference on Very Large Data Bases*, pages 639–650, San Francisco, CA, USA, 1999. Morgan Kaufmann Publishers Inc.

146. R. Kumar, P. Raghavan, S. Rajagopalan, and A. Tomkins. Trawling the web for emerging cyber-communities. In *WWW '99: Proceedings of the eighth international conference on World Wide Web*, pages 1481–1493, New York, NY, USA, 1999. Elsevier North-Holland, Inc.

147. K. Kummamuru, R. Lotlikar, S. Roy, K. Singal, and R. Krishnapuram. A hierarchical monothetic document clustering algorithm for summarization and browsing search results. In *WWW '04: Proceedings of the 13th international conference on World Wide Web*, pages 658–665, New York, NY, USA, 2004. ACM.

148. W. Lam, S. Mukhopadhyay, J. Mostafa, and M. J. Palakal. Detection of shifts in user interests for personalized information filtering. In *Proceedings of the 19th Annual International ACM SIGIR Conference on Research and Development in Information Retrieval (SIGIR'96)*, pages 317 – 325, Zurich, Switzerland, 1996.

149. K. Lang. Newsweeder: Learning to filter netnews. In *in Proceedings of the 12th International Machine Learning Conference (ML95*, 1995.

150. A. N. Langville and C. D. Meyer. Deeper inside pagerank. *Internet Mathematics*, 1(3):335380, 2005.

151. A. N. Langville and C. D. Meyer. *Google's PageRank and Beyond: The Science of Search Engine Rankings*. Princeton University Press, 2006.
152. R. Lempel and S. Moran. The stochastic approach for link-structure analysis (salsa) and the tkc effect. In *Proceedings of the 9th international World Wide Web conference on Computer networks : the international journal of computer and telecommunications netowrking*, pages 387–401, Amsterdam, The Netherlands, The Netherlands, 2000. North-Holland Publishing Co.
153. R. Lempel and S. Moran. The stochastic approach for link-structure analysis (salsa) and the tkc effect. In *Proceedings of the 9th international World Wide Web conference(WWW'00)*, pages 387–401, 2000.
154. B. Lent, A. Swami, and J. Widom. Clustering association rules. In *Proceedings of International Conference on Data Engineering*, pages 220–231, 1997.
155. J. Leskovec, J. Kleinberg, and C. Faloutsos. Graphs over time: densification laws, shrinking diameters and possible explanations. In *KDD '05: Proceedings of the eleventh ACM SIGKDD international conference on Knowledge discovery in data mining*, pages 177–187, New York, NY, USA, 2005. ACM.
156. L. Li, S. Otsuka, and M. Kitsuregawa. Query recommendation using large-scale web access logs and web page archive. In *Proceedings of 19th International Conference on Database and Expert Systems Applications (DEXA'08)*, pages 134–141, Turin, Italy, 2008.
157. L. Li, S. Otsuka, and M. Kitsuregawa. Finding related search engine queries by web community based query enrichment. *World Wide Web*, 13(1-2):121–142, 2010.
158. L. Li, Z. Yang, and M. Kitsuregawa. Aggregating user-centered rankings to improve web search. In *Proceedings of the 22nd AAAI Conf. on Artificial Intelligence (AAAI'07)*, pages 1884–1885, Vancouver, British Columbia, Canada, 2007.
159. L. Li, Z. Yang, and M. Kitsuregawa. Using ontology-based user preferences to aggregate rank lists in web search. In *Proceedings of Advances in Knowledge Discovery and Data Mining, 12nd Pacific-Asia Conference (PAKDD'08)*, pages 923–931, Osaka, Japan, 2008.
160. L. Li, Z. Yang, L. Liu, and M. Kitsuregawa. Query-url bipartite based approach to personalized query recommendation. In *Proceedings of the 23rd AAAI Conference on Artificial Intelligence,(AAAI'08)*, pages 1189–1194, Chicago, Illinois, USA, 2008.
161. L. Li, Z. Yang, B. Wang, and M. Kitsuregawa. Dynamic adaptation strategies for long-term and short-term user profile to personalize search. In *Proceedings of A Joint Conference of the 9th Asia-Pacific Web Conference and the 8th International Conference on Web-Age Information Management*, pages 228–240, Huang Shan, China, 2007.
162. Y. Li, Z. Bandar, and D. McLean. An approach for measuring semantic similarity between words using multiple information sources. *IEEE Trans. Knowl. Data Eng.*, 15(4):871–882, 2003.
163. H. Lieberman. Letizia: An agent that assists web browsing. In *Proc. of the 1995 International Joint Conference on Artificial Intelligence*, pages 924–929, Montreal, Canada, 1995. Morgan Kaufmann.
164. Y.-R. Lin, Y. Chi, S. Zhu, H. Sundaram, and B. L. Tseng. Facetnet: a framework for analyzing communities and their evolutions in dynamic networks. In *WWW '08: Proceeding of the 17th international conference on World Wide Web*, pages 685–694, New York, NY, USA, 2008. ACM.
165. G. Linden, B. Smith, and J. York. Amazon.com recommendations: Item-to-item collaborative filtering. *IEEE Internet Computing*, 7:76–80, 2003.
166. B. Liu. *Web Data Mining: Exploring Hyperlinks, Contents, and Usage Data*. Springer, 2007.

167. B. Liu and K. Chen-Chuan-Chang. Editorial: special issue on web content mining. *SIGKDD Explor. Newsl.*, 6(2):1–4, 2004.

168. F. Liu, C. T. Yu, and W. Meng. Personalized web search for improving retrieval effectiveness. *IEEE Trans. Knowl. Data Eng.*, 16(1):28–40, 2004.

169. C. Luo and S. Chung. Efficient mining of maximal sequential patterns using multiple samples. In *Proceedings of SIAM International Conference on Data Mining*, pages 64–72, 2005.

170. Y. Lv, L. Sun, J. Zhang, J.-Y. Nie, W. Chen, and W. Zhang. An iterative implicit feedback approach to personalized search. In *Proceedings of the 44th Annual Meeting of the Association for Computational Linguistics (ACL'06)*, pages 585–592, Sydney, Australia, 2006.

171. H. Ma, H. Yang, I. King, and M. R. Lyu. Learning latent semantic relations from click-through data for query suggestion. In *Proceedings of the 17th ACM Conference on Information and Knowledge Management, (CIKM'08)*, pages 709–718, Napa Valley, California,USA, 2008.

172. N. Mabroukeh and C. Ezeife. A taxonomy of sequential pattern mining algorithms. *ACM Computing Surveys*, 2010.

173. J. B. MacQueen. Some methods for classification and analysis of multivariate observations. In *Berkeley Symposium on Mathematical Statistics and Probability*, pages 281–297, 1967.

174. S. K. Madria, S. S. Bhowmick, W. K. Ng, and E.-P. Lim. Research issues in web data mining. In *DaWaK '99: Proceedings of the First International Conference on Data Warehousing and Knowledge Discovery*, pages 303–312, London, UK, 1999. Springer-Verlag.

175. H. Mannila and C. Meek. Global partial orders from sequential data. In *Proceedings of ACM SIGKDD International Conference on Knowledge Discovery and Data Mining*, pages 161–168, 2000.

176. H. Mannila, H. Toivonen, and A. I. Verkamo. Discovery of frequent episodes in event sequences. *Data Mining and Knowledge Discovery*, 1(3):259–289, 1997.

177. H. Mannila, H. Toivonen, and I. Verkamo. Efficient algorithms for discovering association rules. In *Proceedings of the AAAI Workshop on Knowledge Discovery in Databases*, pages 181–192, 1994.

178. C. D. Manning, P. Raghavan, and H. Schutze. *Introduction to Information Retrieval*. Cambridge University Press, 2008.

179. C. D. Manning and H. Schütze. *Foundations of statistical natural language processing*. MIT Press, 1999.

180. Q. Mei, D. Zhou, and K. W. Church. Query suggestion using hitting time. In *Proceedings of the 17th ACM Conference on Information and Knowledge Management, (CIKM'08)*, pages 469–478, Napa Valley, California, USA, 2008.

181. P. Melville, R. J. Mooney, and R. Nagarajan. Content-boosted collaborative filtering for improved recommendations. In *AAAI/IAAI*, pages 187–192, 2002.

182. T. M. Mitchell. *Machine Learning*. McGraw-Hill, New York, 1997.

183. B. Mobasher. *Web Usage Mining and Personalization*, chapter Practical Handbook of Internet Computing. CRC Press, 2004.

184. B. Mobasher, H. Dai, M. Nakagawa, and T. Luo. Discovery and evaluation of aggregate usage profiles for web personalization. *Data Mining and Knowledge Discovery*, 6(1):61–82, 2002.

185. B. Mobasher, X. Jin, and Y. Zhou. Semantically enhanced collaborative filtering on the web. In *EWMF*, pages 57–76, 2003.

186. J. K. Mui and K. S. Fu. Automated classification of nucleated blood cells using a binary tree classifier. *IEEE Transactions on Pattern Analysis and Machine Intelligence*, 2:429–443, 1980.

187. R. Nag, K. Wong, and F. Fallside. Script recognition using hidden markov models. In *Proceedings of ICASSP*, pages 2071–2074, 1986.

188. R. Nallapati and W. Cohen. Link-plsa-lda: A new unsupervised model for topics and influence of blogs. In *International Conference for Weblogs and Social Media*, pages 84–92, 2008.

189. N. Nanas, V. S. Uren, and A. N. D. Roeck. Building and applying a concept hierarchy representation of a user profile. In *Proceedings of the 26th Annual International ACM SIGIR Conference on Research and Development in Information Retrieval (SIGIR'03)*, pages 198–204, Toronto, Canada, 2003.

190. M. E. J. Newman. Fast algorithm for detecting community structure in networks. *Phys. Rev. E*, 69(6):066133, Jun 2004.

191. M. E. J. Newman and M. Girvan. Finding and evaluating community structure in networks. *Phys. Rev. E*, 2004.

192. K. Nigam, A. K. Mccallum, S. Thrun, and T. Mitchell. Text classification from labeled and unlabeled documents using em. 2/3(39):103–134, 2000.

193. M. O'Conner and J. Herlocker. Clustering items for collaborative filtering. In *in Proceedings of the ACM SIGIR Workshop on Recommender Systems*, 1999.

194. S. Otsuka, M. Toyoda, J. Hirai, and M. Kitsuregawa. Extracting user behavior by web communities technology on global web logs. In *Proceedings of 15th International Conference on Database and Expert Systems Applications (DEXA'04)*, pages 957–968, Zaragoza, Spain, 2004.

195. L. Pachter, M. Alexandersson, and S. Cawley. Applications of generalized pair hidden markov models to alignment and gene finding problems. In *RECOMB '01: Proceedings of the fifth annual international conference on Computational biology*, pages 241–248, 2001.

196. L. Page, S. Brin, R. Motwani, and T. Winograd. The pagerank citation ranking: Bringing order to the web, 1999.

197. J. Palau, M. Montaner, B. López, and J. L. de la Rosa. Collaboration analysis in recommender systems using social networks. In *CIA*, pages 137–151, 2004.

198. G. Pant and P. Srinivasan. Learning to crawl: comparing classification schemes. *ACM Trans. Information Systems*, 23(4):430?462, 2005.

199. J. S. Park, M.-S. Chen, and P. S. Yu. An effective hash-based algorithm for mining association rules. In *Proceedings of the ACM SIGMOD International Conference on Management of Data*, pages 175–186, 1995.

200. S. Parthasarathy, M. J. Zaki, M. Ogihara, and S. Dwarkadas. Incremental and interactive sequence mining. In *Proceedings of ACM Conference on Information and Knowledge Management*, pages 251–258, 1999.

201. J. Pei, J. Han, B. Mortazavi-Asl, and H. Pinto. Prefixspan:mining sequential patterns efficiently by prefix-projected pattern growth. In *Proceedings of International Conference on Data Engineering*, pages 215–224, 2001.

202. J. Pei, J. Han, B. Mortazavi-Asl, J. Wang, H. Pinto, Q. Chen, U. Dayal, and M. Hsu. Mining sequential patterns by pattern-growth: The prefixspan approach. *IEEE Transactions on Knowledge and Data Engineering*, 16(11):1424–1440, November 2004.

203. M. Perkowitz and O. Etzioni. Adaptive web sites: automatically synthesizing web pages. In *AAAI '98/IAAI '98: Proceedings of the fifteenth national/tenth conference on Artificial intelligence/Innovative applications of artificial intelligence*, pages 727–732, Menlo Park, CA, USA, 1998. American Association for Artificial Intelligence.

204. M. Perkowitz and O. Etzioni. Towards adaptive web sites: conceptual framework and case study. In *WWW '99: Proceedings of the eighth international conference on World Wide Web*, pages 1245–1258, New York, NY, USA, 1999. Elsevier North-Holland, Inc.

205. X. H. Phan, M. L. Nguyen, and S. Horiguchi. Learning to classify short and sparse text & web with hidden topics from large-scale data collections. In *Proceedings of the 17th International Conference on World Wide Web, WWW 2008*, pages 91–100, Beijing, China, 2008. ACM 2008.

206. D. Pierrakos, G. Paliouras, C. Papatheodorou, V. Karkaletsis, and M. D. Dikaiakos. Web community directories: A new approach to web personalization. In *EWMF*, pages 113–129, 2003.

207. A. Pretschner and S. Gauch. Ontology based personalized search. In *Proceedings of the 9th International Conference on Tools with Artificial Intelligence (ICTAI'99)*, pages 391–398, Chicago, Illinois, USA, 1999.

208. F. Qiu and J. Cho. Automatic identification of user interest for personalized search. In *Proceedings of the 15th International Conference on World Wide Web (WWW'06)*, pages 727–736, Edinburgh, Scotland, 2006.

209. J. R. Quinlan. Discovering rules by induction from large collections of examples. *Expert Systems in the Micro Electronic Age*, page 168C201, 1979.

210. J. R. Quinlan. *C4.5: Programs for Machine Learning*. Morgan Kaufmann, San Mateo, CA, 1993.

211. L. R. Rabiner. A tutorial on hidden markov models and selected applications in speech recognition. pages 267–296, 1989.

212. A. M. Rashid, S. K. Lam, G. Karypis, and J. Riedl. Clustknn: a highly scalable hybrid model-& memory-based cf algorithm. In *In Proc. of WebKDD-06, KDD Workshop on Web Mining and Web Usage Analysis, at 12 th ACM SIGKDD Int. Conf. on Knowledge Discovery and Data Mining*, 2006.

213. M. Richardson and P. Domingos. The intelligent surfer: Probabilistic combination of link and content information in pagerank. In *NIPS*, pages 1441–1448, 2001.

214. E. Sadikov, J. Madhavan, L. Wang, and A. Halevy. Clustering query refinements by user intent. In *WWW '10: Proceedings of the 19th international conference on World wide web*, pages 841–850, New York, NY, USA, 2010. ACM.

215. S. R. Safavian and D. Landgrebe. A survey of decision tree classifier methodology. *IEEE Transactions on Systems Man and Cybernetics*, 21(3):660–674, 1991.

216. G. Salton and M. J. McGill. *Introduction to Modern Information Retrieval*. McGraw-Hill, Inc., New York, NY, USA, 1986.

217. P. Sarkar and A. W. Moore. Dynamic social network analysis using latent space models. *SIGKDD Explor. Newsl.*, 7(2):31–40, 2005.

218. B. Sarwar, G. Karypis, J. Konstan, and J. Reidl. Item-based collaborative filtering recommendation algorithms. In *WWW '01: Proceedings of the 10th international conference on World Wide Web*, pages 285–295, New York, NY, USA, 2001. ACM.

219. V. Schickel-Zuber and B. Faltings. Inferring user's preferences using ontologies. In *Proceedings of The 21st National Conf. on Artificial Intelligence and the 8th Innovative Applications of Artificial Intelligence Conference (AAAI'06)*, pages 1413–1418, Boston, Massachusetts, USA, 2006.

220. J. Schroeder, J. Xu, and H. Chen. Crimelink explorer: Using domain knowledge to facilitate automated crime association analysis. *ISI*, page 168180, 2003.

221. J. Scott. *Social network analysis*. London: Sage, 1991.

222. S. Sen, J. Vig, and J. Riedl. Tagommenders: connecting users to items through tags. In *WWW '09: Proceedings of the 18th international conference on World wide web*, pages 671–680, New York, NY, USA, 2009. ACM.

223. C. Shahabi, A. M. Zarkesh, J. Adibi, and V. Shah. Knowledge discovery from users web-page navigation. In *RIDE*, pages 0–, 1997.

224. U. Shardanand and P. Maes. Social information filtering: Algorithms for automating 'word of mouth'. In *Proceedings of the Computer-Human Interaction Conference (CHI95)*, pages 210–217, Denver, Colorado, 1995.

225. X. Shen, B. Tan, and C. Zhai. Context-sensitive information retrieval using implicit feedback. In *Proceedings of the 28th Annual International ACM SIGIR Conference on Research and Development in Information Retrieval (SIGIR'05)*, pages 43–50, Salvador, Brazil, 2005.

226. X. Shen, B. Tan, and C. Zhai. Implicit user modeling for personalized search. In *Proceedings of the 2005 ACM CIKM Int'l Conf. on Information and Knowledge Management (CIKM'05)*, pages 824–831, Bremen, Germany, 2005.

227. A.-Y. Sihem, L. V. S. Lakshmanan, and C. Yu. Socialscope: Enabling information discovery on social content sites. In *CIDR*. www.crdrdb.org, 2009.

228. C. Silverstein, S. Brin, R. Motwani, and J. Ullman. Scalable techniques for mining causal structures. *Data Mining and Knowledge Discovery*, 4(2-3):163–192, 2000.

229. V. Sindhwani, P. Niyogi, and M. Belkin. Beyond the point cloud: from transductive to semi-supervised learning. In *Proceedings of the 22nd international conference on Machine learning*, pages 824–831, 2005.

230. S. J. Soltysiak and I. B. Crabtree. Automatic learning of user profiles- towards the personalisation of agent services. *BT Technology Journal*, 16(3):110–117, 1998.

231. M. Speretta and S. Gauch. Personalized search based on user search histories. In *Proceedings of the IEEE / WIC / ACM International Conference on Web Intelligence (WI'05)*, pages 622–628, Compiegne, France, 2005.

232. R. Srikant and R. Agrawal. Mining sequential patterns: Generalizations and performance improvements. In *Proceedings of International Conference on Extending Database Technology*, pages 3–17, 1996.

233. R. Srikant and Y. Yang. Mining web logs to improve website organization. In *WWW '01: Proceedings of the 10th international conference on World Wide Web*, pages 430–437, New York, NY, USA, 2001. ACM.

234. J. Srivastava, R. Cooley, M. Deshpande, and P.-N. Tan. Web usage mining: discovery and applications of usage patterns from web data. *SIGKDD Explor. Newsl.*, 1(2):12–23, 2000.

235. C. Sun, B. Gao, Z. Cao, and H. Li. Htm: a topic model for hypertexts. In *EMNLP '08: Proceedings of the Conference on Empirical Methods in Natural Language Processing*, pages 514–522, 2008.

236. J. Sun, D. Tao, and C. Faloutsos. Beyond streams and graphs: dynamic tensor analysis. In *KDD '06: Proceedings of the 12th ACM SIGKDD international conference on Knowledge discovery and data mining*, pages 374–383, New York, NY, USA, 2006. ACM.

237. T. Tamura, K. Somboonviwat, and M. Kitsuregawa. A method for language-specific web crawling and its evaluation. *Syst. Comput. Japan*, 38(2):10–20, 2007.

238. A.-H. Tan. Text mining: The state of the art and the challenges. In *In Proceedings of the PAKDD 1999 Workshop on Knowledge Disocovery from Advanced Databases*, 1999.

239. B. Tan, X. Shen, and C. Zhai. Mining long-term search history to improve search accuracy. In *Proceedings of the 12th ACM SIGKDD International Conference on Knowledge Discovery and Data Mining (KDD'06)*, pages 718–723, Philadelphia, PA, USA, 2006.

240. F. Tanudjaja and L. Mu. Persona: A contextualized and personalized web search. In *Proceedings of the 35th Hawaii Int'l Conf. on System Sciences (HICSS'02)*, pages 67–75, 2002.

241. J. Teevan, S. T. Dumais, and E. Horvitz. Personalizing search via automated analysis of interests and activities. In *Proceedings of the 28th Annual Int'l ACM SIGIR Conf. on Research and Development in Information Retrieval (SIGIR '05)*, pages 449–456, Salvador, Brazil, 2005.

242. W. G. Teng, M. Chen, and P. Yu. A regression-based temporal pattern mining scheme for data streams. In *Proceedings of International Conference on Very Large Data Bases*, pages 93–104, 2003.

243. M. Toyoda and M. Kitsuregawa. Creating a web community chart for navigating related communities. In *Proceedings of the 12th ACM Conference on Hypertext and Hypermedia (HT'01)*, pages 103–112, Århus, Denmark, 2001.

244. M. Toyoda and M. Kitsuregawa. Extracting evolution of web communities from a series of web archives. In *Proceedings of the fourteenth ACM conference on Hypertext and hypermedia(HYPERTEXT'03)*, pages 28–37, 2003.

245. M. Toyoda and M. Kitsuregawa. A system for visualizing and analyzing the evolution of the web with a time series of graphs. In *Proceedings of the sixteenth ACM conference on Hypertext and hypermedia(HYPERTEXT'05)*, pages 151–160, 2005.

246. M. Toyoda and M. Kitsuregawa. What's really new on the web?: identifying new pages from a series of unstable web snapshots. In *Proceedings of the 15th international conference on World Wide Web(WWW'06)*, pages 233–241, 2006.

247. P. Tzvetkov, X. Yan, and J. Han. Tsp: Mining top-k closed sequential patterns. In *Proceedings of IEEE International Conference on Data Mining*, pages 347–358, 2003.

248. V. Vapnik. *The Nature of Statistical Learning Theory*. Springer-Verlag, 1995.

249. W. Wang and J. Yang. *Mining Sequential Patterns from Large Data Sets*, volume 28. Series: The Kluwer International Series on Advances in Database Systems, 2005.

250. S. Wasserman and K. Faust. *Social Network Analysis: Methods and Applications*. Cambridge University Press, 1994.

251. S. Wasserman and J. Galaskiewicz. *Advances in Social Network Analysis*. Sage Publications, 1994.

252. F. Wei, W. Qian, C. Wang, and A. Zhou. Detecting overlapping community structures in networks. *World Wide Web*, 12(2):235–261, 2009.

253. J.-R. Wen, J.-Y. Nie, and H. Zhang. Query clustering using user logs. *ACM Trans. Inf. Syst.*, 20(1):59–81, 2002.

254. J.-R. Wen, J.-Y. Nie, and H.-J. Zhang. Clustering user queries of a search engine. In *WWW '01: Proceedings of the 10th international conference on World Wide Web*, pages 162–168, New York, NY, USA, 2001. ACM.

255. D. H. Widyantoro, T. R. Ioerger, and J. Yen. Learning user interest dynamics with a three-descriptor representation. *JASIST*, 52(3):212–225, 2001.

256. J. Xiao, Y. Zhang, X. Jia, and T. Li. Measuring similarity of interests for clustering web-users. In *ADC '01: Proceedings of the 12th Australasian database conference*, pages 107–114, Washington, DC, USA, 2001. IEEE Computer Society.

257. G. Xu, Y. Zhang, J. Ma, and X. Zhou. Discovering user access pattern based on probabilistic latent factor model. In *ADC*, pages 27–35, 2005.

258. G. Xu, Y. Zhang, and X. Zhou. A web recommendation technique based on probabilistic latent semantic analysis. In *Proceeding of 6th International Conference of Web Information System Engineering (WISE'2005)*, pages 15–28, New York City, USA, 2005. LNCS 3806.

259. J. Xu and W. B. Croft. Query expansion using local and global document analysis. In *Proceedings of the 19th Annual International ACM SIGIR Conference on Research and Development in Information Retrieval (SIGIR'96)*, pages 4–11, Zurich, Switzerland, 1996.

260. G.-R. Xue, D. Shen, Q. Yang, H.-J. Zeng, Z. Chen, Y. Yu, W. Xi, and W.-Y. Ma. Irc: An iterative reinforcement categorization algorithm for interrelated web objects. In *the 4th IEEE International Conference on Data Mining(ICDM'04)*, page 273?280, 2004.

261. X. Yan, J. Han, and R. Afshar. Clospan: mining closed sequential patterns in large datasets. In *Proceedings of SIAM International Conference on Data Mining*, pages 166–177, 2003.

262. J.-M. Yang, R. Cai, F. Jing, S. Wang, L. Zhang, and W.-Y. Ma. Search-based query suggestion. In *Proceedings of the 17th ACM Conference on Information and Knowledge Management, (CIKM'08)*, pages 1439–1440, Napa Valley, California,USA, 2008.

263. Z. Yang, Y. Wang, and M. Kitsuregawa. Effective sequential pattern mining algorithms for dense database. In *National Data Engineering WorkShop (DEWS)*, 2006.

264. Z. Yang, Y. Wang, and M. Kitsuregawa. Lapin: Effective sequential pattern mining algorithms by last position induction for dense databases. In *Int'l Conference on Database Systems for Advanced Applications (DASFAA)*, pages 1020–1023, 2007.

265. D. Yarowsky. Unsupervised word sense disambiguation rivaling supervised methods. In *Proceedings of the 33rd annual meeting on Association for Computational Linguistics*, pages 189–196, 1995.

266. H. P. Young. Condorcet's theory of voting. *American Political Science Review*, 82(4):1231–1244, 1988.

267. K. Yu, S. Yu, and V. Tresp. Soft clustering on graphs. In *in Advances in Neural Information Processing Systems*, page 05, 2005.

268. M. J. Zaki. Scalable algorithms for association mining. *IEEE Transaction on Knowledge and Data Engineering*, 12(3):372–390, 2000.

269. M. J. Zaki. Spade: An efficient algorithm for mining frequent sequences. *Machine Learning Journal*, 42:31–60, 2001.

270. M. J. Zaki, S. Parthasarathy, M. Ogihara, and W. Li. New algorithms for fast discovery of association rules. In *Proceedings of ACM SIGKDD International Conference on Knowledge Discovery and Data Mining*, pages 283–286, 1997.

271. S. Zhang, R. Wang, and X. Zhang. Identification of overlapping community structure in complex networks using fuzzy c-means clustering. *Physica a-statistical mechanics and its application*, 374(1):483–490, 2007.

272. X. Zhang and W. S. Lee. Hyperparameter learning for graph based semi-supervised learning algorithms. In *Advances in Neural Information Processing Systems 19*, 2006.

273. Y. Zhang, G. Xu, and X. Zhou. A latent usage approach for clustering web transaction and building user profile. In *ADMA*, pages 31–42, 2005.

274. Y. Zhang, J. X. Yu, and J. Hou. *Web Communities: Analysis and Construction*. Springer, Berlin Heidelberg, 2006.

275. D. Zhou, O. Bousquet, T. N. Lal, J. Weston, and B. Scholkopf. Learning with local and global consistency. In *Advances in Neural Information Processing Systems 16*, 2004.

276. Y. Zhou, X. Jin, and B. Mobasher. A recommendation model based on latent principal factors in web navigation data. In *in Proceedings of the 3rd International Workshop on Web Dynamics*, 2004.

277. Z. Zhou and M. Li. Semi-supervised learning by disagreement. *Knowledge and Information Systems*.

278. X. Zhu. Semi-supervised learning literature survey. Technical Report 1530, Univ. of Wisconsin, Madison, 2005.

279. X. Zhu, Z. Ghahramani, and J. Lafferty. Semi-supervised learning using gaussian fields and harmonic functions. In *Proceedings of the Tenth International Conference on Machine Learning*, pages 912–919, 2003.